The Ultimate Computer Buyer's Guide

Greg Metz Thomas Jr.

Wordware Publishing, Inc.

Library of Congress Cataloging-in-Publication Data

Thomas, Greg Metz.
The ultimate computer buyer's guide / Greg Metz Thomas, Jr.
p. cm.
Includes index.
ISBN 1-55622-446-X
1. Microcomputers--Purchasing. 2. Title.
QA76.5.T535 1994
004'.029'7--dc20 94-42631
CIP

1506 Capital Avenue
Plano, Texas 75074

Printed in the United States of America

ISBN 1-55622-446-X
10 9 8 7 6 5 4 3 2 1
9508

All inquiries for volume purchases of this book should be addressed to Wordware Publishing, Inc., at the above address. Telephone inquiries may be made by calling:

(214) 423-0090

Contents

Disclaimer

Acknowledgments

This book is a labor of love. Thanks to:

Julian Adams, Ada Agusta, Larry and Virginia Andrews, Jim Asiano, Joe Asiano, Charles Babbage, Tiffany Biggs, Jett Black, Spencer Brownstone, Zelig Chua, Nick Desin, Fredrico Fellini, Aaron Ferguson, Josh Ferguson, Flora Fong, Bill Gates, Hilary Goodkind, Lane Goodkind, Bob Hambrecht, Eric Hartouni, Neil Hickey, Agustin Huneeus, Harry Hunt, Young Ihm, Maca Jarmillo, Skip Johnson, Iming Jung, Robert Knox, Akira Kurosawa, Joe Leong, Matt Levy, Martin Luther King Jr., John Lynch, John Miliken, Wolfgang Mozart, Greg Munson, Nicholas Negroponte, Odwalla, Steve Pomerans, Kelly Quon, Jim Rutherford, Sydney Saidy, Heather Schwabe, Elizabeth Scott, the Scotts, the Sibleys, Jay Sycip, Erin Sodden, Scott the Import, Thayton Towner, Michael Tsang, Mel Valdez, Sid Vicious, Wired, Jeff Wood, Simon Yeo.

Special Thanks

Thanks to Mom, Dad, Elizabeth, Caroline, and my grandparents for all their support.

Foreword

The revolution will not be televised, it will be digitized. In 1993, computers outsold televisions. Thirty-three percent of all U.S. households have a computer, and ten percent of the populace are wired to the world by modem. The holders of power in this next generation are those who know the boundaries of technology and are able to manipulate it to the desired effect. The digiratti hold the reins on communication and thus information and ideas. Enhanced communication via the Internet and other networks is essentially the democratization of information.

Where are we going in this post-post-modern age? As an optimist, I argue toward the path of enlightenment. As humanity learns how to make machines think for themselves, we learn more about ourselves. To know oneself is to have a better understanding about the universe and its *raison d'être*.

I know almost too much about technology and its capabilities and read incessantly about technology for about eight hours every day, so why did I write this book? Many people have turned to me for advice about computers without the slighest notion of what computer technology is and what it can do for them. I wanted to refer these curious people to an excellent book which would gracefully launch them into the information age. After an exhaustive search I concluded there weren't any books available that did justice to the subject matter.

The Ultimate Computer Buyer's Guide holds your hand through the computer buying process. This book is not overly complex, but it goes deep enough into the important issues allowing you to make intelligent buying decisions. Its design includes **bold** and *italic* text to help you find key areas of importance.

Everyone buying computers, including first-time computer buyers, computer consultants, and computer resellers, can benefit from the guidance inside *The Ultimate Computer Buyer's Guide*. One empowering chapter contains a list of recommended computer system configurations for real-life software applications like spreadsheets, databases, desktop publishing, and more. This book helps you understand what is best suited for your current and future needs.

The tables and graphics in the book help you visualize computer concepts and performance issues. A look at microprocessors stops the confusion over what each chip does and which one you really need. In the explanation of computer terminology this book incorporates many non-computer metaphors, enabling long-lasting understanding.

Get ready to explore the possibilities computer technology has to offer.

Chapter 1

Introduction

Congratulations! You have decided to learn how to buy the best personal computer to suit your needs. Personal computing power has increased in the last few years and with the recent declines in price, personal computers are now extremely affordable.

You are ready for a great voyage into the future. The computer is a tool of the information age, and machine computing is vast in comparison to the computing lifespan of an individual. The computer keeps the world literally at your fingertips with just about any topic pertaining to human existence hidden somewhere in the wide network of computers that together are known as the Internet.

Become the Guru

Reading this book will give you the power to make the right buying decisions. A survey conducted by Channel Marketing Corporation (Dallas, Texas) of 1,000 buyers of IBM-compatible computers showed that nine out of ten consumers wished they had made a different choice when they bought their computer system. The changes the consumers wished for included better monitors, more expansion capabilities, more memory, and a larger hard drive. It is often hard for novices to discern what is needed for common uses, and that is why you will find this book a helpful guide.

Computers that use the operating systems DOS, Windows, and OS/2 are commonly referred to as PCs. This is an abbreviation of "personal computer" which technically is a much broader category of computers including the Amiga and Macintosh, NeXT, and a few other computers. The name PC has been usurped by the IBM and IBM-compatible machines, and that is what PC refers to in this book.

The widest assortment of software is available on the PC computing platform. There are about 35,000 commercially available software titles for PC computers vs. 6,000 commercially available titles for the Macintosh. The titles range from cooking and recipe software to high level math and everything in between. There is a plethora of peripherals, items you add to your computer to enhance its capabilities, available for the PC.

In the past, the Macintosh was known for its ease of use because the Mac had a graphic user interface, a screen that is intuitive and easy to use, while PCs were still using cryptic commands to run the computer. Microsoft Windows elevated the PC to the level of ease that previously only the Mac users enjoyed. The Mac was also known as the artist's platform of choice because most of the excellent artistic software was first available only on the Mac platform. This has changed as most software manufacturers have realized they have much to gain by developing software for the PC platform because there is a much bigger market using this platform. The fixed costs of developing and marketing a product are recovered much faster when it is made to run on a PC instead of a Mac because there are many more PC users.

Computers are like Lego kits. The main computer is like the Lego board that acts as the foundation for the rest of the Lego creation. In computer lingo the parts added to enhance the main system are called peripherals. Adding peripherals to a computer system will give it new features it did not have before. Adding peripherals to Macintoshes has generally been an easier process than adding new peripherals to a PC. Adding new items to the PC will be just as easy as with the Macintosh when computers arrive standard with "plug-and-play" designs. If installing a new device inside the computer case sounds like something that is not in your nature, it probably is a good idea to have a computer consultant or computer service center install it for you.

Both the Macintosh and PC are excellent computers to enhance everyday life, and it may be hard to decide which platform to buy. The following story might help you decide which platform would be best for you.

You are in a room with ten doors and each of the doors are identical. Behind each of those doors is an enlightened guru who is ready to tell you the meaning of life. Eight of the gurus know only how to speak Swahili, the ninth guru can speak Mandarin, and the last guru speaks a couple of different languages but can only remember one at a time. You want more than anything else to learn the meaning of life, but you are only allowed to open one of the doors to meet a guru. You do not know any of the languages that the gurus speak and you have the choice to learn one more language before opening a door. Which language would you choose to learn?

You are probably wondering what this means. Of all the personal computers currently owned, eight out of ten are PCs, one out of ten are Macintoshs, and the remaining are a small variety of lesser-known computers.

When you budget for a computer, remember to include the cost of the software programs. Some programs are as inexpensive as $10, but other specialized programs cost $1,000 or more.

When buying a computer, keep in mind that there will always be new technology coming out. It is generally a good idea not to buy the newest technology when it is first available because there are often problems that still need fixing. The price of the newest technology is always sky-high, too. The one-year plan is the best route to take; let a new product remain on the market for one year before buying it. This ensures the product is updated to fix any major problems that surfaced during the initial release. After one year the price will be much more palatable too.

The Basics

The fun of exploring with computers never ceases as long as the initial investment provides you with the power to run the programs you want to use. Just as people can specialize to become accountants or doctors or hang gliding instructors, computers can be configured to accomplish various tasks in the best possible manner. That is where this book comes in handy, as it explains how the different parts of hardware combine to make a complete computer system. Computers are somewhat like a wardrobe; you have shirts and pants and it is best to make sure your socks match or you will look silly. Computer hardware that does not match will make you feel silly for wasting money. **Hardware** consists of the physical parts of your computer. Examples of hardware include circuit boards, keyboard, monitor, chips, and connectors. This hardware needs to be properly matched to work effectively.

In a stereo system, if your speakers go bad you usually do not have to replace the whole stereo, just the speakers. This is a modular design. Each component or module combines to form a whole synergistic system. Like stereo systems, the personal computers are very modular. They generally come as separate and somewhat interchangeable parts.

Software consists of the instructions given to your computer and is stored on various types of media like floppy disks and hard disks. Comparatively speaking, an audio CD player is hardware, while the music it plays that is stored on the CD is equivalent to software. Some examples of popular software programs are PageMaker, WordPerfect, Lotus 1-2-3, and Windows. Each software program gives you the ability to accomplish unique tasks. Common tasks are word processing, drawing, painting, creating spreadsheets, and information storage and retrieval.

The two main operating environments used are Microsoft Windows (for PCs) and System 7 (for Apple computers). These environments are known as GUIs (graphical user interfaces) and they have pull-down menus, icons, use a mouse for easy interaction, and are very intuitive; making them easy as pie to learn and use. Many of the GUI programs are similar in concept, so once you learn how to use one program it is easy to learn and use other programs. The GUI was pioneered by Xerox and subsequently developed by Apple and Microsoft. The GUI offers a great advantage over the previously used command prompt because the user does not have to memorize hundreds of commands. This feature brought computers out of the hands of specialists and into the laps of the proletariat.

The first physical part of the computer you should be aware of is the **central processing unit**, which is commonly referred to as the **CPU**. The CPU is at the core of every computer and often predicates the rest of the abilities of the computer.

A computer essentially is comprised of millions of tiny electronic circuits or gates that can be open or closed. In a circuit there are essentially two states of being conditioned, one by the presence of electricity and the other by the absence of electricity. The two simple states—on or off—can be theorized to mean yes or no, true or false, 1 or 0. Electronic circuits essentially use logic theory, full of conditional statements, to result in predictable answers.

The smallest piece of information used in a computer is a "bit," which is short for **b**inary dig**it**. A bit represents one of the two states and is denoted by either of the digits 0 or 1, which are used in binary notation corresponding to the off or on of electric pulses inside the computer circuitry. Binary is a system of counting that, instead of using ten symbols (0, 1, 2, 3, 4, 5, 6, 7, 8, 9), uses only the two symbols 0 and 1 to represent all possible numbers. This allows information to be processed in the machines' language.

A byte is a unit of data or memory that is universally taken to mean 8 bits. So there are 8 bits in a byte, and 1,024 bytes in a kilobyte, and 1,024 kilobytes in a megabyte. Once again:

1 bit = 0 or 1		
1 bit x 8 = 1 byte	or	1B x 8 = 1 b
1 byte x 1024 = 1 kilobyte	or	1 b x 1024 = 1 Kb
1 kilobyte x 1024 = 1 megabyte	or	1 Kb x 1024 = 1 Mb

How Much Is a Megabyte?

Abbreviation	*Unit of Measure*	*Number of Bits*
B	bit (**bi**nary digi**t**)	1 (represented by a 0 or 1)
b	byte	8 bits
KB	kilobits	1,024 bits
Kb	kilobytes	8,192 bits
MB	megabits	1,048,576 bits
Mb	megabyte	8,388,608 bits
GB	gigabit	1,073,741,824 bits
Gb	gigabyte	8,589,934,592 bits
TB	terabit	10,995,116,277 bits
Tb	terabyte	87,960,930,222 bits
Bps	bits per second	1 bit each second
bps	bytes per second	8 bits each second
KBps	kilobits per second	1,024 bits each second
Kbps	kilobytes per second	8,102 bits each second
MBps	megabits per second	1,048,576 bits each second
Mbps	megabytes per second	8,338,608 bits each second

Common Measurements

Common Words	*Abbreviation*	*Measurement*
millisecond	ms	0.000,1 of a second
nanosecond	ns	0.000,000,001 of a second
Hertz	Hz	One complete cycle per second
kilohertz	kHz	1,000 cycles per second
Megahertz	MHz	1,000,000 cycles per second

The Computer System

The computer system is comprised of a number of independent elements, just like the human body is a collection of different organs. These include the CPU, FPU, case, I/O ports, monitor, motherboard, power supply, RAM, hard disk, keyboard, mouse, and video controller card. These elements are explored in the following chapters.

Chapter 2

The Motherboard and Operating System

The motherboard (also known as the systemboard or main circuit board) is the junction where all the hardware components meet and connect. The motherboard is a "grand central station" where all the circuits get to talk to one another. There are many different options and configurations possible on a motherboard. The design of the motherboard has a large impact on the longevity and performance of the computer system as a whole. The components installed on the motherboard determine the computer's speed and capabilities.

Diamond motherboard

The CPU

The central processing unit (CPU), also called a microprocessor or main processing unit, is a silicon chip and is the main brain of the computer. These chips don't look like tortilla chips but more like a small square bug with lots of metal legs. There are people with different IQs and cars with different amounts of horsepower, and similarly there are CPUs with different levels of computing power. CPUs have evolved from Neanderthal-like chips of yesterday to record-breaking high-speed chips of today. Some companies that make CPUs are Intel, Cyrix, Advanced Micro Devices (AMD), Chips & Technologies, IBM, Texas Instruments, and DEC.

CPUs are organized into different models. The lower-powered CPUs are slow performers and therefore obsolete (i.e., 8088, 8086, 80286 and 80386 CPUs). These Intel chips were at the forefront of technology years ago but they currently don't offer the power to effectively run Windows or many of the great programs that are out on the market now. From this point in the book these chips will be ignored, may they rest in peace.

When a microprocessor manufacturer describes a CPU, the chip family number generally comes first and the clock speed in MHz comes last. Often there is another descriptor like DX, SX, SLC, DLC, DLX, DX2, or Overdrive that is squeezed between the two. These extra letters are not there to confuse you. The letters help explain performance factors that further differentiate the available chips. These differences will be explained in the following sections that feature the different chips available on the market.

Each chip has a **clock speed** that is measurable by its megahertz (MHz). Megahertz is a notation of millions of clock ticks per second. The clock of the computer is on the motherboard and acts much like a coxswain on a crew boat who shouts out the pace that the rowers pull the oars. Having a microprocessor set at a fixed MHz is like having the coxswain shouting at regular intervals. As the speed of the oars is not the only measure of strength of the rowers, the clock speed is not the only thing affecting the power of the CPU.

Just as some boats are built to go faster, more advanced CPU families run faster than their predecessors. For example, the 486-33 MHz contains nearly twice the power of a 386-33 MHz even though they sport the same clock speed. The external clock speed is the speed at which the motherboard is running, the speed at which the microprocessor accepts information from the world outside itself. The internal number of instructions per second is the speed the microprocessor is running inside. This is the speed at which it moves information around its internal registers.

All other things being equal, a microprocessor that runs at a higher clock speed than a similarly designed microprocessor is going at a speed that is almost in direct proportion to its clock speed. For example, a 486-50 MHz chip runs about twice the speed as a 486-25 MHz chip.

It is recommended that you invest wisely and buy from the family of 486 chips or faster instead of older chips like a 386 or 68030. The only possible exception is if you have very special needs and know you will not need the extra power.

The new microprocessors available are called **RISC** (Reduced Instruction Set Computing) processors and are faster, simpler, and cheaper to produce than processors that are built on **CISC** (Complex Instruction Set Computing) architecture. RISC chips generally consume less power and give off less heat than CISC processors with the same computing power. The CISC design allows the microprocessor to do more functions than a RISC chip. Traditionally, the RISC design is capable of parallel execution of multiple instructions, but CISC chips are edging into these areas. RISC processors perform the more complex instructions by building from a combination of basic instructions.

RISC chips tend to excel over CISC chips when doing floating point operations, which are commonly used by computer aided design programs and scientific programs. Faster floating point operations do not usually speed up the abilities of more general use programs like word processors.

A typical RISC chip has 128 or fewer instructions it can perform, whereas a CISC chip typically can perform about 200 to 300 instructions. Because a CISC chip can handle so many instructions, it is more complex and less efficient than a RISC chip. The next generation of CPUs is based on VLIW (Very Large Instruction Word) technology. These chips will be extremely fast but will require specially designed software programs in order to run.

The **Arithmetic and Logic Unit** (ALU) is the core workhorse of the CPU. It is the part that performs the main decisions for the computer. The **internal instruction and data buses** are the highways that information flows on inside the CPU. These can be different than the external instruction and data buses that are on the motherboard.

A **heat sink** is provided on some of the faster CPUs. A heat sink is a metal device that looks like a small waffle iron. It is designed to absorb and dissipate heat away from the chip. Having a heat sink on the CPU could extend its life and the life of motherboard by preventing excess heat stress. Some heat sinks are coupled with a fan that increases its effectiveness. Heat sinks can get in the way for hard drive upgrades or expansion cards if the motherboard was not designed with this in mind. When buying a computer with a heat sink, ask to pop the hood and check whether the heat sink is an obstacle for future upgrades.

Registers, like memory, store data and instructions in the CPU. This storage space is small compared to the main system RAM (Random Access Memory). For the CPU, using a register is like having scratch paper to help take notes while doing math problems. To augment the registers, many CPUs have an integrated level one cache.

An **internal cache** or level one cache (L1) in a microprocessor helps it run faster by storing information that it needs to access next. This super fast memory is contained inside the chip, and the cache sits between the registers and the external bus on the motherboard. The cache speeds up the functioning of the CPU by containing the information it will probably need to "think" about next.

Internal caches generally range in size from 1 kilobyte to 32 kilobytes. Most motherboards provide an **external cache** or level two cache (L2) that sits between the microprocessor and the main memory. External caches generally range in size from 64 kilobytes to 1 megabyte. An internal cache is preferred to an external cache because it is usually better designed.

The **pipeline** consists of the path that data takes through the CPU while it is being worked on. A pipeline has many stages, like an automotive assembly line. In general, a pipelined chip can process more instructions per clock cycle than a non-pipelined chip running at the same speed. The newer chips have more than one pipeline for data to flow through. Having more than one instruction being performed at one time is parallel processing and adds speed to a computer. A chip that has two or more pipelines will require software optimized to make use of this feature. A chip with the ability to process more than one instruction per clock tick is called **superscalar**. Multiprocessing is done by using more than one pipeline and sending instruction pairs down these pipelines simultaneously.

A **Floating Point Unit** (FPU), also called a math-coprocessor, is a component dedicated to processing floating point arithmetic. This means it rapidly processes math equations that have decimal points. Some CPUs have an FPU built in; some others allow for an external FPU, and some do not. An internal FPU is a little better than an external FPU because it gains performance from access to the internal cache memory and instruction pipeline. An FPU speeds up math- and science-based programs, graphics programs, and high-end spreadsheet operations, like 10,000 cell recalculations. Some programs require the computer system to have an FPU in order to run. Check the software manual for the answer.

Clock doubling is a technique that allows the microprocessor to run two or more times faster inside than the speed of the rest of the motherboard. An address bus is the path the microprocessor takes to communicate with the system memory. The data bus is the path the information from the rest of the computer follows to get to the CPU. A bus that is 32-bit can transmit more information than a 16-bit bus, like a 32-lane highway can handle more traffic than a 16-lane highway.

Microprocessors have an **operating voltage**, which is the amount of current that needs to be supplied to make the chip run. Most chips manufactured before 1993 ran at 5 volts, but these days there are many 3.3-volt chips available. The 3.3-volt chips are especially desirable in portable computers where power consumption off the battery is always an important issue. Many microprocessors used in portable computers have power management features integrated into the chip. This allows the CPU to put parts of the computer into a sleep mode when the computer is idle after a specified amount of time. Power management features can shut down modems, hard disks, ports, and other peripherals to prolong the life of the battery.

There are several measures of performance for CPUs including SPEC, MIPS, and iCOMP. The **SPEC** (Standard Performance Evaluation Corp.) benchmark was designed by a group of manufacturers, users, and industry analysts. It is based on real world performance that measures integer speed and floating point speed separately as SPECint92 and SPECfp92, respectively. **MIPS** rating measures the number of millions of instructions per second a microprocessor can perform. The **iCOMP** performance rating is provided by Intel as a measure of its chips' performances.

The Intel iComp Index

Microprocessor	*iComp Rating*	*Microprocessor*	*iComp Rating*
Pentium 100	815	486DX2-50	231
Pentium 90	735	486SX2-50	180
Pentium 66	567	486DX-33	166
Pentium 60	510	486SX-33	136
486DX4-100	435	486DX-25	122
486DX4-75	319	486SX-25	100
486DX2-66	297	486SX-20	78
486DX-50	249		

A rating of the relative performance of Intel microprocessors

Specific CPU Chips

The following is a list of Intel and competitive chips.

Intel

Intel is the big daddy of CPU manufacturers. It sells chips in PGA (Pin Grid Array), which means the contact pins stick out of the bottom of the chip, and in PLCC (surface-mounted Plastic Leaded Chip Carrier), where the chip fits into a socket that comes up and surrounds its sides.

80486SX 25/33

The Intel 80486 (also known as the i486SX or 486SX) has a more advanced design than the 386 chip. An 8K cache is built-in, allowing it faster access to data. The chip executes more instructions in fewer clock cycles than the 386 chip. Motherboards with these chips usually are upgradable to a 486DX. The upgrade chip is actually a real 486DX that when in place takes over as the CPU and disables the 486SX.

The Cyrix **Cx486S2/50** is a clock-doubled chip running at 50 MHz internally and 25 MHz externally and is 486SX compatible.

80486DX

The Intel 80486DX (also referred to as i486, 486DX, or 486) has an FPU, which the 486SX lacks. It has a fast RISC (Reduced Instruction Set Code) core, an 8-kilobyte write-through memory cache plus cache controller, and an enhanced 387-compatible FPU math coprocessor built in. The FPU addition helps speed up graphics programs, spreadsheet programs, and other number-intensive programs. The 486 is a RISC and CISC hybrid chip.

The Silicon Graphics **R4200** is pin-compatible with Intel 486DX chips and contains 1.3 million transistors. This is a low-powered, 3.3-volt chip that performs similarly to the 66 MHz Pentium chip.

486SL 25/33 MHz

This is a low power consumption version of the 486DX-25 MHz chip drawing only about 30 percent of the power. It apparently is a bit faster because it is based on a newer generation of improved algorithms that allow some calculation to be done in fewer clock cycles. It is equipped with an 8K cache and coprocessor.

The Cyrix **Cx486SLC/e** is competition for Intel's 486SL. It has a programmable space on the chip that allows for hardware virtualization. This is the ability to create peripherals, like modems, by programming the chip. The Texas Instruments **TI486SXLC** is competition to the Intel 486.

80486DX-2 and Overdrive

The 80486DX-2 chip, also marketed as an Overdrive (also called ODP486), is based on the 486DX but is turbocharged with a dual clock. A normal 486DX internally runs at the same clock speed (MHz) set by the system's clock chip. The 486DX-2's internal speed is twice that of the system clock. It comes in two versions: the 486DX-2 25/50 MHz and the 486DX-2 33/66 MHz. This chip is meant to fit in the 486SX system socket designed for the 487SX FPU coprocessor. It is pin compatible with the 486DX and will work in the majority of systems that originally housed the 486DX chip. All you have to do is make the swap, but it is recommended that you consult your retailer just to make sure it will work.

The increased internal clock speed of these chips translates to a 30- to 70-percent speed increase with most business applications. Because they have an FPU built-in, these chips, when handling number intensive applications, are about 350 percent faster than the 486SX. The 486DX2-66 is rated at delivering about 54 MIPS (Millions of Instructions Per Second), a measure of computing power.

To install an overdrive chip you need a special Overdrive socket, or a 169-pin Intel 486SX or 487 socket or a 168-pin Intel 486DX socket on your motherboard. The Overdrive is available in 16 MHz, 20 MHz, 25 MHz, and 33 MHz external clock speeds.

Cyrix makes the **CxDRu2**, which competes against the 486DX-2. The Cyrix **Cx486DX** and **CX486DX2** are Intel 486DX-2 compatible chips. Texas Instruments **TI486SXL** and **TI486SXL2**, and AMD **Am486DX2** are competition for the Intel 486DX-2.

486DX4

The name is a little misleading, as these are really clock-tripled chips. These chips are running internally at 2, 2.5, and 3 times the speed the motherboard is running externally. The DX4 is a 3.3-volt chip and contains a 16-kilobyte cache. They use 0.6

micron technology. The 486DX4 33/110 MHz has an iCOMP rating of 435.

The IBM **486SLC25/75** and **486SLC 33/100** are clock-tripled like the Intel 486DX4, but they lack some features, making the Intel a better performer. The IBM **Blue Lightning D466BL** is a clock-tripled chip that closer rivals the Intel chip but lacks an FPU.

Pentium

Next in line is the Intel 80586 (also called the 5P or 586) which Intel has named the "Pentium." This chip was first released in 1993 and is faster than the IBM R400 chip set. The Pentium has 3.2 million transistors, which is about three times that of the 486. It uses 5-volt BiCMOS or 3.3-volt technology. The Pentium has a 64-bit internal data bus and a 32-bit address path. It is rated at 100 MIPS (Millions of Instructions Per Second) which is more than twice as fast as 486 chips and will not fit into a 486 socket. It has a 64-bit external data path and a 16-kilobyte write-back primary cache split into two separate 8-kilobyte caches for instruction and data. It has internal parity checking that will catch errors in the data, a nice feature. The Pentium is able to perform about 112 million instructions per second (MIPS). This is more than twice the rated speed of a 486DX2-66 which is rated at 54 MIPS. The Pentium at 66 MHz rates a SPECint92 of 67.4 and a SPECfp92 of 63.6.

The Pentium FPU (floating point unit) is five to ten times faster than the FPU on a 486DX-33 MHz. The Pentium is superscalar, able to process more than one instruction per clock cycle. This is because it has two integer-execution units allowing it to execute two instructions in a single clock cycle. (The 486 can only process one instruction per clock cycle.) The Pentium is backwardly compatible with the existing PC software, but software has to be rewritten to take full advantage of this new chip. Without rewriting, even a 16-bit application runs twice as fast on a Pentium as on a 486DX2-33/66 MHz chip. Once applications have been rewritten to take advantage of the Pentium architecture, the programs will run an additional 25 to 35 percent faster on the same chip.

Cyrix makes a chip called the **Cyrix M1** that competes with the Pentium. The **K5** is AMD's rival to Intel's Pentium chip.

NexGen is an Intel rival with their Nx586, which is competition against the Pentium. The Nx586's floating point unit is external to the chip and the chip is not pin compatible with the Pentium.

Pentium II These chips are based on a 0.6 micron process instead of the 0.8 micron process of the original Pentium. This allows Intel to compete better against the Power PC chip by reducing manufacturing costs.

P54C Released in 1994, this Pentium runs at 90 MHz internally and 50 MHz externally. It offers 150 MIPS performance. It uses a smaller die size, reducing heat problems. The P54C uses a 3.3 volt power supply and rates at 78 SPECint92 and 85 SPECfp92.

P54CT This is a Pentium-to-Pentium upgrade chip.

P54M This chip offers 300 MIPS performance.

Pentium Overdrive There will also be a chip based on the same technology as the Pentium that will fit into the 238-pin ZIF sockets that are available on some 486 motherboards. This relative of the Pentium (also called the 566SX) will not be quite as powerful as a genuine Pentium chip. It operates at 64 bits internally and 32 bits externally.

80586SL This chip has power saving properties.

80686 Also called the P6, it houses 10 million transistors. The 486 and 586 have only 1.2 million and 3.1 million transistors respectively. The MIPS rating of the P6 is expected to be at 200 MIPS.

80786 This chip is the next generation after the 80686 and contains advanced VLIS (Very Large Instruction Word) technology.

Other CPU Manufacturers

Higher-end processors that outperform the Pentium are made by Silicon Graphics, Integrated Devices Technology, and Toshiba, Sun, DEC, and Wietek. These processors are not completely compatible with PC software and therefore are only used for specific applications.

SPEC Ratings

Microprocessor	*SPECint92*	*SPECfp92*	*Microprocessor*	SPECint92	SPECfp92
Intel P54C 100 MHz	100	81	DEC Alpha AXP 21064 200 MHz	130	184
Intel P54C 90 MHz	90	73	DEC Alpha AXP 21064A 275 MHz	170	290
Intel Pentium 66 MHz	67	62	DECchip 21066 166 MHz	70	105
Intel Pentium 60 MHz	60	56	MicroSparc II 85 MHz	57.2	49.5
Intel 486DX4-100 MHz	51	25	Sun SuperSPARC 60 MHz	89	103
Intel 486DX2-66 MHz	36	16	hyperSPARC 110 MHz	111	135
Intel 486DX-33 MHz	28	13	MIPS/NEC R4200 80 MHz	55	30
Intel 486SX2-50 MHz	21	N/A	MIPS R4400 200 MHz	117	131
PowerPC 601 80 MHz	85	105	MIPS R4400 150 MHz	94	105
PowerPC 601 66 MHz	73	91	MIPS R4600	92.1	82
PowerPC 601 50 MHz	60	70	HP PA-7100LC	80	84
PowerPC 603 80 MHz	75	85	HP PA-7150 125 MHz	135	201
PowerPC 603 66 MHz	60	70	IBM Power2 71.5 MHz	126	260
PowerPC 604 100 MHz	160	165			

Floating Point Unit

The Floating Point Unit (often called an FPU, math coprocessor, or Numeric Processing Unit (NPU)) is designed to complement a CPU that lacks one internally. These chips are placed in their appropriate sockets on the motherboard and deliver added computing power for graphic, spreadsheet, mathematical, and scientific programs. These chips are becoming rare because most newer chips have a floating point unit built into the chip (with exception of the NexGen 586). The older chips like the 286 and 386 lack an internal floating point unit.

Clock Speed

The board speed is measured in clock cycle times, which is the amount of time it takes the microprocessor to perform a basic operation such as moving a number from one internal area to another. The **clock** tells the system how fast to operate and is measured in megahertz (MHz), millions of cycles per second. The range of clock speeds is 20 MHz to 250 MHz, the latter being the fastest. On many previously manufactured motherboards the clock is stuck at a specified speed and cannot be changed, but on some newly designed models the clock speed can be changed to different MHz rates providing for the possibility of upgrading the CPU in the future without having to buy a new motherboard. The usual way the clock speed of the motherboard is changed is either through toggling DIP (dual in-line package) switches or by completely replacing the clock chip.

The Bus

The add-on options available with motherboards these days have grown tremendously with the arrival of new technologies. The motherboard **Bus** is a system component that has been constantly evolving to offer better performance and greater standardization. The motherboard bus is not like a big yellow school bus with screaming children hanging out the windows, but instead is similar to a highway of information connecting the CPU with other hardware. Examples of hardware that can be connected to the bus include the video adapter, sound card, modem, or hard disk controller.

Just as a highway with more lanes can handle more cars, a wider bus path can transmit more information at a time than a smaller bus at the same clock speed. The greater the speed limit on a highway, the faster the cars can arrive at their destinations. Consequently the higher the MHz or clock speed a bus can handle, the quicker the flow of data from one point to another.

Most motherboards generally sport six to eight expansion slots. Each slot allows you to plug in a new feature to the computer.

The expansion slots may all be of the same design or the motherboard may contain a mix of designs. The most common bus architectures are ISA, EISA, VL-Bus, and PCI bus.

Bus Standards Compared

Bus Architecture	*ISA*	*EISA*	*MCA*	*VL-Bus*	*VL-Bus 2.0*	*PCI*
Maximum bandwidth in bits	16	32	32	32	64	32 or 64
Maximum clock speed in MHz	8	8.3	10	33	33	33
Maximum sustained data thoughput in Mbps	16	32	40	132	264	120 or 240
Max. number of peripherals supported	12	12	12	3	3	10

An **ISA** (Industry Standard Architecture, also called ATA) bus consists of 16-bit "lanes" and the speed limit is 8 MHz. ISA is limited to a theoretical maximum of 8 megabytes per second in burst mode as the top data transfer rate, which is a little slow by today's standards. The ISA sustained transfer rate is near 3 Mb to 5 Mb per second. A video display that has a better resolution than 800 x 600 and more than sixteen colors will bottleneck on an ISA bus, slowing the transfer of data.

The **ISA Plug and Play** standard is an upgraded version of the original ISA standard. It enables users to install expansion cards with ease because the expansion cards are self-configuring. This means a card can be installed without needing to set jumpers or dip switches or add software drivers. The Plug and Play ISA standard allows for hot docking. A portable can be removed from a docking bay without first needing to be turned off. To take advantage of Plug and Play ISA, the operating system must be compliant with the standard. Windows version 4 is Plug and Play compliant.

The next better standard to ISA is called EISA. An **EISA** (Expanded Industry Standard Architecture) bus has 32-bit "lanes" with an 8.33 MHz speed limit. It is limited to a theoretical transfer rate of 32 megabytes per second. Future advanced releases of EISA boards will be able to transfer up to 66 megabytes per second.

A little-used bus standard is called MCA. The Micro Channel Architecture, **MCA**, is a 32-bit bus with a 10 MHz speed. It can transfer data at 20 megabytes per second, or 40 megabytes per second in burst mode. The advantage of EISA over MCA is that it is backwardly compatible with ISA boards all the way back to 8-bit cards. MCA adapter cards are rare and expensive, which makes EISA an even more desirable alternative.

The VESA (Video Electronics Standards Association) **VL-Bus** standard, also referred to as VESA local bus, has a 32-bit data path and runs at the microprocessor's external clock speed. VL-Bus can theoretically handle speeds up to 66 MHz. On a computer with a 33 MHz CPU clock speed, the 32-bit VL-Bus can sustain a transfer rate of 132 megabytes per second in burst mode. This is a whopping twenty-six times more data than the ISA bus can transfer. The 386 and 486 CPUs speak in 32-bit chunks so it is best to have a bus that will convey this amount of information. VL-Bus uses the same style 112-pin slot that MCA uses. VL-Bus can support bus mastering but only one master can be in control of the bus at one time. A bus mastering card can control and access other parts of the computer without the intervention of the CPU, effectively reducing overhead on the CPU and overall speeding up the computer system. This prevents bus mastering cards from running simultaneously with the CPU.

The VL-Bus is an extension of the internal bus used in the 486 chip. It can offer an eight times greater transfer of information than an ISA bus. Due to engineering limitations there can effectively be only three or less VL-Bus slots in a machine running at 33 MHz, two slots in a machine running at 40 MHz, and no slots in a 50 MHz or faster machine. There can be up to two VL-Bus devices on 40 MHz or 50 MHz systems, but they need to be hardwired to the motherboard. For maximum flexibility with this bus design it is recommended that you buy a 33 MHz VL-Bus motherboard and run a 486DX2-33/66 for maximum performance, or opt for a PCI Pentium based system.

VESA has expanded the initial VL-Bus capabilities. The Video Electronic Standards Association has increased the maximum total possible number of motherboard VL-Bus slots from three to ten. VESA is also working on improving the bus mastering capabilities. VL-Bus 2.0 allows for expansion cards on the motherboard at clock speeds up to 50 MHz. In the works for the VL-Bus is to increase the bus width handling from 32-bit to a 64-bit transfer that will make the VL-Bus useful with the Pentium.

A 64-bit VL-Bus 2.0 is expected to be able to transfer at 264 megabytes per second. *Mezzanine bus* is a buffered design that will allow speeds up to 80 MHz. Buffering slows things down about 15 percent because it adds wait states when addressing a device. PCI and VL-Bus hybrid motherboards were both available on the market in 1994.

Intel released **PCI** (Peripheral Component Interconnection) in 1993, a standard that is perhaps a little better than VL-Bus. It uncouples peripherals from the CPU and has layers that manage and route data. This extra control overhead does limit the maximum transfer rate of 32-bit PCI to 76 megabits per second, a bit slower than VL-Bus at the same clock speed. PCI technically is not really a local bus since it operates at a fixed 33 MHz and communicates with the CPU via a controller chip. The signaled buffered design will make it more expandable, and although it was eclipsed for the time being by VL-Bus' head start of 10 to 14 months, PCI is sure to catch on fast. PCI allows ten devices to be connected to the bus and supports both 32-bit and 64-bit data transfers. The extra circuitry required by PCI requires more processing than VL-Bus, so the real world transfer rates are a little slower than VL-Bus.

PCI is compatible with bus mastering, which allows several devices to make a direct memory address circumventing the CPU. This is called multimaster concurrency and it speeds things up. For 32-bit PCI the maximum transfer rate is about 132 megabytes per second. A 64-bit transfer will double the possible transfer rate to a theoretical rate of 264 megabytes per second. PCI runs independently of the CPU, which ensures fewer compatibility problems with future improvements. Considering the price, PCI is a bit more expensive than VL-Bus, but it allows easier upgradibility, so it may save you money in the long run. Because PCI separates the CPU from the rest of the motherboard, it will allow upgrading the CPU without the need to replace the motherboard. Another good feature of PCI is it will make installing expansion boards easier; they will be auto-configuring.

Some peripherals cannot make performance gains with the increased transfer rates that PCI and VL-Bus use. Modems, fax-modems, printers, film recorders, and sound cards do not have performance gains with a faster bus than ISA.

CPU Sockets

The way the CPU is attached to the motherboard can affect the future usefulness of the motherboard with regard to CPU upgrades. On some systems the CPU is housed on a separate circuit board, called a daughterboard, that is attached to the motherboard by a slot. A more common design has the CPU located directly on the motherboard itself. Some CPUs are hardwired to the circuit board and therefore are not removable. This design is a limiting option because it does not allow easy replacement of the CPU. The system will need to be able to accept a processor card to remain upgradable.

Some sockets on the motherboard allow the CPU to be unplugged and replaced. A **LIF** (low insertion force) socket requires a special chip pulling tool to effectively remove the CPU. **ZIF** (zero insertion force) sockets are the newest and better because they allow easy removal. The ZIF socket has a lever on its side that when flipped will loosen or tighten the grip on the chip pins. Intel has released two ZIF sockets. One is a 169-pin version that will accept the 486SX and 486DX chips but will not accept the DX2 or a Pentium chip. The other is a 238-pin ZIF socket that will accept DX2 and Overdrive chips and will accept a Pentium-related chip that has a 32-bit bus. To run a real Pentium CPU you must have a motherboard with a 64-bit data bus.

Other Features

The other items on the motherboard you should be aware of are the maximum amount of DRAM you can install and what type of DRAM it takes; the type of math coprocessor that the motherboard will support; what the upgrade path is for the CPU; and the size case the board will fit in (usually classified as AT, baby-AT, XT, or tower). You should also know how many expansion slots total and available there are on the motherboard. Expansion slots are where peripherals like modems and network cards are plugged in. Find out what architecture the slots on the motherboard feature (i.e., ISA, EISA, MCA, VL-Bus).

Look for motherboards that allow **symmetric multiprocessing** capabilities. This allows the computer the advantage of using more than one CPU. Like tandem bicycling, this method can greatly improve system performance. Many of the new motherboards that allow symmetric multiprocessing will make use of the upgrade socket. The original chip and the upgrade CPU will work as a team, giving more boom for the buck.

Before buying a computer, pop off the computer case cover and check for **tracer wires** on any of the circuit boards. These are small wires that indicate either the board contains faulty circuits that needed repair or indicate the board has been cheaply updated from an inferior design.

Bus Mastering

To be able to use the best peripherals the motherboard needs to support **bus mastering**. This is an advanced method of moving data while taking the burden off the CPU. The "smart" adapter cards that support bus mastering will help speed up your system altogether. Bus mastering cards are capable of DMA (direct memory access) thereby accessing DRAM while bypassing the CPU. This can speed up the communication of the expansion card and the rest of the computer. Some ISA motherboards only allow one DMA channel. Other motherboards usually have seven channels available for use by adapter cards. Without bus mastering not all adapter cards will work compatibly with your motherboard.

The Cache

The system cache, as explained before, makes access to information quicker for the CPU, and this speeds up the operation of the computer. A system with a 1 megabyte cache can work about twice as fast as a computer without a Level 2 cache. The 486 has about a 15-percent performance increase over the 386, but in conjunction with its 8-kilobyte internal cache the performance of a 486 doubles to a 30-percent increase in performance. The 8-kilobyte cache built into the 486 is comparable to having a 32-kilobyte cache external to the chip since the 8-kilobyte cache is four-way set-associative and the external cache is two-way set-associative. The 32-kilobyte cache size provides a 90 percent chance that the data will remain in the cache until requested by the CPU. If the data needed is in the cache, this is called a hit; if the data is not in the cache this is called a miss. The cache built into the 486 is not big enough for the maximum hit rate, and that is why an external cache is used.

An external cache, also called a Level 2 (L2) cache, is comprised of static random access memory (SRAM) and is coupled with a cache controller which anticipates the data the microprocessor will require. SRAM has no refresh overhead unlike the conventional dynamic random access memory (DRAM). SRAM is rated as fast as 12 nanoseconds, which is equivalent to about 83.3 MHz.

Although a larger cache size is generally better, the performance gain of an increased cache size does not progress in a linear fashion; that is, more is not always better. To gain additional performance above a 90 percent hit rate, the size of the cache has to be doubled. That is why the smallest external cache for the 486DX is 64 kilobytes. The next size up is a 128-kilobyte cache, then a 256-kilobyte cache, and some systems offer up to a 512-kilobyte cache. If you plan on using 8 megabytes of RAM or more and multitask, that is, if you plan on using many programs simultaneously, you will get the best performance with a 128-kilobyte or 256-kilobyte cache. If you plan on using OS/2 or Windows NT, a larger cache size is recommended.

A better-designed 64-kilobyte cache can give better performance than a 128-kilobyte cache that is poorly designed. There are three categories of **cache write design**. A *write-through* cache only reads from memory. Better is the *posted write-through* cache that buffers all writes until the memory system bus is free before completing them. The best is a *write-back* cache which can cache data read from and written to memory.

There are three types of **cache architecture**. A *direct-mapped cache* is not divided and is the least costly. Better is a *two-way set associative cache*, which has the cache divided into two separate blocks. The best design is a *four-way set-associative cache*, which divides data into four separate blocks. This type of design is used in 486 chips.

The cache is read by the CPU in one of two ways. The slower design is the **look through cache** which sits in serial between the CPU and the system memory causing the CPU to "look through" to DRAM. This is a simpler design than the look aside cache and therefore is cheaper to produce. All memory requests first pass through the cache and then to DRAM. Only if there is a cache miss will a request be made to the main system memory. This causes the request to be delayed, slowing information retrieval from DRAM.

A **look aside cache** is designed on the bus in parallel with the main system memory. This is the better cache method. All memory requests are sent simultaneously to the cache and main system memory. If a cache hit occurs, the cache tells the CPU to cancel the main system memory request and the cache sends the requested information to the CPU. This type of cache does not slow the CPU down because the memory and the cache are both trying to locate the requested information simultaneously. A system with a look aside cache can be bought without the cache and upgraded with a cache later.

The RAM

RAM is the place the computer puts information the CPU needs to access. The hard disk is where information is stored long-term; this is analogous to having a library to store books. The RAM is used like an office desk. The bigger the desk, the more information at immediate disposal. Similarly the more RAM a computer has installed, the faster the CPU can work because it has quick access to the information it needs.

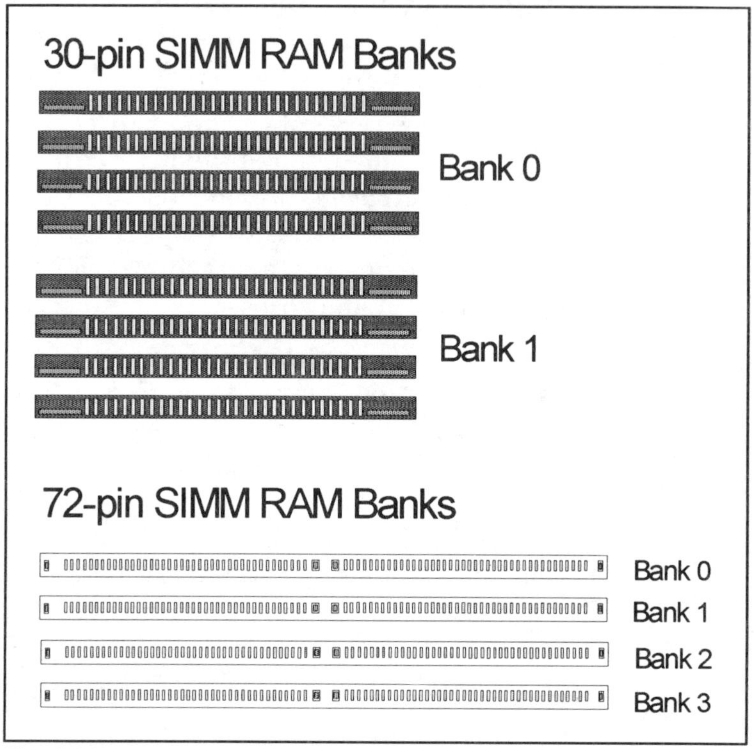

The RAM

RAM (Random Access Memory) is volatile memory. You will lose anything stored in RAM, like your exam paper, the silly picture you drew of your boss, or the latest spreadsheet figures, when you turn off the power. Dynamic RAM is cheaper and slower than static RAM, which is used for cache memory. To retain information, DRAM (Dynamic RAM) has to be refreshed or recharged by a pulse of electricity many times a second. This slows performance. Static RAM (SRAM) does not need to be refreshed and therefore is much faster, at about 20 nano seconds. SRAM is used in a computer cache.

Memory Storage Comparison

Memory Type	Cost	Erasable	Volatile	Access Time
Hard Drive	Low	Yes	No	24,000 ns
ROM	Medium	No	No	120 ns
SRAM	Highest	Yes	Yes	15 ns to 20 ns
VRAM	High	Yes	Yes	20 ns
DRAM	High	Yes	Yes	60 ns to 100 ns
EPROM	Medium	Yes	Under UV light	150 ns
EEPROM	High	Yes	No	150 ns
Flash Memory	High	Yes	No	70 ns

The speed of RAM is measured in nanoseconds; this is 1/1,000,000,000 of a second. **DRAM** usually rates between 80 ns (nanoseconds) to 60 ns. Don't you wish your car was this fast going zero to 60 MPH? The smaller the number, the faster the DRAM. The faster the RAM a system uses does not necessarily mean the computer will be faster. A system that can use 70 ns RAM may not be faster than if it uses 60 ns RAM unless the system is designed to handle the speed better. It is a good idea to keep all the memory used in the computer matched at the same speed, or quirky problems may arise.

These days DRAM usually comes packaged on a **SIMM**, which stands for Single Inline Memory Module. SIMMs come in two different pin-out flavors: 30-pin and 72-pin. The 30-pin SIMM design is the older and more prevalent of the two. The 30-pin SIMMs used for PCs are 9-bit devices and SIMMs used for Macs are 8-bit chips. The extra bit on the PC SIMM is used as a parity check for each byte of information. This helps ensure the data that is being moved is not accidentally corrupted. 30-pin SIMMs are usually installed in a bank on the motherboard two or four at a time. To work, the memory bank must be completely full with SIMMs or completely empty. This type of memory does not take up much space on the motherboard and is usually measured in amounts of 512 kilobytes, 256 kilobytes, and 1, 4, 8, 16, 32, and 64 megabytes.

The 72-pin SIMM is a 32-bit device and is used in newer, high-end system motherboards. The bank for a 72-pin SIMM usually consists of one or two sockets and allows you to mix and match different combinations of memory more easily than with 30-pin SIMMs. The 72-pin design makes it easier to upgrade your memory.

To run Windows 3.1, a computer system needs at least 4 megabytes to 8 megabytes of DRAM. For keeping more than one program open at a time, like a spreadsheet, a personal information manager, and word processor, 8 megabytes to 16 megabytes of DRAM is recommend. For working with graphics programs it is recommended to install 16 megabytes to 32 megabytes or more DRAM. The version of Windows called NT (New Technology), released in 1993, requires a minimum of 16 megabytes of DRAM. It is recommended that a Windows NT system have 20 megabytes of RAM as a minimum.

If adding RAM to a computer system, it is best to buy the fewest number of memory modules to accomplish the job. For example, if you are upgrading from 4 megabytes to 20 megabytes, it is better to buy one 16-megabyte SIMM instead of four 4-megabyte SIMMs. Using this technique will make future memory upgrades easier and more cost-effective.

Multitasking is an advantage that Windows offers. A computer is multitasking when there are two or more programs running at the same time, a technique allowing the user to jump quickly from one program to the another while the rest of programs operate in the background. For example, you can have a fax program sending faxes and a spreadsheet doing calculations in the background while at the same time you are typing a letter to a friend. The optimal setup for multitasking requires a generous amount of RAM, although computers lacking the extra RAM can use virtual memory. Virtual memory is a method allowing the computer to use free space on the hard drive as though it were RAM. Hard disks are about 1,000 times slower than real RAM, and while using virtual memory your computer session is noticeably slowed down.

To tell whether your computer has enough RAM, open a typical document and examine whether the hard disk is being constantly accessed while using the document. Another method to test is to turn off virtual memory, restart the computer, and open a typical document. If the document does not open due to insufficient RAM, consider upgrading.

New varieties of RAM are breaking slowly into the market. The Rambus DRAM (RDRAM) is thirteen times faster than normal DRAM. Ramtron's Enhanced DRAM (EDRAM) and Mitsubishi's Cache DRAM (CDRAM) both incorporate a SRAM cache within the chips. These designs eliminate the need for an external SRAM cache for the CPU. Another form of RAM is Synchronous DRAM (SDRAM), which promises faster speeds and enhanced performance.

The BIOS

When you were born you had all the "hardware" needed to function: your lungs, eyes, brain, heart, etc. In order for you to survive, your subconscious instinctively tells your lungs to breathe and you heart to beat. This instinct is similar to the function of the BIOS (Basic Input/Output System) in a computer system. The BIOS contains the basic information for the computer system to "wake up" when you turn it on. It performs some basic diagnostic tests, sends and receives information to and from components connected to your computer, and does other low-level tasks.

Most BIOS are paired with a setup program that lets you change the CMOS settings. This information, specific to your computer, is stored in a battery powered chip. When the battery runs out of charge, the settings will be lost, so be sure to make a backup of the settings to restore the CMOS after replacing the battery.

The BIOS is stored in **ROM** (Read Only Memory), which is nonvolatile memory. Nonvolatile memory is not erased when it loses power. The BIOS is sometimes found in flash memory, which has a combination of ROM and RAM attributes. Flash memory can be erased and is fast like RAM. Flash RAM is also volatile like RAM but does not require much energy to keep its memory. A reason flash memory is not too common is because it is expensive.

Another type of ROM is called **PROM**. This stands for Programmable ROM. A PROM chip is burned-in with instructions sometime after it is manufactured. Once the instructions are coded they cannot be changed. This is a nonvolatile type of memory and like most ROM is fairly slow. **EPROM** is Erasable Programmable ROM and is loaded with instructions after it is manufactured. EPROM chips' instructions can be changed by exposing them to ultraviolet light. The light erases the memory, allowing the chip to be reprogrammed with new instructions. **EEPROM** is Electrically Erasable Programmable ROM and is erased by exposing it to a stronger electrical current than it normally requires. After it is erased it can be reprogrammed again with new information.

If the PC you buy has a BIOS that replicates the functions of an IBM BIOS, you then can run the same software that runs on an IBM personal computer. A new computer system should have the latest BIOS chip included to ensure compatibility with other products on the market. A system with a flash memory BIOS can be updated with software to keep the BIOS current. To upgrade a ROM BIOS, the entire chip will have to be replaced. It is a good idea to write down the BIOS brand and version for later reference in case incompatibility problems arise. Some popular BIOS manufacturers are Phoenix, AMI, DTK, and Award.

The Operating System

After you are born you need to learn a language like Spanish, English, Arabic, etc., so you can communicate with other people and, for example, go to the bank and say "hello" to the bank teller and request to withdraw $100,000,000. An operating system gives the computer a basic "language" with which to communicate.

The operating system is a software program which carries out certain tasks such as loading instructions when you turn on the computer, relaying information typed at the keyboard, formatting disks, opening and closing files, creating and naming files, memory management, and input/output functions. The operating system acts as a liaison between the applications you use and the system hardware. The operating system is usually stored on a hard disk, although it can be located in flash RAM or on a floppy disk.

An operating system links the main computer with its peripherals and devices, for example CD-ROM, printer, or fax-modem. These peripherals usually come with *device drivers,* software that supplies the operating system with information to control the device. Drivers essentially tell the computer what kind of device is attached to it. For example, if you connect a Hewlett-Packard printer to a computer it will not know what is attached until you install the printer drivers that come with the printer on a floppy disk.

MS-DOS (Microsoft Disk Operating System), Windows NT, Windows 95, Solaris, System 7, PowerOpen, UNIX, XENIX, and OS/2 are the most popular PC operating systems. It is recommended that you use the latest version available of an operating system to take advantage of its advanced and enhanced features.

CPUs and Operating System Compatibility

Chip Type	DOS and Windows 3.1	Windows NT	OS/2.2	NeXT	Solaris	System 7	UNIX
PowerPC	No	Yes	Yes	Yes	Yes	Yes	Yes
Intel 386	Yes	Yes	Yes	No	No	No	Yes
Intel 486	Yes	Yes	Yes	Yes	Yes	No	Yes
Intel Pentium	Yes	Yes	Yes	Yes	Yes	No	Yes
DEC Alpha	Yes	Yes	No	No	No	No	Yes
MIPS R4000	Yes	Yes	No	No	No	No	Yes
MIPS R4400	Yes	Yes	No	No	No	No	Yes
HP PA-7100	No	No	No	Yes	No	No	Yes
SPARC	Yes	Yes	No	No	Yes	No	Yes
Macintosh 68000	No	No	No	No	No	Yes	Yes

Chapter 3

Drives and I/O Ports

Floppy Disk Drives

The floppy disk is the most popular way of adding or removing data and software from the hard disk. Floppies generally come in two physical sizes, the 3.5-inch and the obsolete 5.25-inch. Even though the 5.25-inch floppy is an obsolete media, a 5.25-inch drive is needed if you want to exchange data with friends or coworkers who do not have the newer 3.5-inch floppy drive. The 3.5-inch drive is currently the standard floppy format, and most software sold in retail stores comes in the 3.5-inch format.

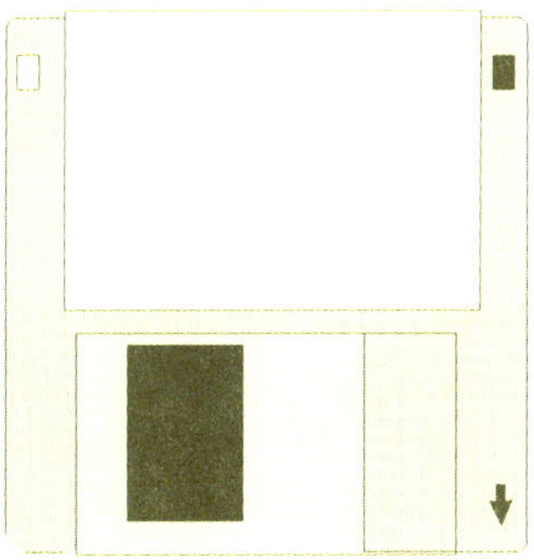

3.5-inch Floppy

5.25-inch Floppy

Typical Floppy Disks

Some new floppy drives accept both the 5.25-inch and the 3.5-inch floppies. These combo drives are great if you want to conserve space for other peripherals in your case. The drawback is that if one of the two drives breaks down you have to replace the entire unit.

Another property of floppy disk drives to consider is their density capabilities. The 3.5-inch floppies come in double density and holds 720 kilobytes. The 3.5-inch also comes in high density, which holds 1.44 megabytes. The new ultra high density 3.5-inch disks hold 2.88 megabytes.

A good floppy drive will give a noticeable click when the floppy slides into place inside the drive. The 3.5-inch floppy drives should have a eject button that propels the floppy out far enough to be easily removed.

Hard Disk Drive

The hard disk acts like library for software programs. The hard disk is where all the programs, documents, and goofy pictures of your cat you scanned in are stored. Hard disk sizes are measured in megabytes (Mb). Generally speaking, a bigger hard drive allows the computer to store more programs.

It is sort of an unwritten law that no matter how big your hard disk is it will somehow fill all the way up before you are ready to buy a new hard drive. Software programs these days keep getting bigger and bigger because they are packed with new features. To keep pace with today's software, the minimum recommended hard disk size is 300 megabytes. This may seem big at first, but with Windows NT, which is around 50 megabytes, and a few programs your disk will already be at capacity. Even if you just use Windows 3.1, a 15+ megabyte chunk is already taken from the hard drive.

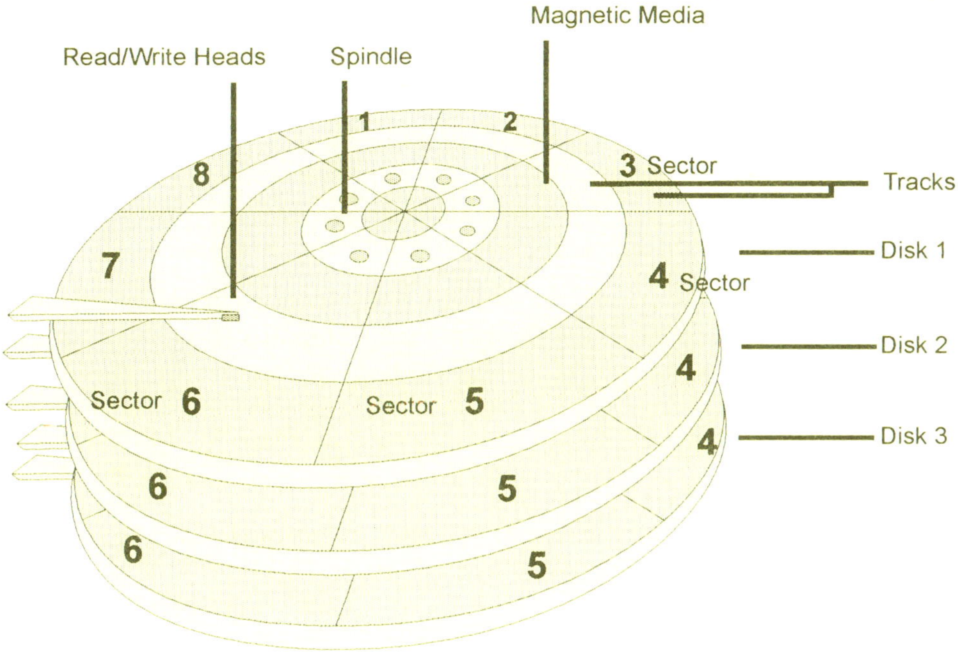

A Look Inside a Hard Drive

As a general rule, graphics programs are larger than most other programs. To estimate the hard disk space your computer will need, allocate 25 megabytes for each program you will use and then double the total megabytes, and add extra room for the operating system. An alternative way to estimate hard disk storage needed is to take the total amount of disk space actually required by the programs and multiply by 1.5 to get the minimum recommended hard disk capacity.

Remember when shopping for a hard drive that the formatted capacity of a drive is about 5 percent less than the advertised capacity of the drive. Data on a hard drive is stored in concentric tracks which are equally divided into sectors. The tracks and sectors do not physically exist, but their locations are marked when the hard disk is low-level formatted. To be used, a hard disk must then be high-level formatted by the operating system that will be used, like DOS or System 7. This second formatting contains information regarding the space where data is to be stored on the disk. The formatted area is used only by the operating system and is not made available for storing programs and documents. The space leftover after the formatting is done is the space available to store programs and data. Most hard drive vendors rate their drives at their unformatted capacity, allowing them to state the largest possible value. When you purchase a hard disk, ask if the stated hard disk capacity is the unformatted or formatted size.

Some advertisers are claiming larger capacity than the drives are rated. They do this by listing the capacity using software compression. It is a good idea not to use compression unless it is an unavoidable necessity, because compression slows the computer down and makes it harder to retrieve data on a damaged hard drive.

Hard disks are either external or internal to the computer system case. An **internal hard disk** is found in most computers. It sits inside the computer case and stores the programs you will need to use. An **external hard disk** is located in a self-contained case that is connected to your computer by a cable. These hard disks are not as common as internal hard disks but are often added as a second hard drive. The advantage of having an external hard disk is that they generally can be connected and disconnected in a simple manner. This means the hard disk can be reconnected to many different computers allowing quick access to the data on the drive.

Hard drives come in varying physical sizes. Their dimensions are measured by their height. **Standard height** drives are 3-inch, **half height** drives are 1.5-inch, and **third height** drives are 1-inch high. The diameters of the drives are usually 5.25-inch, 3.5-inch, or 2.5-inch. The smaller hard drives are usually found in portable computers. Hard disk capacities vary from a small 20 megabytes to 1 gigabyte (Gb) or larger. When you purchase a hard drive, ask about its formatted capacity. Sometimes the unformatted capacity is advertised, which is larger than the formatted capacity. Knowing the formatted capacity of a hard drive will allow you to figure out if the programs you intend to use and the data you will create will fit onto the disk.

Quantum 2 ½-inch hard disk

Hard disks have read and write heads flying over rapidly spinning platters of magnetic media. You normally never get to see these platters because they are sealed in a dust-free chamber which is placed inside the computer case. Hard disk platters are made of aluminum-nickel or chemically hardened glass. A new variety is made of glass-ceramic, which is stronger and stiffer than the aluminum-nickel disks. Glass-ceramic platters get their basic shape from glass upon which ceramic crystals are grown, making the disks stronger than ordinary glass disks.

Glass platter disks have several advantages over aluminum. Glass is more stable than aluminum, and that makes it more resistant to shock. If the drive happens to be dropped it has less chance of being damaged by coming in contact with the head. The glass is smoother than aluminum, allowing the read/write head to fly closer to the platter. This increases the amount of data that can fit onto the drive. Glass is stiffer than aluminum and therefore can be made thinner. This translates into reduced weight and height. The drawback is that glass platters are more expensive to produce than aluminum.

The hard disk platter is coated with a ferrite solution, most often barium ferrite. The magnetic media platters rotate inside at 3,600 rpm (revolutions per minute) or faster. This is known as the **spindle speed**. Newer technology drives spin at 5,600 rpm to 7,200 rpm. For disk-intensive applications like video or databases, a disk with a faster spindle rate is desirable because information can be written or read from these disks at faster rates.

There are different varieties of hard drive controllers to be considered. The hard disk controller is the circuitry that positions the heads on the drive to read or write information and transfers the information to and from the computer system. MFM, RLL, and ESDI drives are obsolete and should not be considered. The two main hard disk types in use are SCSI and IDE.

Today's hard drives have access times of 18 ms (milliseconds) or less. **Access time** is the time it takes the read heads in the hard disk to locate the information for which it is searching. Disks that spin faster place the needed information under the read-write head faster and therefore have faster access times. The access time is a combined factor of the **average seek time**, the time it takes to position the head over the specific track, and the **average latency**, the time it takes the drive to make one-half rotation. The **sustained data transfer rate** is the rate at which the hard disk can continuously read and write data. This rate should take access time, average latency, seek time, and real computing factors into account. The important types of hard drive controllers to consider are the **IDE** (Integrated Device Electronics) and the **SCSI** (Small Computer System Interface).

The **IDE** hard drives have the controller built right in to the hard drive so there is no need to buy an extra controller card. An IDE connection on the motherboard can control one or two drives but data can only be transferred to one drive at a time. An IDE drive is dependent on the computer's CPU to write and gather data from RAM. IDE drives are in about 80 percent of the PCs on the market. The controller sits between the computer and the hard drive and allows the two to communicate. This eliminates the need to buy an expensive hard drive controller card for inside the computer. All you need is an adapter card. Some IDE drives plug directly into the motherboard if the motherboard has the necessary connectors. IDE drives are cheap, durable, and usually have good access times, but their transfer rates peak at about 5 megabytes per second. If your hard disk needs are 500 megabytes or less, an IDE drive will do the trick.

Peak Peripheral Interface Transfer Rates

Disk Interface	*Megabytes Per Second*	*Disk Interface*	*Megabytes Per Second*
MFM (ST-506)	0.63	SCSI-2 (Fast)	10
RLL (ST-506)	0.94	SCSI-2 (16-bit, Wide)	10
ESDI (10 MHz)	1.25	SCSI-2 (16-bit, Fast-Wide)	20
ESDI (20 MHz)	2.5	SCSI-2 (32-bit, Wide)	20
IDE (8-bit)	4	SCSI-2 (32-bit, Fast-Wide)	40
IDE (16-bit)	8	SCSI-3 (16-bit)	20+
EISA (DMA)	13	SCSI-3 (32-bit)	40+
SCSI-1	5		

New enhanced IDE controllers will support up to four IDE drives and will offer additional support for CD-ROMs, SyQuest drives, scanners, and other peripherals. The enhanced IDE will increase the current IDE rate of 2 to 5.5 megabytes per second to a much faster 9 to 13 megabytes per second using local-bus. The enhanced IDE standard should be able to handle up to 8.4 gigabyte drives, which is much higher than the old 528 megabyte limit.

SCSI hard drives are great for larger drives, 500 megabytes or more. A SCSI (pronounced "scuzzy") controller can connect up to seven additional SCSI devices. Each of the devices is assigned an ID number selected from the range of 0 through 7 which allows data and instructions to be routed to the correct device. The SCSI ID numbers are usually set by switches or jumpers on each SCSI device, and the SCSI controller is usually defaulted the ID of 7. When more than one SCSI device tries to talk at the same time, the SCSI device with the higher assigned SCSI ID is given priority. Since the SCSI adapter gets SCSI ID 7, it is the boss. Hard disks on a SCSI chain are usually assigned number 0 for the first disk and number 1 for the second hard disk.

The SCSI device at each end of a SCSI chain must have a terminator attached to it. A terminator is an electrical resistor that keeps the impedance of the SCSI bus constant; in essence a terminator cancels electrical echoes so they do not confuse the SCSI controller. A SCSI controller can send or receive data from one device while another SCSI drive is reading or writing data. Many SCSI controllers have their own control chip which can make direct access to RAM. This direct access frees the computer's CPU to do other work while the SCSI controller handles transfer of data. SCSI hard drives generally have better access times (15 ms or better) and better transfer rates (up to 20 megabytes per second) than the IDE drives. SCSI drives are more expensive than IDE drives, and you also need an SCSI adapter card for the computer to interface with the drive. These controller cards are priced at $100 and up. The good side is, after you have an SCSI adapter card installed, you can connect up to seven devices—hard disks, tape drives, scanners, CD-ROMs—together in a daisy chain.

When buying SCSI devices, make sure they support SCSI parity to ensure that bad transmissions are caught and fixed. For SCSI parity to work, all devices on the SCSI chain must support parity checking. Good manufacturers of SCSI adapter cards are Always Technology, Trantor, and Corel Systems. Good manufactures of hard drives are Maxtor, Conner, and Seagate. If you plan on using more than one SCSI card in a computer, minimize the possibility of conflicts by using two of the same cards.

If you do go with SCSI, make sure it conforms with the newer SCSI-2 standard. It is more advanced than the older SCSI-1 specification, which only transferred 1.5 megabytes to 5 megabytes per second. SCSI-2 will allow data transfer of 10 megabytes to 40 megabytes per second. SCSI-2 speeds up the flow of data and clears up some incompatibility problems that were inherent with SCSI-1. Devices that are SCSI-1 can be hooked up to a SCSI-2 chain as long as you use the right drivers.

The host adapter must follow either the ASPI (Advanced SCSI Programming Interface) or ANSI CAM (Common Access Method) standard for SCSI software interface. These two standards cannot be mixed. The ASPI standard allows different devices to communicate better with one another.

A SCSI controller can have an 8-bit or 16-bit ISA interface, a 16-bit or 32-bit EISA interface, or a super fast 32-bit or 64-bit PCI or VL-Bus interface. **Fast SCSI-2** can achieve a data throughput of up to 10 megabytes per second over an 8-bit (narrow SCSI) or 20 megabytes per second over a 16-bit data path, and for a 32-bit path it supports 40 megabytes per second. This is twice the speed of SCSI-1. Wide SCSI-2 can transfer 20 megabytes to 40 megabytes per second over a 16-bit (half wide) or 32-bit (full wide) interface. The best SCSI cards have on-board caches and are bus mastering. Some SCSI adapters contain a boot ROM allowing you to boot from an attached device. Floppy drive controllers are found integrated on some SCSI cards.

SCSI-3 allows for fiber optic media, which can transfer data over longer distances. In addition to longer cables, SCSI-3 allows for more devices to be chained together. SCSI-3 allows up to 256 devices to be linked together, a great improvement over SCSI-2. SCSI-2 limits the overall cable length of the SCSI devices to 19 feet 10 inches. For the best results keep the cables as short as possible.

It is important to know the **MTBF** (Mean Time Between Failure) rating for a hard drive. Since hard drives have moving parts they are prone to breaking down at a indefinite time in the future. The MTFB is the average number of hours before the disk will have a serious problem; the higher the MTBF the better. IDE drives are rated up to 250,000 hours, while some SCSI drives have MTBF ratings of 750,000 hours or better. Another way to find out how long the drive will last is to inquire about the hard disk's warranty. This is a representation of confidence in the product. The warranties generally range from one year to five years.

Most hard drives have a built-in **buffers**, and the fastest drives are usually those with the biggest buffers. Buffer sizes range from 64 kilobyte to 512 kilobyte. This buffer will read ahead of the data requested by the operating system. The assumption is the data in the buffer will be the information the operating system needs next. A **segmented buffer** divides the cache into smaller sections in order to store information from multiple reads. **Adaptive segmented buffering** is a better method which allows the drive to change the size and number of these cache buffers to optimize data retrieval.

If the applications you will be using are disk intensive, like databases or video editing, it may be invaluable to add a **hard disk caching controller** to speed up information retrieval. These expansion cards usually house one to several megabytes of RAM. They operate on a cache type of theory and can make access time as quick as 0.3 ms. Now that is almost faster than Speed Racer. A caching controller is a great way to increase system performance.

The cost of hard drives on a per megabyte basis is usually between $1.50 and $3. Smaller hard disks cost more per megabyte than the larger disks. Bigger hard disks have a kind of economy of scale where the cost of the last few added megabytes is less than the initial megabytes.

In cases where data loss is extremely risky, a Redundant Array of Inexpensive Disks (RAID) is an intelligent answer. A RAID is essentially a bunch of hard disks working together in one computer system. RAIDs are used in multimedia or networking applications and can ensure the integrity of valuable data. There are different levels of RAID used for different situations. **RAID 0** is not really a redundant form of storing data. The files are spread across disks and allow fast access. **RAID 1** uses two disks and mirrors the data. The exact same information is written on each disk. If one disk stops working, the data can be accessed from the other disk. This is the most widely used form of RAID but also the most inefficient form. **RAID 3** uses two or more disks. If one of the disks fails, the data can be recovered from the other disks. This RAID method provides the fastest access to data and therefore is commonly used in CAD and multimedia. **RAID 5** uses two or more drives and has parity information spread across all drives. RAID 5 is slower than RAID 3 but lost information is restored faster.

I/O Ports

When you buy a stereo receiver there are connectors on the back of the unit for hooking up a cassette deck, CD player, and speakers via cables. The I/O ports (Input/Output) serve the purpose of providing connectors to hook up the computer to its peripherals. The I/O card usually fits in one of the motherboard expansion slots and provides the ports on the back of the computer.

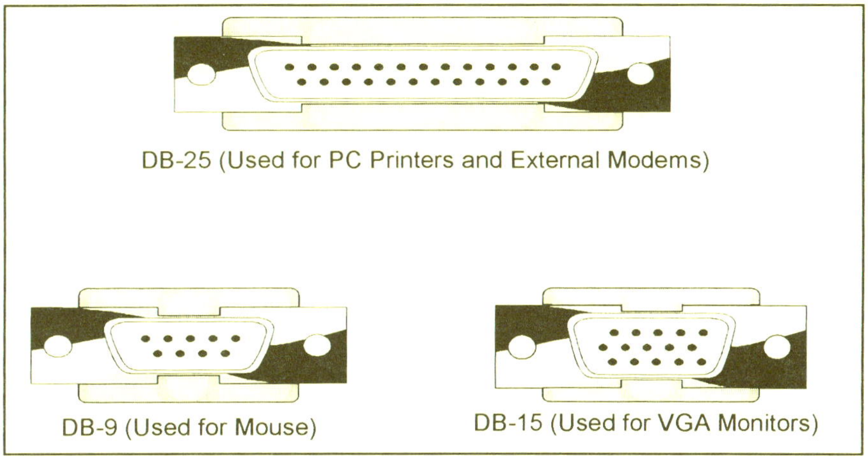

A Look at Common Cable Connectors

On some computers the I/O ports are integrated into the motherboard itself, which frees up an extra expansion slot for other uses. The Centronics **parallel port**, which usually has 25 pinholes, is where a printer is connected. The normal parallel port is slow, from 50 kilobits per second to 100 KBps. An Extended Capabilities Port (ECP), also known as IEEE 1284, operates bi-directional at 2.4 megabits per second. Printers that are ECP enabled are able to receive data at much faster rates from your computer. Older printers can receive data from an ECP-enabled computer at 500 KBps. That is four times the data rate. Windows 95 includes drivers for this enhanced port.

Microsoft and Hewlett-Packard are at work designing a faster bi-directional parallel port. The new parallel port will be capable of data transfers up to 10 Mbps (megabytes per second), a substantial jump over today's transfer rate of 2.4 megabits per second.

The **serial port** consists of either 8, 9, or 25 pinholes and is where the mouse and modems can be plugged in. It is sometimes called the Reference Standard number 232 revision c (RS-232c) serial port. It is widely used and is closely related to the CCITT V.24 standard, but only permits transfer of 50 feet (15.25 meters) or less. RS-423, another variety of serial port, allows data transfer over distances up to 1,000 feet (305 meters). This is an asynchronous communication signal meaning, unlike most of the computer, it does not conform to a clocking signal.

A serial port transmits data in a single file line, but the computer processes data in parallel. Processing in parallel is comparable to a marching band that is 16 or 32 people wide, and serial data is like a marching band in a single file line.

The **keyboard connector** is often round with 5 pinholes. Some IBM computers use a PS/2 connector for the keyboard. The **video connector** which attaches the computer to the monitor has 9 or 15 pinholes.

A computer system should have at least one parallel port and two serial ports: a parallel port for a printer, one serial port for a mouse, and another serial port for an external modem. If you wish to use a joystick for games it will need a game port. Many sound cards include a game port. The standard port configuration that most computers come with is two serial, one parallel, and one game port.

The **PCMCIA** (Personal Computer Memory Card Industry Association) is another connection specification that is becoming popular. It is a small 68-pin slot that connects the bus to tiny credit card-sized peripherals like fax-modems, hard drives, SCSI ports, and network connectors. It has a raw transfer rate of up to 8 megabytes per second. Its first use was with portable computers but can now be found on some desktop models. To ensure compatibility, make sure the slot is a PCMCIA release 2 standard so the devices you use will be easily interchanged. With a PCMCIA port on a desktop computer you could pop out the hard disk in your office computer and connect it to a

PCMCIA slot on your portable computer. This means no more time-consuming file transfers between your portable and desktop computers.

For ease of use the PCMCIA slot should probably be located on the front of the computer case so you can swap cards effortlessly with your portable computer. The PCMCIA card can be inserted or removed with the computer's power on without damaging your computer or the card; this is known as *hot swapping*.

There are also two PCMCIA technical standards. Release 1.0 came out in 1990 and made standards for flash RAM, static RAM, and EPROM memory cards. Release 2.0 was set up in 1991 and is backwardly compatible with the prior standard. Release 2.0 makes standards for modems, faxes, and network adapters. Additionally the Execute In Place (XIP) specification lets applications and operating systems run directly on the card instead of first being loaded into the system RAM.

PCMCIA Card Standards

PCMCIA Type	Type I	Type II	Type III
Connector	68-pin	68-pin	68-pin
Width	54 mm	54 mm	54 mm
Height	85.6 mm	85.6 mm	85.6 mm
Thickness	3.3 mm	5.0 mm	10.5 mm
Typical Uses	Flash memory, RAM, EEPROM, programmable memory	LAN adapter, modem, I/O device	Removable mass storage, memory upgrades, radio communication device

Chapter 4

Power Supply and Case

Power Supply

The computer power supply needs to produce enough wattage to run your system, and not all computers draw the same amount of power. A computer that is used for a file server that contains many hard drives and network cards needs a bigger power supply than a home computer that sports only one hard drive. Most computer power supplies range in power from 200 watts to 300 watts, although the power supplies in file servers can be closer to 900 watts.

A power supply usually works best when providing 25 to 75 percent of its maximum capacity. With the growing supply of the lower power consumption 3.3-volt computer products, the power requirements of computers will drop to about half when compared to the 5-volt systems that are currently being sold.

When purchasing a computer system, find out how many power connectors there are coming off the power supply for future upgrades. If you need to add a hard disk, tape backup, and CD-ROM, the system will need extra power connectors. If the power supply does not have extra power connectors, a Y-cable can be used to split the power to feed more devices.

Most power supplies house a fan that has the job of keeping the computer system cool. In the standard computer setup the fan blows air out of the case, producing a slight vacuum inside the computer case. Air in the case is replaced by leaking through the holes and vents in the case. If the computer is to be used in a harsh environment with a lot of smoke or airborne particles, a forced air fan is recommended to prevent damage to the computer. Forced air systems have filtered air sucked into the case which then leaks out through vents and crevices. The fan's filter has to be changed when it gets dirty, but that is fairly easy to do.

If international travel is in your future you will want to know if your computer has universal, frequency independent, or frequency dependent power requirements. Products equipped with **universal power supplies** can be used internationally without major changes. They can accept a range of voltages and frequencies and only need a plug adapter to work at their destination. Some equipment containing a universal power supply requires a switch to be manually toggled to adjust to the specific locale, while other power supplies are autoswitching—you just plug them in and they adjust automatically.

Frequency independent gear can be used internationally but requires a voltage transformer. If you buy a 120-volt computer and want to use it in Europe, you will need a step-down isolation transformer to adapt the voltage, plus a plug adapter, unless the transformer has one already. When buying a transformer make sure it provides a third prong for ground, and the wattage it provides should equal 150 percent of the total wattage the products will draw. For example, if the computer's power draws 200 watts, get a transformer that handles at least 300 watts.

Frequency dependent products cannot be used internationally unless the target country uses the same frequency as the country of origin. This is due to the fact that transformers only change the power voltage and not the frequency. If your gear contains a frequency dependent power supply, you may want to have the power supply replaced if that is an option.

The Case

Computer cases come in a variety of styles, shapes, sizes, and colors. The usual color is a kind of eggshell white but there are now cases that come in practically all shades of the rainbow. If you are a purple lover or need everything black to match the room's decor, with a little footwork you should be able to find the case of your dreams. Computer cases sit either horizontally on your **desktop** or vertically on the floor, which is called a **tower** case. The desktop case sizes are AT, baby AT, or slim-line.

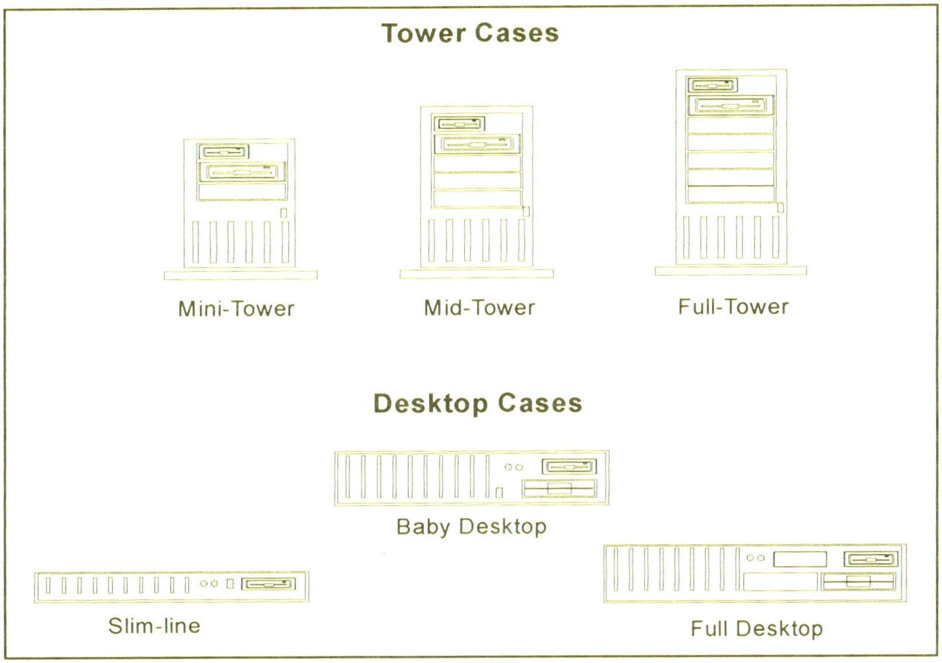

A Look at Computer Cases

The case footprint is the amount of space it takes up on the desktop. The smallest cases are called slim-lines and are about two inches high and about as big as a notebook. Slim-lines leave little room for expandability. There is not much space to add hard disks, expansion boards, or CD-ROMs. Avoid buying a small footprint computer case unless it is absolutely essential, because a slim-line has extreme limitations for future upgrades.

A baby AT case has more room for expansion but not as much as a regular AT case.

Tower cases come in super-tower, full-tower, mid-tower, and mini-tower. Tower systems free up valuable desktop space and leave plenty of room for expandability. A mid-tower is good enough for most regular users, but a power user might want a full-tower case. Super-tower cases are primarily used for network servers, computers that are accessed by other computers linked together on a computer network.

A bay in the computer case is a holding area for items that are attached to your computer. A bay is like a garage for floppy drives, hard drives, tape drives, and other devices. Note the total number of bays in the case including the bays already filled and the number of unfilled bays in the computer case. Some bays are accessible from the front and usually hold floppy drives, CD-ROMs, and tape drives. Other bays are internal to the case and often hold hard disk drives.

Most cases have a small display on the front that shows the CPU's operating speed in megahertz. Cases also need an on-off power switch plus a light to indicate the power is on. Make sure the power and reset buttons are spaced far away from the floppy drive eject button. This will prevent the computer from accidentally being turned off. Some cases have covers that protect the power and reset buttons. This is great for tower cases because they can be near the foot area. Without a cover, if you move a foot in the wrong direction the computer could accidentally be turned off. Often there is a light indicating that the hard drive is being accessed. The keyboard lock on cases prevents the keyboard from being used. Sometimes a keyboard port is included on the front of the case to plug in the keyboard. This plug allows the keyboard cable to easily reach the case depending on whether the case will be placed on the tabletop or on the floor.

Most people think of turbo as a way to make things go faster, but here is what it really means: some computer cases provide a "turbo" switch that toggles the system from its normal speed to a slower speed. The slower speed is infrequently needed to make some older programs run correctly. The programs that need some slowing down were written when the slower speeds were the standard and the high-speed computers of today are too fast for them.

Open the computer case and make sure the CPU is in line with ventilation holes which keep cooler air circulating over it. The case should have plenty of these ventilation holes for ample air circulation. The CPU should not be obstructed by an expansion card or disk drive or it may overheat. The case should contain a support bar that crosses the middle for extra structural stability. Try pushing the case with your hand near the floppy drive bays. If the case flexes too much or bends out of shape, it is cheaply made. Look at the quality of the paint on the case. It is no fun to have a case with paint chips falling off. Inspect the edges of the case. Cheap cases have straight edges which are prone to cutting hands with their sharp edges. The better cases have rolled-over edges which makes them safer and stronger. Every time a floppy disk is put in the case it puts wear and tear on the case, and with a flimsy case this could cause damage to the drive bays. Look at the motherboard. It should be attached to the case with three or more metal screws. Bigger motherboards need at least four screws. All the power cables that lead from the motherboard to the power supply should be neatly aligned. Make sure the case has enough room for expansion cards to stand upright and unimpeded. If there are cards installed they should be spaced apart to allow a cooler air flow to the circuitry.

Opening the case is something everybody eventually has to do. Some cases offer easier access to the inside of the case. Thumbscrews alleviate the need for screwdrivers when opening the case, but they do not necessarily make opening the case easier.

Chapter 5

The Display

The Monitor

The monitor (also called a display, or cathode-ray tube) is an important and integral part of a computer system. The monitor is your port into the world of computers. When buying a stereo you are supposed to pay close attention to the quality of the speakers, and when you buy a computer it is wise to pay close attention to the quality of the monitor. This notion holds especially true if the monitor is going to be in your face most of the day.

Monitors are available in **monochrome**, which means only one color is displayed, generally amber, green, or white, with a black background. A **paper white** monitor is a screen that has black text on a white background. Monitors also come in **grayscale**, and this mode presents various intensities of the same color to give the appearance of different shades on the screen. Grayscale monitors usually can present 16 or 256 shades on the screen including black and white. Color monitors are available which are capable of displaying from 16 colors to 16.7 million colors. If you are unsure whether you need a color or grayscale screen, get a color one. When you bought a television, did you buy a black-and-white or a color TV?

Monitor **sizes** vary from a small 9-inch to large 21-inch screen. The standard size that most people buy is a 14-inch monitor. The screen measurement is made by calculating the diagonal length of the screen. The actual measurement of the active screen, the area that shows the image, is somewhat shorter. The diagonal measurement published by the manufacturer often includes the glass that is covered by the plastic bezel frame that surrounds the screen.

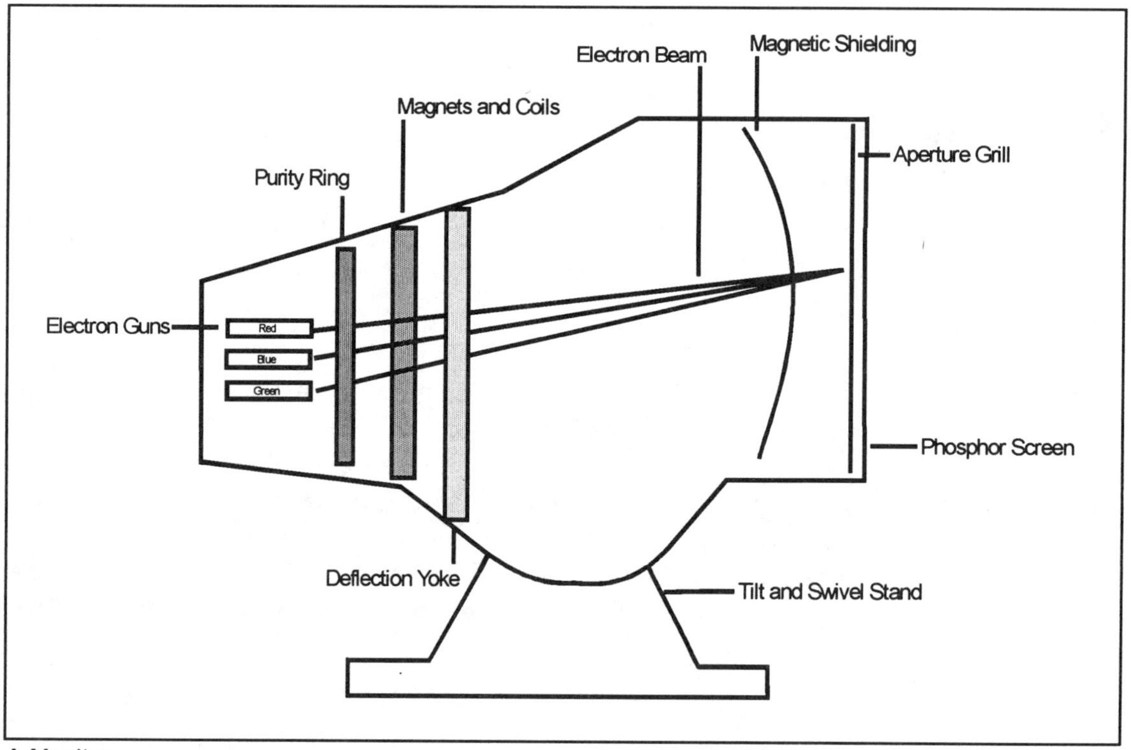

A Monitor

The average active screen size of a 14-inch monitor is really closer to 13 inches to 13.8 inches when measuring the exposed screen. For 15-inch monitors the exposed screen size ranges from 13.4 inches to 14.2 inches on the average. On some screens the picture does not even cover the total part of the screen that shows. There often is a black border between the viewable image and the plastic bezel at the screen's edge, but this usually can be eliminated by using the sizing and centering controls. The best way to find how the screen is measured is to go see for yourself. Monitors whose viewable image fills the whole screen without a black border are called edge-to-edge displays.

A 14-inch monitor can effectively be worked to handle most basic computing, but a larger screen can show more detail and more image. Larger screen sizes give greater visibility, especially if you need to do full page editing or are working with big spreadsheets or graphic programs. If you are using page layout, spreadsheet, or graphics programs, the extra cost of a 19-inch, 20-inch, or 21-inch monitor pays off in saved time and frustration. To edit a page on a 14-inch monitor, the page has to be scrolled up and down to edit. To see a full page the image must be shrunk to fit on the screen, and this leaves the type too small to read. A 21-inch monitor is a wonderful thing to have if you are using it for computer-aided design, computer-aided engineering, mapping, animation, imaging, and multimedia. Some of these big monitors offer BNC connectors which provide a separate shielded connection for each of the primary colors—red, blue, and green—and separate signal wires for horizontal and vertical sync signals. This provides for less distortion of the video signal in comparison to the widely used DB-15 connector.

Monitor Size and Recommended Resolutions For Display

Resolution	14-inch	15-inch	17-inch	19-inch	21-inch
640 by 480	Great	Great	Good	Poor	Poor
800 by 600	Good	Great	Good	Marginal	Marginal
1024 by 768	Poor	Poor	Great	Great	Good
1280 by 1024	Poor	Poor	Poor	Good	Great

The screen size and resolution of the image must be matched for the best results. Higher resolutions place more information on the screen. VGA resolution is 640 vertical lines by 480 columns. SVGA is a higher resolution that offers 800 by 600 lines. For a VGA display a 14-inch monitor is the minimum recommended size. For SVGA the minimum recommended size is 15 inches which offers about 20 percent more screen space than a 14-inch monitor. With a 15-inch display you should be able to show about 30 percent more rows and columns in a spreadsheet or another paragraph in a word processor than a 14-inch monitor. For a higher resolution display a 17-inch monitor is the minimum recommended size. This provides about 40 to 65 percent more screen space than a 14-inch monitor. Bigger screens display larger type that is easier to read and reduces the amount of scrolling needed to move the text around on the screen. Bigger screens are also great for running more than one application simultaneously side by side.

Some monitors will pivot from portrait mode to landscape mode. You could get the same effect if you took a TV and turned it on its side and then adjusted the picture to be displayed upright. In **portrait mode** the screen is taller than it is wide—this is the position paper is viewed from when writing a letter. In **landscape mode** the screen is wider than it is tall, like turning a piece of paper 90 degrees sideways. A few monitors are available that only display in portrait mode, which would be good for a user who only works with text, but most screens are fixed in landscape mode.

Forcing a 14-inch screen to display a high resolution such as 1,280 by 1,024 will force the pixel spacing below the screen's dot pitch, resulting in a fuzzy picture. To show 1,024 by 768 on a 14-inch monitor the dot pitch would have to be less than .25 mm and everything would appear very, very tiny. The usual accepted minimum screen size for a resolution of 1,024 by 768 is 17 inches. For resolutions of 1,280 by 1,024 the screen size should be 19 inches or bigger. Although 19- and 21-inch screens are often called two page screens, this is a misnomer. A 19-inch monitor can effectively display an area of 1,024 by 768 pixels. This is about two inches short on each side and an inch short on the top. The 21-inch screens usually display 1,152 by 870 pixels, which is short about an inch on each side.

Maximum Recommended Dot Pitch For Each Resolution

Monitor Size	*640 x 480*	*800 x 600*	*1024 x 768*	*1280 x 1024*
14-inch	0.31	0.28	0.22	0.18
15-inch	0.31	0.3	0.24	0.19
17-inch	0.35	0.31	0.27	0.22
20-inch	0.35	0.35	0.31	0.25

Monitors come with a power cord which is plugged into a wall outlet or into an outlet in the back of the computer case. Monitors usually have a 9-pin or 15-pin data cable that connects to the video adapter at the rear of your computer. This cable sends the image information from the computer to the monitor.

The **video adapter** communicates the graphical information from the computer in a format that can be shown on the monitor. The great painter George Seurat, who was a pioneer of the style of painting known as pointillism, used tiny dots of paint that when viewed up close just appeared as random spots of color, but when viewed at a distance came together to form scenes of people in parks or other subjects. The video monitor uses dots called pixels to create images (with the exception of Trinitron monitors which use vertical phosphor stripes). In color monitors there are three different colored phosphors that are red, blue, and green arranged in triads. These triad groupings are known as **pixels**, which is short for picture element. The **dot pitch** (aperture pitch for Sony Trinitron) represents the proximity of the phosphor dot to its nearest neighbor of the same color and is measured in millimeters. Sony Trinitron monitors have stripes of phosphors, and the distance between each like-colored stripe is called the **aperture pitch**. The smaller the dot pitch, the sharper the image will be. The video display should have a dot pitch of no greater than 0.31 mm. Any greater and the picture will seem fuzzy.

Inside a monitor is a gun that shoots an electron beam at the phosphors. Monochrome monitors use one gun and fire at phosphors that glow one color. Color monitors usually have three electron guns, one for green phosphors, one for red phosphors, and one for blue phosphors. To paint the screen, the electron gun starts at the top row and works its way down. This is done similarly to the way you are reading this page. The screens with short persistence phosphors require a faster redraw than a screen with long persistence phosphors. If the pixels are not refreshed quickly enough the screen will appear to flash on and off. This flicker causes eyestrain and headaches.

The inside face of the display screen is coated with thousands of tiny **phosphor** dots. These dots are categorized by their persistence, the length of time they glow before fading away. The phosphor ratings are those with long, medium-long, medium, medium-short, and short persistence. The older monitors that displayed only one color had medium-long persistence phosphors, causing them to glow for a while after the monitor's electron beam hit them. If the image on the monitor changed there would be a ghosting of the previous image left on the screen. To avoid the ghosting of images, monitors made now use medium-short persistence phosphors. As phosphors degrade over time they become dimmer. If you use a screen saver program it is best to use a dark screen saver to prolong the monitor's life. If you are leaving your monitor for a break, turn it off to save the phosphorus life and to conserve electricity.

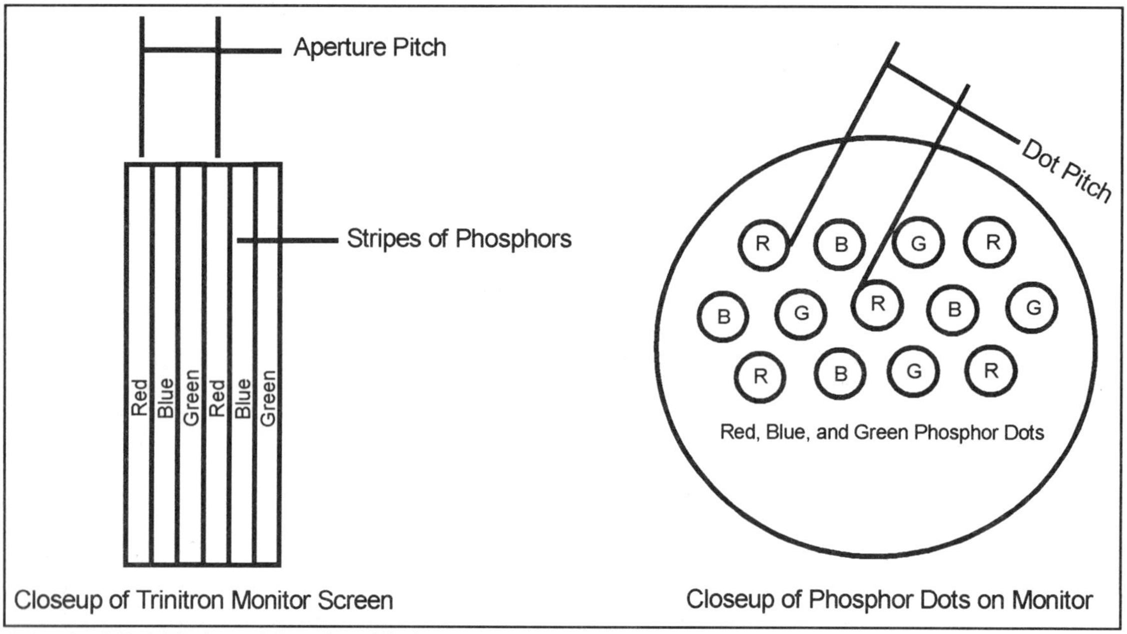

A Look at Dot Pitch and Aperture Pitch

To guide the electron guns so they focus on only one phosphor dot at a time there is a metallic foil that has tiny holes or stripes called a shadow mask. The shadow mask prevents the surrounding phosphors from being hit by a stray electron. The shadow mask must be able to withstand the heat created by the electron beam. The better ones are made out of Invar, which has a good heat resistance.

The number of pixels on a monitor is called the **resolution**. The **pixel** is a small unit of the display that can be turned on or off or can display a color on a color monitor. A monitor with many pixels is capable of showing high-resolution images. The resolution for a **SuperVGA** (Video Graphics Array) is 800 by

600. The first number is the amount of pixels horizontally across the screen (left to right) and the latter number is the amount of pixels vertically down (top to bottom) the screen. Therefore the total number of pixels on a SuperVGA screen is 480,000. The higher the graphic resolution the crisper the picture. For **VGA** text resolution, 600 by 480, use a dot pitch of 0.31 mm. For SuperVGA graphics resolution of 800 by 600 or **Extended SuperVGA**'s 1,024 by 768 resolution, use a dot pitch of 0.28. For the resolutions of 1,024 by 768 or greater, use a 0.26 mm dot pitch.

To find the maximum resolution of a monitor within about 15 percent accuracy, multiply the monitor's diagonal measurement by 20, then divide the result by the dot pitch. A 20-inch monitor with a .28 dot pitch should be able to display a resolution of about 1,428 by 1,428: (20 x 20)/ .28 = 1,428.57

The dot pitch is tied to contrast and brightness in a monitor. Contrast is the difference between the dark and light areas of the screen. The brighter the white, the greater the contrast of the monitor. A smaller dot pitch means a smaller opening in the shadow mask is used. The smaller opening allows fewer electrons to land on the phosphors, thereby reducing the total contrast of the monitor. Turning up the brightness will only compensate to a fixed degree before overcompensating, which makes the pixels bleed and the image distort.

As the resolution of a screen is increased you can see more of the spreadsheet or letter you are writing, but the size of the image on the screen becomes smaller. Let's pretend you are using a 14-inch screen to view the letter "M", which measures half an inch tall in 640 by 480 resolution. If you double the resolution on the screen the letter "M" will now appear a quarter of an inch tall. Everything on the screen is now twice as close together as before. If you take this same resolution and apply it to a bigger screen, say a 17-inch screen, everything on the screen will appear bigger again. It is like stretching the image back out. Compare the screen image to having a balloon with the word "Paradise" written on it. Before the balloon is blown up the writing may be too small to read, but when the balloon is filled with air the word is clearly visible.

The monitor is repainted, or scanned, several times a second. One type of scanning called **interlaced** occurs when the frame is repainted, that is, refreshed by scanning the screen with two passes. On the first pass the even lines are refreshed and on the second pass the odd lines are refreshed. This method can cause a screen flicker that is bothersome to the eyes. With the preferred method, called **non-interlaced**, every line on the screen is refreshed in one pass. To compare, the way you read a book is non-interlaced. If you read every odd line on the page and then every even line, this would be called interlaced reading.

The **vertical refresh rate** (also called the vertical scanning frequency, vertical frequency, vertical scan rate, or scan rate) is the number of times each second the electron beam in the monitor can repaint the screen and is measured in cycles per second, or hertz (Hz). A monitor with a 72 Hz vertical refresh rate is repainted 72 times a second, so the vertical refresh rate should be 72 Hz or faster. Slower than that and you are likely to have unwanted screen flicker which over extended periods of time can be annoying and lead to eyestrain. Screen flicker is most easily seen on a white screen while looking off to the side of the monitor. A buying hint: Make sure the refresh rate of the monitor corresponds with the resolution you will be using most of the time. The refresh rate of monitors often changes when showing a different resolution.

Minimum Recommended
Vertical Refresh Rate for Monitors

Screen Resolution	VESA Standard
640 x 480	72 Hz
800 x 600	72 Hz
1024 x 768	70 Hz
1280 x 1024	70 Hz

The **horizontal refresh rate** (also called the horizontal frequency or horizontal scanning frequency) is closely related to the vertical refresh rate. It is the amount of time it takes the monitor to draw just one line. The horizontal refresh rate is measured in megahertz (MHz). If you use a higher vertical refresh rate the horizontal refresh rate will have to be higher. The vertical refresh rate is the horizontal refresh multiplied by the number of horizontal lines plus a small amount of time for the electron beam to get from the bottom right of the screen to the top left so the beam can start drawing again.

A helpful analogy to refresh rates is comparing the amount of time a typist takes to type one line (horizontal refresh rate) and the time it takes to type a whole page (vertical refresh rate).

Decide what resolution you want to display and then make sure the monitor you buy will be able to show the fastest vertical refresh rate that the video adapter card can output. This will ensure you get the least amount of screen flicker. Make sure the monitor can handle the highest bandwidth that your video card will output so the image will be as sharp as it can be. Bandwidth is the total information transferred from one point to another, or a measure of how many pixels can be painted onto a screen in one second. VGA monitors typically have a bandwidth in the range of 25 to 28 MHz.

Video Bandwidth

Display Mode	*Minimum Recommended Bandwidth For Monitor*
VGA 640 x 480	30 MHz
SVGA 800 x 600	60 MHz
EVGA 1024 x 768	90 MHz
1280 x 1024	147 MHz

Multifrequency (also called multiscanning or multisync) monitors allow great flexibility due to their ability show many different screen resolutions. As the resolution increases so does the scanning rate. A multifrequency monitor detects when the scan rate changes and adjusts the frequency accordingly. **Fixed-frequency multiscanning** monitors are capable of displaying signals from a video card that sends frequencies in the monitor's specific range. For example, a monitor that can display vertical scanning rates of 62 Hz, 70 Hz, and 72 Hz requires a video card that will send signals with these scan rates. A **variable-frequency multiscanning** monitor is one that will support a video display of several different resolutions within a given range such as 60 Hz to 90 Hz. Variable-frequency monitors are better equipped to accept future video card upgrades. Some of the better multifrequency monitors automatically adjust the sizing and centering positions of the picture on the screen when you change resolutions to get the best screen image.

It takes a certain amount of data to describe to the monitor what it should display. It takes one bit of information to describe if a pixel should be on or off. This is how a monochrome monitor operates. To display four colors it takes two bits of information per pixel. For sixteen colors it takes four bits per pixel.

The **bandwidth** of a monitor affects how effectively the monitor can display the image that is fed to it. Bandwidth is a measurement of how much information the electron beam is capable of handling. It indicates the amount and speed of information that the monitor is capable of handling. The image quality deteriorates if a monitor tries to show a signal that exceeds its bandwidth. The bandwidth is measured in megahertz, and a higher rating is better. Typical bandwidths fall between 35 MHz and 130 MHz. To find an estimate of bandwidth, multiply the number of pixels displayed by the vertical scan rate and add 50 percent more to the result for head room.

For example, at VGA mode 640 by 480 pixels multiplied by a 72 Hz vertical refresh rate times 1.5 calls for a bandwidth of 33.2 MHz. For a SVGA 800 by 600 display with a 72-Hz vertical refresh rate you need a minimum of 51.8 MHz bandwidth. A 1024 by 768 with a 70-Hz vertical refresh rate requires a 97.1 MHz minimum bandwidth. To be on the safe side the minimum bandwidth should be doubled for a good display because response falls off at higher frequencies.

The entry level VGA supports graphics in 16 colors at a resolution of 640 by 480. Today's prices on SuperVGA are so competitive it is strongly recommended you buy one for basic computing needs. To be able to position the monitor, it is a good idea to have a monitor that features a **tilt and swivel base**.

That way the screen can be turned side to side or up and down for the optimal viewing position.

Another feature to consider is **edge to edge image** display. Some monitors leave black edges of unused screen space and by doing so effectively reduce the screen real estate. Some monitors require manual screen sizing and adjustments. Other monitors have auto-sizing and auto-centering of the screen image for optimal viewing. The monitors that do are usually higher priced, so if you want the best get ready to shell out a little extra.

The shape of a monitor can affect the picture quality. Traditional monitors are bubble-shaped as if they were cut from a large globe. This is not the best for artists who need see straight lines drawn on the surface of the monitor. This curved surface also reflects the most glare because light from any angle will be reflected off the screen and onto your face. Sony Trinitron tubes are curved on the horizontal axis and straight on the vertical axis. They appear to be cut from a cylinder. Newer picture tubes are called flat-square, and although they are not completely flat they are considerably better than their predecessors.

If the monitor does not have automatic adjustment make sure the front mounted control panel has **vertical size and position adjustments** and **horizontal size and position adjustments**. The better monitors have digital controls instead of analog controls. The digital controls can let you save specific settings that will be needed when changing resolutions. If you plan to switch from DOS to Windows and back again often, you will want a display with automatic sizing and centering to take care of adjusting the screen every time to gain a maximized viewing area.

Monitor control panels can be found recessed, in the open, in a compartment, or hidden on the side or even the back of the monitor. Adjusting controls on the back can be a pleasant experience if you are a yoga master; otherwise get them on the front. To extend the life of the monitor look for a **degaussing** switch. By pressing this button once a month you will dissipate magnetic buildup that accumulates in the monitor. Degaussing will also remove color distortions that occur with magnetic buildup.

A microprocessor controlled monitor, also known as a digitally controlled monitor, is able to tell when the video mode has changed. When the mode changes it will adjust the image on the screen automatically. This is great for someone who changes resolutions often because it eliminates the need to fuss with the sizing and centering controls every time the screen resolution is changed. Some units allow the adjustments the monitor makes to be set by the user; other monitors have factory preset values.

For those of you who are health-conscious about VLF (Very Low Frequency) and ELF (Extremely Low Frequency), there are low-radiation emission monitors out there that will meet the stringent Swedish SWEDAC low emissions standard. The **Swedish Board for Technical Accreditation or SWEDAC** (formerly MPR II) standards allow for 2.5 milliGauss (a unit of measure of magnetic field intensity) for ELF fields and 0.25 milliGauss VLF fields at 20 inches from the monitor. Note that the earlier MPR I standard did not account for ELF emissions. An even more stringent standard than the Swedish MPR II is the TCO standard. **TCO** allows only 2 milliGauss at 12 inches for ELF fields. Companies selling these monitors include Compaq, IBM, Nanao, NEC, Wyse, and Sony. At this writing the lowest emission monitor on the market is the Ultra 7000 from Safe Technologies Corp. At 20 inches it emits only 0.55 milliGauss ELF and 0.008 milliGauss VLF radiation.

Due to uncontrollable ambient light there can be unwanted glare on the computer screen. Ambient light is caused by the light streaming through the window or from the fluorescent lights on the ceiling, or any other light source. For those of you who plan to spend a great amount time in front of the monitor it is recommended that the one you chose has **glare reduction**. This is an extremely important feature because glare reduction can reduce eyestrain and improve image quality. The drawback to glare reduction is that although it reduces strong reflections on the screen it also cuts down on the amount of light emitted from the monitor. It is good to have a monitor with a brightness control that will compensate for this loss of light due to glare reduction methods. A luminance level of 15 foot-lamberts (fl) is the minimum acceptable brightness for a good monitor.

Some of the best monitors now have **color correction** to correct the luminescence, white point, and gamma of a monitor. Color correction is an important feature for people who work with color output, like desktop publishers and graphic artists. Color correction is essential if the color on your screen needs to be close in hue and saturation to the color the printer produces. Most color correctors base their standards on CIE XYZ color space, which was developed in the 1930s by the Commission International de l'Eclairage (CIE).

Monitors and printers use different methods to produce color. Monitors use the additive color method which has three colors (red, blue, and green) blended together to produce the spectrum of colors. Printers use the color subtractive method in which dyes and pigments are used (Cyan, Yellow, Magenta, Black) to absorb or reflect different colors. To achieve color correction the monitor must have controls for adjusting the intensity of the red, green, and blue pixels and for storing different color settings. Monitors generally need to be recalibrated every month or so because of phosphor degradation, electronic component drift, and other age-related changes that affect the monitor.

Remember that external factors affect the color on the screen. The color of the room will skew the perception of color on the screen, as will the lighting in the room. Incandescent bulbs cast a yellowish to orange light, and halogens cast a bluish light. The truest light is fluorescent light, but these lights flicker at 60 Hz. The best setup for accurate color manipulation would be to work in a black room without lights or windows, and for checking printed output you want a pure white painted room with fluorescent lighting.

Luminescence is the brightness of the screen, and this can vary from point to point on the same monitor. Adjusting the luminescence with a calibrator to the right balance will ensure the monitor has the most accurate level of brightness. The white point is the monitor's color temperature when each input of red, blue, and green is at the maximum voltage level. The white point is measured in degrees Kelvin and is referenced to other light sources. Most graphic artists work with 5,000°K light, the same intensity as natural daylight. Most monitors come set at 9,300°K, which is hotter and bluer than daylight. Many monitors aimed for sale in the desktop publishing market are set to 6,500°K, which approaches a truer white point.

Gamma is the relationship between the monitor and the video card that controls it. Gamma takes into account color, brightness, contrast, and saturation. For each incremental change in signal from the video card there should be an equal change in luminescence of the image on the screen. This relationship ideally should be a 1:1 balance, which rarely happens in real life. Calibration can optimize the relationship between the video card and the monitor. For making color correction, additional support hardware usually is required, although some less expensive methods use software calibrators. Software calibration is less precise because it allows you to adjust your monitor using colored paper swatches to match images on the screen. This works only as well as the eye's perception of color.

Hardware color correction is a more accurate method. This uses a sensor that is held up to the screen that measures the image. Single channel calibrators measure brightness only and therefore are good for measuring grayscale but not all that good for color. For the best color calibration you need three channel calibrators that can separately read green, red, and blue output on the monitor's screen.

To make use of these calibrators it is best to have a calibrating monitor which can adjust voltages inside the monitor. This allows a precise adjustment of color and luminescence. Without an adjustable monitor, color correction is done on the video board, a less precise method. Usually this control has a tradeoff of correct white balance for decreased contrast, brightness, and reduced number of available colors.

There are two major **glare reduction** techniques. The first is a *roughened screen surface*. The etches diffuse the reflections but also diffuse the video image and reduce the contrast. The better method is a *thin anti-glare coating* that is bonded to the screen to allow emission of the video light but reduce the outside glare. This coating can be damaged by regular glass cleaners, so it is best to use a cleaner that will not harm it. To further reduce glare try moving the lighting and adjusting the angle of the screen. Direct light sources like lamps or sunlight should be shielded from the monitor. Features that help in conjunction with glare reduction techniques are **brightness** and **contrast** controls on the monitor. A monitor that has better brightness control will also add longer life to the monitor because as the monitor ages the phosphor dots are not as responsive to light as they were when new and you can adjust the brightness to compensate for the deficit.

Keep an eye out for monitors that "sleep" when they are not being used. This will be a important power saving extra promoted by the Video Electronics Standards Association. The sleep mode will start after a set period of non-use and power down the monitor until the computer is used again.

Images on monitors can show geometric distortion due to imperfections in design. Most monitors have a screen that is not completely flat. The screens appear like they were cut from a sphere or from a cylinder. The spherical shaped monitors curve around all four edges and the cylindrical monitors appear to curve on two edges while remaining flat along the other two edges. *Blooming*, also called *defocusing*, and *halo* distortion occur when images become less focused as they become brighter. This is especially noticeable when viewing a dark image next to a bright image. Blooming can often be controlled to some degree by using the contrast control on the monitor. Haloing specifically affects solid images. *Bowing* is a geometric distortion that causes the sides of the screen to bend in the same direction.

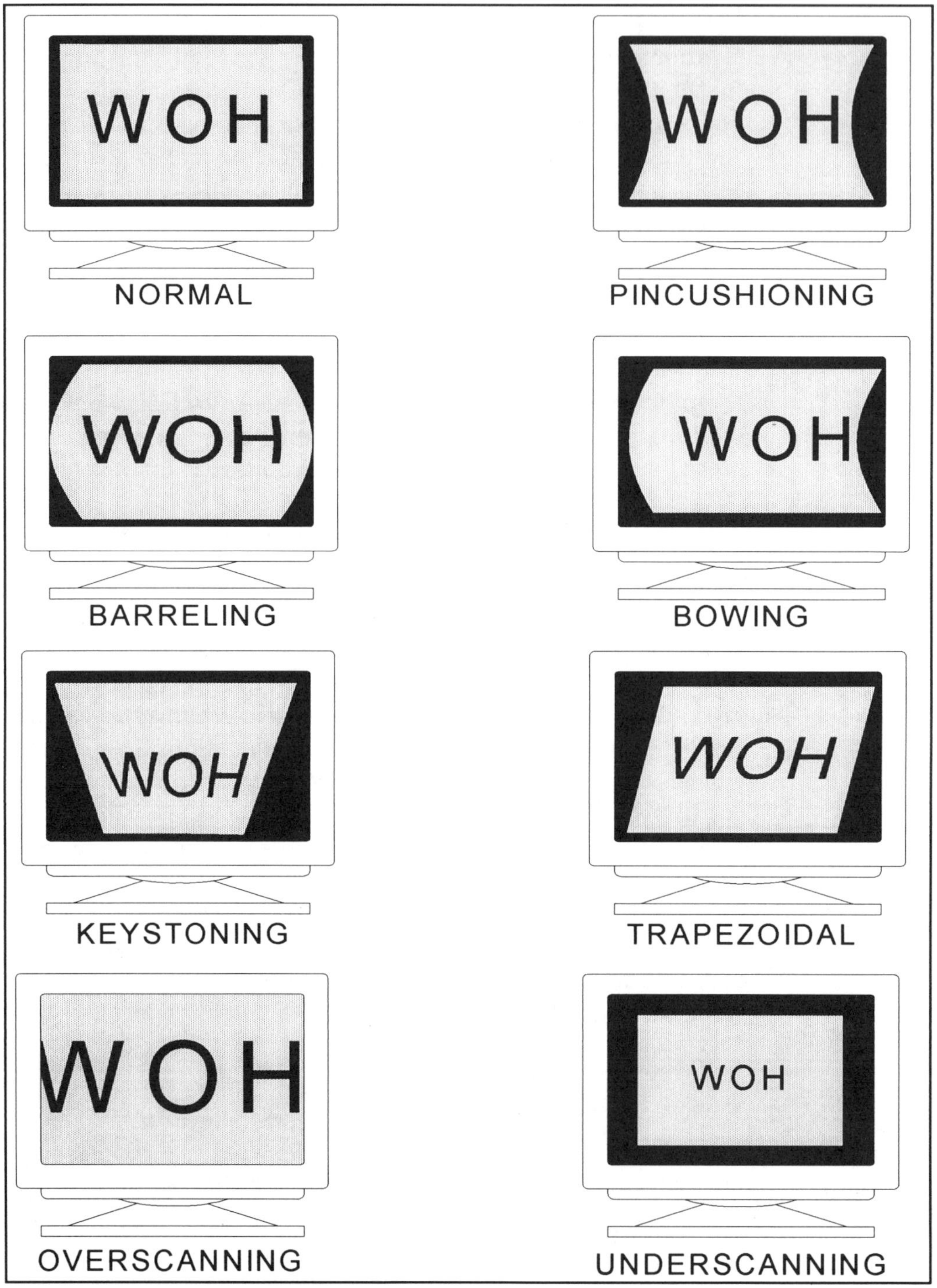

Monitor Geometric Distortions

Misconvergence occurs when the monitor is unable to align the individual color components correctly on the screen, causing images to lose detail and appear fuzzy on the screen as a result of bleeding between adjacent colors and colored halos around white objects on the screen. A quick way to check a monitor for misconvergence is to call up some white text on a colored background. If the monitor has a problem the white text will appear fringed with color. Some monitors have control over convergence. *Flicker* happens when the refresh rate is too low. *Non-linearity* is the distortion of lines and images that should appear straight but the screen displays them bent or jagged.

Pincushioning is a reference to an inward curvature of the top, sides, or both. This can be controlled by adjusting the size of the image using the horizontal and vertical sizing and positioning controls, but reducing the image size is not the best solution. Some better monitors have pincushioning controls. The new flat-square screens used on some of the higher-end monitors are known to have fewer problems with barreling and pincushioning. To assure your monitor will not have geometric distortions you need to examine it before buying it. The better models usually have less distortion.

Barreling is a geometric distortion that causes the screen image to bulge out at the sides, the top and bottom, or both. *Keystoning* is a distortion that causes one side of the screen to be smaller than the other end. This can affect the top, bottom, or sides. These distortions are sometimes reduced by controls on the monitor. A *moiré pattern* is a typical problem seen on television sets when someone wears a small checkered or striped pattern. The pattern will appear to wave back and forth in a mesmerizing way. This is usually caused by a misalignment of the display shadow mask and the phosphor dots on the screen at various resolutions.

Some monitors have a detachable signal cable which makes it easy to replace if it ever becomes damaged. A monitor cable that is not detachable has to be serviced by a technically gifted person if it ever becomes damaged. The length of the power cord can affect how easy it is to position and attach the monitor to the computer. A longer cord is usually more desirable. The size of the monitor should be of concern, especially if you are buying a monitor that is 17 inches or larger. These monitors will take up a great deal of space and will often extend back fairly deeply. Height might also be a concern in cramped quarters. The monitor weight is an important factor because some larger monitors may be too heavy to be supported by a desktop case or a flimsy desk. Keep in mind that you want to stay at least 18 inches away from the monitor for optimal viewing to minimize eyestrain.

A monitor's image can be affected by magnetic fields of nearby objects. Do not place unshielded speakers next to a monitor or the image will distort. Even the earth's magnetic field can affect a monitor. For best viewing, position your monitor with the earth's magnetic field. In the northern hemisphere face the monitor west, and in the southern hemisphere face the monitor east. This should interest anyone involved in Feng Shui, the ancient Chinese art of placing things to be in harmony with earth and nature.

Fluorescent lights flicker at 60 Hz and can make a monitor flicker noticeably. The best thing to do is to replace the lighting with incandescent lighting or to combine the two. Controlled lighting can make the colors on the screen appear truer, so do not overlook this important feature.

VESA has created a power-down standard called Display Power Management Specification (DPMS). This standard operates compliant monitors in four modes: on, standby, suspend, and off. Each of these states correlates to a different power consumption mode. To work correctly you need a DPMS graphics card or a system that contains the DPMS standard integrated into its BIOS.

The Video Adapter Card

The **video adapter** is the unit that connects the computer with the monitor. It translates the digital video data produced by the CPU into analog signals that are painted with the electron guns onto the pixels on the monitor screen. The display circuitry can be located on an expansion card or on the motherboard. Some motherboards have the video adapter **hardwired** on the board, which means the video adapter is built into it. A hardwired design is often faster than an expansion card, but if the hard-wired video cannot be disabled then there is no way to upgrade the video system.

The more common video scenario is a computer system with a separate video adapter that plugs into one of the motherboard expansion slots. With this design the speed at which the video adapter transmits is affected by the bus interface (ISA, EISA, VL-Bus, PCI) of the motherboard. The best type of video board for use with Windows has a PCI or VL-Bus connection. To use one of these video cards you need a motherboard with a PCI or VL-Bus slot.

It is important to buy a video card that supports the refresh rates at the monitor resolution you plan to display. The ultimate vertical refresh rate is 110 Hz, which is visually analogous to looking at paper. Low refresh rates cause the monitor to flicker, and this leads to headaches and eyestrain. Screen flicker is most noticeable on a white background, like in a word processor, and via peripheral vision. If you are checking out monitors in a store, face the monitor and then turn sideways, or 90 degrees, from the monitor and view the screen with peripheral vision. This will make the screen flicker more noticeable.

Typically, a video card can operate at a higher refresh rate when showing lower resolutions. To minimize flicker, make sure the video card refresh rate is VESA-compliant or better. The VESA standard for resolutions of 800 by 600 calls for a refresh rate of 72 Hz, and for resolution of 1,024 by 768 it calls for a refresh rate of 70 Hz. Some video cards handle higher resolutions by interlacing the video image. As stated previously, interlacing can cause the screen to noticeably flicker so it is best to find a non-interlaced video board. Make certain the system's monitor bandwidth can handle the highest resolution and refresh rate that the video board can run or the monitor will not be able to display the video in that mode. When a monitor's bandwidth is exceeded, the image on the screen generally becomes unreadable.

The horizontal refresh rate is the speed at which the video card refreshes each line on the screen. If you know the vertical refresh rate, the rate at which all the lines on the screen are refreshed, you can use that information to determine the horizontal refresh rate. To do so take the vertical refresh rate and multiply it by the vertical resolution, and multiply the result by 1.09. The .09 allows for the time it takes the electron beam to return from the bottom right corner of the monitor to the top left of the monitor at the end of the scan. For example, let's take a 72 Hz refresh rate with a resolution of 800 by 600. To use the formula, multiply 72 by 600, which equals 43,200. Then multiply 43,200 by 1.09, which equals 47,088, or a 47 kHz horizontal refresh rate.

72 x 600 = 43,200
43,200 x 1.09 = 47,088
47,088 = 47.088 kHz.

One of the previous limitations of the PC was that the color it could display was not up to par with that of the Macintosh computers. This is no longer relevant, as "true color," which is the display of 16.7 million colors, is now readily available for the PC. This number of colors displayed is kind of overkill, as the best human eyes can discern only about 190,000 different colors.

To make things even more jumbled, there is more than one standard for video cards and monitors. Many of these are not compatible with each other, so the video system needs to match the monitor to run properly. The common video display standards used are VGA, SVGA, EGA, CGA, and XGA. Things that differentiate the standards include the range of colors that can be displayed, the refresh rate, the resolution, and whether color or monochrome is used. Let's explore the different video display standards.

VGA (Video Graphics Array) was introduced in 1987 and is compatible with EGA and CGA software applications. VGA is an 8-bit technology, so it can show 256 colors with a 640-by-480 resolution. For every pixel on the screen there are 8 bits that describe the color. This is done by assigning a specific color from a palette of 256,000 colors to each of the 256 numbers that can be described with 8 bits. The video adapter then, using a digital to analog converter, translates these signals to a mix of red, green, and blue that displays on the monitor. Because of the limited number of colors in VGA, dithering technology is used to simulate other colors and tones. The result is an approximation of the real thing. The SuperVGA standard extends the resolution to 800 by 600 pixels. There are many manufacturers that offer VGA video boards with extended features that allow the display of higher resolutions and more colors.

Video Mode Resolutions

Video Mode	Horizontal Rows of Pixels	Vertical Columns of Pixels
Color Graphics Array (CGA)	640	200
Enhanced Graphics Adapter (EGA)	640	350
Hercules (Herc)	720	348
Monochrome Display Adapter (MDA)	720	350
PGA	640	480
Video Graphics Array (VGA)	640	480
NTSC Television	672	525
PAL Television	767	575
SuperVGA (SVGA)	800	600
Mac	832	624
XGA 8514/A	1024	768
ExtendedVGA (EVGA) or High Resolution (HR)	1024	768
Super High Resolution (SHR)	1152	864
Mac	1152	870
SPARC	1152	900
Two Page Display (2PD)	1280	960
WYSIWYG two page display (2PWYSIWYG)	1536	1152
Super Desktop Publishing (SDTP)	1600	1200
High Definition Television (HDTV)	1920	1080
Ultra High Resolution (UHR)	2048	1536
Air Traffic Control (ATC)	2048	2048

VGA and SVGA adapter cards are the most commonly used in computers today. The following display standards are outdated and rarely used anymore. **XGA** (eXtended Graphics Array) video board is compatible with VGA monitors. It has accelerated performance and can show 15-bit or 16-bit color. **CGA** (Color Graphics Adapter) was released in 1981 and can simultaneously display four colors from a possible 16 colors with a resolution of 320 by 200. With the higher resolution of 640 by 200, only one color can be shown at a time. **EGA** (Enhanced Graphics Adapter) is an improved version of CGA and was developed in 1984. EGA can display 16 colors out of a total of 64 colors in a resolution of 640 by 350. **MDA** (Monochrome Display Adapter) has been available since 1981. The MDA can show text but not graphics, in one color at a resolution of 640 by 350 pixels. **HGA** (Hercules Monochrome Adapter) was introduced in 1982 and allows monochrome monitors to display graphics and text. The resolution of HGA is 720 by 348 pixels.

Total Colors in Different Color Modes

Color Mode	*Bits Per Pixel*	*Number Of Colors*
Low Color	4	16
Pseudo Color	8	256
High Color	15 or 16	32,768 or 65,536
True Color	24	16,777,216

The number of colors a video card can display is important because it can affect the ability of the computer to effectively run graphics applications. **Low color** video boards are also called 4-bit boards and are capable of showing a maximum of 16 colors on the screen. These boards are uncommon in new computer systems because they are archaic by today's standards. **Pseudo color** video boards are the next step up in quality. They allow for 256 colors to be displayed.

High color boards show more colors on the screen using 15 or 16 bits per pixel to define the color. A 15-bit adapter can display 32,768 colors and a 16-bit adapter can display 65,536 colors. These are still not enough colors to work with high-end graphics.

True color is the king of the mountain for color display. Using these adapters, each pixel is assigned 24 bits. Each color receives 8 bits, resulting in a possible intensity of 256 for each color on each pixel. This translates into a possible 16,777,216 color display. That many colors on a display is kind of overkill because the human eye is capable of differentiating only about one-tenth that amount of colors.

A **DAC** is the digital-to-analog converter. It is also referred to as the **LUT-DAC**, which is short for Look Up Table Digital to Analog Converter. It changes the digital signal the computer produces into an analog signal that the monitor can display. The LUT-DAC controls the color depth and resolution on the screen. On color monitors there are three DACs, one for each display phosphor color: red, blue, and green. For a 24-bit true color display, each DAC must be able to handle 8 bits. The other DACs are capable of 6-bit or 4-bit manipulation.

Video adapters need to have memory to display these bits of color, and the more complex images usurp more RAM. The memory used on most video adapter cards is called **VRAM** and is much quicker than the DRAM that is used on the motherboard. VRAM is faster because DRAM has only one connection to the rest of the computer. DRAM can either be written to or read from but not both at the same time. This allows only one function to occur at one time. VRAM has dual ports allowing for simultaneous reading and writing, which is a much faster way to transfer data. VRAM is more expensive than DRAM, so some of the cheaper video cards use the slower DRAM instead. The video cards that use DRAM usually are not up to standard when delivering high-resolution images.

Video Memory Needed At Each Color Depth

Color Mode	640 x 480	800 x 600	1024 x 768	1280 x 1024	1600 x 1200
Low Color	150 kb	234 kb	386 kb	640 kb	938 kb
Pseudo Color	300 kb	469 kb	768 kb	1.3 Mb	1.9 Mb
High Color	562.5 kb	879 kb	1.41 kb	2.35 Mb	3.44 Mb
High Color	600 kb	938.5 kb	1.5 Mb	2.6 Mb	3.8 Mb
True Color	900 kb	1.4 Mb	2.3 Mb	3.8 Mb	5.6 Mb

You can determine how much VRAM a video adapter needs with some simple math. Now is the time to break out the calculator. In determining the memory requirements for the video RAM, multiply the screen resolution by the number of bytes needed to attain the color depth you want to display on the monitor.

Here is an example just for the fun of it; get ready to put your thinking caps on:

> First, multiply the horizontal resolution by the vertical resolution to get the total number of pixels on the screen. For example, let's use a resolution of 1,024 x 768 = 786,432 pixels on the screen.
>
> Second, multiply the bits by the pixels.
>
> Figure out how many colors will be shown.
>
> > For 16 colors there are 4 bits per pixel.
> > For 256 colors there are 8 bits per pixel.
> > For 32,768 colors there are 15 bits per pixel.
> > For 65,536 colors there are 16 bits per pixel.
> > For 16,777,216 colors there are 24 bits per pixel.
>
> For true color we multiply 786,432 x 24 = 18,874,368.
>
> Third, divide the last number by 8 to arrive at the total number of bytes.
>
> 18,874,368/8 = 2,369,296
>
> Fourth, divide the number of bytes by 1,024 to obtain the total number of kilobytes.
>
> 2,369,296/1,024 = 2,304
>
> Fifth, divide the number of kilobytes by 1,024 to arrive at the number of megabytes.
>
> 2,304/1,024 = 2.25 Mb of VRAM needed to display true color at 1,024 by 768 resolution.

Video boards made today are classified into a few distinct groups according to the way they can handle graphics, which affects their speed. The most plain of the bunch are called **frame buffers** or dumb frame buffers. They just manage the display memory while the CPU does all the work such as drawing the picture and keeping track of the pixels. These are good for DOS applications which generally are not graphically demanding of the CPU.

The Windows environment uses a limited number of processor commands to rearrange the graphics on the screen. When using Windows the CPU's resources are taxed by having to perform the graphic commands, which tell the video board what to display. **Fixed function graphic accelerators** intercept these graphic commands from the CPU and perform them instead with the video board. Fixed function graphic accelerators are good to use with Windows because they can take most of the graphics load off the system CPU by providing the ability to perform graphics functions on the video card, like BitBlt operations, off-screen caching, hardware cursor, and line draws. Next to text, lines are the next most common elements that appear on the screen. Fixed function graphic accelerators perform the graphic commands faster than the CPU because they are especially made to handle these commands. On the average, accelerated graphics are about 25 percent faster than a dumb frame buffer.

In Windows there are lines that combine to form all the boxes on the screen. A BitBlts operation occurs when you grab one of these boxes and move it to another point on the screen. This happens when moving an icon, scrolling, or displaying menus. This process copies the rectangle box pixel by pixel from one point on the screen to another. Another operation that some graphic accelerators handle is rectangle fills. This is the filling of the boxes with their specified colors. Using a graphics coprocessor or accelerator decreases the graphics workload for the CPU and frees it up for other computing functions.

Some graphics cards use caching and other methods to enhance graphic performance. Off-screen caching is used to store fonts and drop-down menus. This speeds up scrolling through documents. A hardware cursor maintains the cursor as a separate element on the screen, so when the cursor is moved the screen does not need to be drawn, nor does the cursor.

Graphic accelerators handle many graphics functions, allowing the performance to climb to three times that of a dumb frame buffer, but have little impact on display of randomly patterned images such as a scanned photograph or design. **Programmable graphic accelerators** are designed specifically to handle certain applications, such as CAD programs, and therefore can be faster than fixed function graphic accelerators. **Graphics coprocessors** are by far the best type of video cards for graphics. They have their own microprocessors that are dedicated to processing graphics and take the full burden off the system's CPU, which allows the system to achieve top performance.

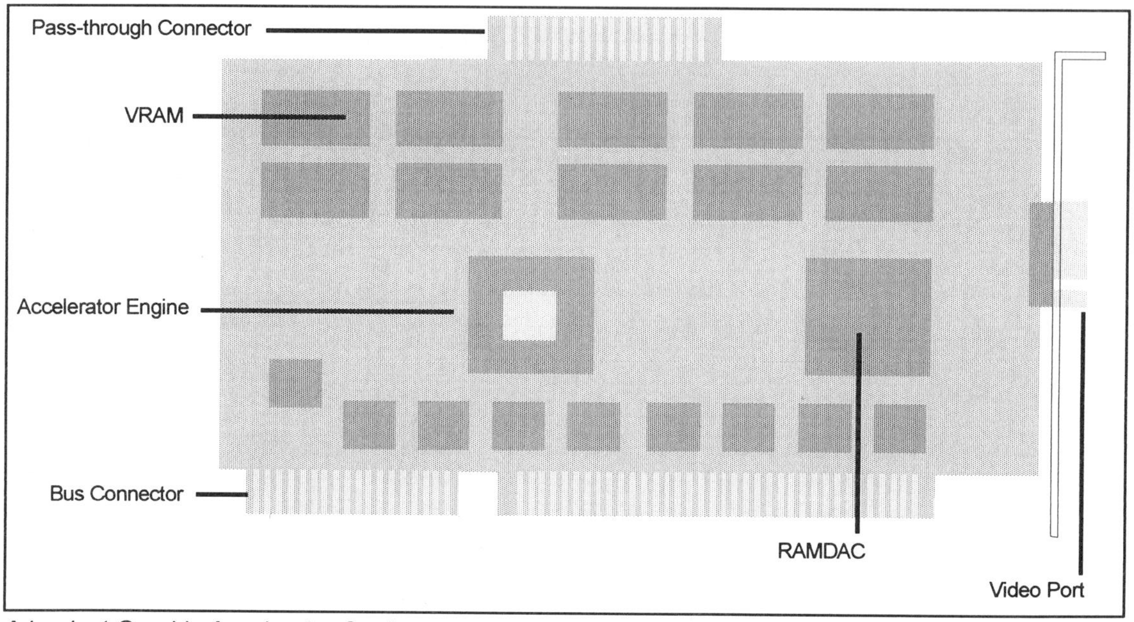

A Look at Graphic Accelerator Cards

The Windows program comes with a bunch of **video drivers** that you can use with the computer's video card. The video drivers are software that allow you to set the video mode the monitor will display. The different drivers let you choose the resolution and the number of colors displayed. For the best performance you want to get the latest drivers to run your video card. The quality and efficiency of the video drivers can make a big impact on overall display performance. These drivers let you choose the mode of display, such as the number of colors and the display resolution. Drivers are usually updated periodically, and you can obtain the new set of drivers directly from the manufacturer through the mail or by using a modem to call a computer bulletin board system. Buying from a well-established video card manufacturer usually means the drivers that support the hardware will be upgraded from time to time. There is nothing worse than a company that does not support its products with new drivers, because when a new release of Windows is sold the video may not work unless the drivers are updated.

An extra bonus included with some video cards is a utility that allows you to switch video resolutions and colors without restarting Windows. This feature can save you time and hassle and should be a prime consideration when buying a new video board.

The video adapter and monitor need to be properly matched in order to take advantage of their respective features. A fast video board that displays ultrahigh resolutions is not worth buying unless your monitor can match those specifications. Remember, even if your video card can display 16.7 million colors, you don't always need to run the video in that mode. More colors on the screen and higher resolutions will slow the video system down. If you do not need the extra colors, like when using a word processor, load a video driver that only displays 256 colors so the computer system delivers better overall performance.

Chapter 6

Input Devices

The Keyboard

The keyboard is often overlooked as an important player on the team. The keyboard is invaluable for communicating with the computer, and there are a variety on the market to suit different tastes. There are a few characteristics that differentiate one keyboard from another.

Keyboards differ in their *throw*, which is the distance a key has to travel to make a character appear on the screen. The greater the throw, the harder the key hits the bottom of the stroke. Everyone has different tastes, so try out the keyboard to see how it feels. The spaces between the keys vary from one keyboard to another. Some keyboards have large spaces between keys, and portable computer keyboards have small spaces between keys. Most keyboards have a standard 84-key layout or a 101-key layout and have the familiar QWERTY key arrangement that graces most typewriters. The QWERTY keyboard is so named because of the arrangement of keys on the upper left row of the keyboard. There are alternatives to the QWERTY keyboard on the market which group commonly used letters for more efficient typing. These keyboards have unusual key layouts to reduce movement and make typing faster. The Dvorak keyboard is an example of this. These redesigned keyboards may be great in the long run, but a touch typist will face a long learning curve to remaster this new layout.

The 84-key keyboard has a numeric keypad on the right of the board. This keypad also doubles as a cursor controller and moves the cursor position on the screen. The 84-key keyboard has ten function keys on the left side of the keyboard that are usually assigned to different actions in each program. Common function key actions include exiting a program, bringing up a menu on the screen, or cutting, pasting, and copying text or graphics. Most PC keyboards have the same basic layout; however, some keyboards have the punctuation keys located in different places.

PC keyboards contain their own microprocessors and attach to the computer through the keyboard port that is usually located at the rear of the computer case. If you are buying a keyboard for an older computer, make sure the keyboard has the right pinout on its plug.

The 101-key keyboard, also called an *enhanced keyboard*, is the standard keyboard bundled with new computers. Differences among the 101-keyboards and the 84-keyboards include the shape of the Enter key and the position of the backslash key (\). These keyboards have twelve function keys along the top of the keyboard and have separate cursor control keys that lie just to the right of the main lettered keys.

The cable on the keyboard should be long enough to reach the computer case. Many keyboards have replaceable cables to facilitate a change in the cable length. Most keyboards have adjustable feet on the bottom to offer good height and stability for the keyboard.

There are four major varieties of keyboard technologies on the market: mechanical, capacitive, conductive rubber dome, and membrane. The **mechanical** key has a contact between two conductive materials. A spring maintains the tension of each key, which when depressed completes the circuit. These keyboards are reliable and have a long life. An advantage with mechanical keys is they make an audible clicking sound upon contact and have a very good feel to them when typing.

Capacitive keys have a dielectric cushion at the end of the plunger which, when pushed down, forces the conductive elements apart, thereby creating a closed circuit. Capacitive keyboards are expensive to manufacture but are very reliable and have a long lifespan. These keyboards are not ideal for harsh environments where there is a great amount of particulate matter in the air because dirt can cause the board to malfunction.

Conductive rubber dome keys have a carbon dot under a raised rubber dome. When the key is pushed down the dome collapses, allowing the carbon dot to make contact, and this action completes the circuit between two contact pads. A conductive rubber dome keyboard can feel good depending on the quality of rubber used. These keyboards are fairly inexpensive and do offer spill protection because liquid is stopped by the rubber layer. A problem with conductive rubber dome keyboards is if one of the keys on the board goes bad, the whole rubber pad has to be replaced.

The **membrane** key consists of two layers of polyester film. Each layer has a pattern of silver-carbon silkscreened on one side. The layers are separated by a membrane that has gaps in it, so when the plunger pushes the cushion onto the top membrane it forces it to contact with the lower membrane resulting in a completed circuit. Membrane key technology is the least expensive but it is hard to repair and has the shortest lifespan. Membrane keyboards are quiet and have very little tactile feel to them. They are a good choice for harsh environments and are found on exercise equipment, ATMs, and other public access terminals.

Try out a variety of keyboards before the purchase because a bad keyboard can cause keyboard operators to suffer injury from typing known as repetitive stress injury. Cushioned pads can be attached to the keyboard which give you a place to rest your hands and let you maintain a better contact angle with the keyboard. There are a variety of ergonomic keyboards on the market that are designed to eliminate wrist strain and reduce finger travel. Many designs use a split keyboard that keeps your wrists at a more natural angle than traditional keyboards. Some have angled the split keyboard in a vertical fashion so your hands are opposed to each other as they are when clapping. This design takes the tension off the wrist muscles and tendons caused by the pronation on a traditional keyboard.

Ergonomic Keyboard

In conclusion, the keyboard is a highly personalized part of the computer that can make a big impact on the utility of the computer. Since the keyboard is the main path of communicating with the computer, make sure you get a keyboard that will make you a happy camper. Keyboards are not a very expensive investment, and buying the right keyboard can keep you away from injury and big medical bills. Many new computer systems come bundled with a keyboard. If the keyboard is not right for you, start shopping for a new one.

Pointing Devices

These days millions of desks have a **mouse** scurrying around on the tabletop. They are usually cream-colored and have long tails. Unlike the furry rodents, the computer mouse is made of plastic and has one or more buttons to click and fits in the palm of your hand like a bar of soap. The tail is a cord that, on a serial mouse, plugs into the serial port at the back of the computer, and for a bus mouse, comes with a circuitboard that fits into an expansion slot inside the computer on the motherboard. The mouse controls the cursor on the computer display that can be moved and pointed at objects to carry out commands with the computer. The mouse can be used to do things that would be hard to do with the keyboard, like draw a picture or drag icons across the screen.

Pointing Devices Compared

Pointing Device	Mouse	Trackball	Portable Trackball	Stylus	Digitizer
Cost	$10 to $150	$70 to $250	$50 to $150	$50 to $350	$100 to $10,000
Control	Handheld	Finger operated ball	Thumb operated ball	Held like pen	Sensor pad and puck or stylus
Application	General use	General use	Portable computing	Graphics, CAD, portable computing	Graphics, CAD
Size	Like a bar of soap	Fits under hand or thumb	Fits in palm or attached to computer	Like oversized pen	12 by 12 inches and larger
Function Keys	1 to 3 buttons	1 to 3 buttons	1 to 3 buttons	1 to 3 buttons	1 to many buttons
Pros	Easy to use, simplistic	More precise than mouse, needs little desk space	Can attach to portable, good for travel	Fine control, good for design and graphics	Sharp resolution for detailed work
Cons	Low resolution, not precise for drawing	Low resolution, not as easy as mouse	Not as good feel as full size trackball	Low resolution, must be picked up to use	Clumsy for general applications, takes lots of desk space

There are many types of pointing devices used with computers, such as digitizers, trackballs, stylus, and touch-sensitive monitors. The mouse is the most popular pointing device used with the computer, and there are three basic types of mice. The common **mechanical** mouse is inexpensive and does a great job for general computer use where pointing precision is not necessary. The mechanical mouse has a ball inside it that rolls when the mouse is moved. The movements of the ball move trackers in the mouse, which is interpreted as movements on the computer screen.

The **opto-mechanical mouse**, like the mechanical mouse, has a little ball underneath it that rolls when the mouse is moved. The movement of the ball is sensed by a phototransistor that reads the light that bounces off the ball. The movements are correlated as a change in the cursor position on the screen. Both of these mice use a mouse pad that provides a good tracking surface for the little rubber ball in the mouse to roll on.

The uncommon mouse is called an **optical mouse**. It has lights on the bottom and travels over a light-sensitive pad, thus doing away with the ball, which means fewer parts that can foul up. The mouse moves over a special optical mouse pad that has a fine grid on it. The mouse can sense when it passes over lines on the grid and translates the movement to the cursor position on the screen. The optical mouse is the most precise of the three mouse designs but is also the most expensive.

All mice have at least one button that acts as a select button when you position the cursor over items on the computer screen. It is common for mice to have two, three, or even more special purpose buttons. A three-button mouse is highly recommended because many programs make use of all three buttons and make the programs easier to use. Some mouse drivers let you assign the mouse buttons to activate different functions. This type of customization can be a great help for getting work done faster.

Two popular manufacturers of mice are Logitech and Microsoft. The Logitech MouseMan is a particularly well-made mouse that is ergonomically designed in two styles to fit either the left hand or the right hand. It also has three buttons which can come in handy and is not as limited as models that feature only one or two buttons.

There is also a **cordless mouse** for those who do not like to be restricted by the wire attached to the mouse. A cordless mouse is either infrared or radio-controlled. Radio-controlled mice are better than infrared mice because infrared needs to have line-of-sight transmission, just like your television remote control, and this can make the mouse act quirkier than a radio controlled model. Make certain the radio-controlled mouse has a choice of channels it can transmit on to avoid interference by other radio-controlled devices in your neighborhood. Many things can cause radio interference including cordless phones, computers, ham radios, microwaves, and even electrical wiring. Some manufacturers of the cordless mouse are Numonics, Logitech, Practical Solutions, and Lightwave Technologies.

The **mouse pen** is another pointing device and operates on the same theory as a regular mouse but is shaped and held like a pen. Some people prefer to use a mouse pen with their portable computers because it can operate on a variety of surfaces like airplane armrests and pant legs. Other people prefer the mouse pen because they like using a pen instead of a puck-shaped mouse. The pen mouse is great with graphics programs because it feels more natural to paint with a pen than a bar of soap. Manufacturers of the pen mouse include Appoint and International Machine Control Systems.

Summagraphics Graphics Tablet with puck

The **trackball** is kind of like an upside-down mouse. Trackballs have a ball that can be rolled around with a hand, or with the smaller trackballs with a thumb. Some video arcade games use a trackball type of controller. There are some advantages to this design. Unlike the mouse, which needs plenty of desktop space to move around, the trackball case does not move around the desk and therefore takes up less desktop real estate. The trackball is handy to use with portable computers and is often a built-in feature because it does not need a surface to push around on. Trackballs can be good for people with tendonitis or

RSI and are adversely affected when using a mouse. The trackballs come in different sizes. Models with larger ball often give greater control than those with a small ball. The buttons on the trackball should be placed so they are easily pushed while using the ball. Misplaced buttons can be a real drag. Some manufacturers of trackballs include Kraft, Kensington, Appoint, Logitech, Microwave, and Microsoft.

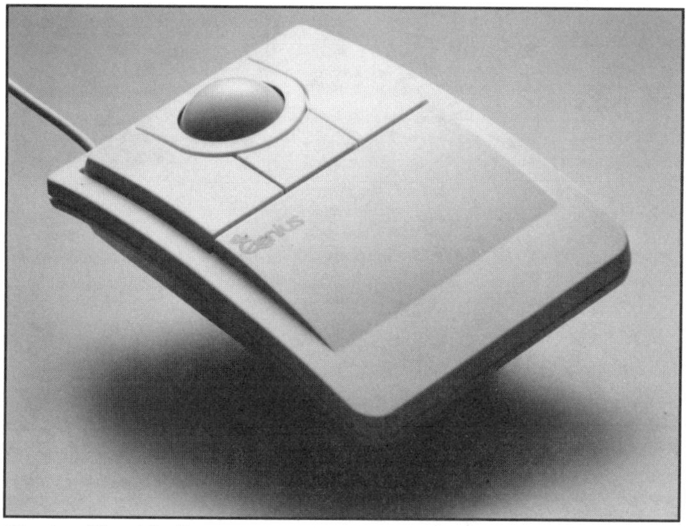

Genius Trackball

Games often use a pointing device called a **joystick** which usually enhances the ability to maneuver in flying games and run about in arcade games. A joystick can simulate better control over many flying games, therefore helping you to shoot down the Red Baron. Some joysticks are shaped like flying yokes used to steer airplanes, and these can be great for the home pilot. Joysticks vary in quality, and the cheap ones usually do not feel as good as the mid- to high-priced joysticks. In short, you get what you pay for.

Kraft Joystick

Yet another incarnation of the pointing device is the **mouse tablet** which is used with a stylus or finger on a sensitive pad. A *stylus* is a pointing instrument that looks like a pen and is used to point the cursor at the desired location on the screen. **Digitizer tablets** have the ability to be programmed to perform several functions that will transpire when a certain part of the tablet is touched. CAD (Computer Aided Design) programs make use of digitizer tablets to make architecture schematics and engineering designs. Some digitizer tablets are touch-sensitive—this is a great feature when used with a painting program so you can vary the pressure that the painting medium, like charcoal, Crayon, or pencil, applies to the artwork. For example, if you are using a computer-simulated pastel tool with a touch-sensitive pad, you can press lightly for faint color or you can press hard to make dark imprints in the artwork. Summa Sketch, Ace Cad, Wacom, and Micro Touch Systems make mouse tablets and digitizers.

Tablets have a lattice of wires arranged horizontally and vertically that correspond to points on the screen. They sense the position of the stylus and relay the information to the computer. The position of the stylus or puck is an absolute position, which means the center of the digitizer pad correlates to the center of the drawing space and the edge of the pad is the edge of the drawing space.

Because of this absolute relation, the digitizer is used by draftspeople and cartographers for tracing paper objects into the computer. An example of an image to be traced is a map or architectural blueprint. Artists can use the digitizer to trace in preliminary sketches. Using the pen-like stylus and a paint program can produce excellent results. For keeping the paper attached to the pad some tablets use clamps or overlays to hold the paper in place. Another method on some pads is an electrostatic surface which causes the paper to cling to the surface. If you are going to trace transparencies, blueprints, film, or X-rays you will need a translucent tablet which can be backlit.

Digitizer tablets range in size from a small active range of 12 by 12 inches to huge formats. Often the digitizer must be large enough to handle the paper size that is used for your business. For tracing E-size paper the tablet must have an active area of 36 by 48 inches. For D-size it is 22 by 34 inches. Most digitizers support a tracking resolution of at least 1,000 lines per inch and go up to about 5,000 lines per inch. The minimum accuracy remains about 0.02 inch. If you need to trace aerial satellite photographs or do other detailed work, a digitizer accuracy of at least 0.005-inch is recommended. A high-end digitizer to do this detailed work usually has an optional magnifier with super fine etched crosshairs and an oversized glass sight to help with the accuracy of the drawings. The technology most often used in a digitizer consists of a grid of wires under the tablet's surface that detect the proximity of the coil which is inside the puck or stylus. Cordless pucks and batteryless pens are the easiest to work with, as there is no cumbersome cord to get in the way.

Most digitizers come with special utilities that let you map the active area to a specialized portion of the pad. This allows you to use templates that fit on the tablet to make activating commands within the application you are using easier. To be able to set these commands, the software design application used must be able to program the tablet's free regions.

You have probably seen **touch screen displays** before. You can point with your finger or stylus at the screen to activate commands. Touch screen displays are popular in public use areas. The downside to the touch screen is that the monitor becomes dirty from being touched and the finger is too clumsy and large for refined operations. Touch screens usually have a lag time of 8 ms to 40 ms.

An important feature to be considered when looking for a pointing device is its resolution, which is reference to the fineness and precision of control that the device can achieve. People who work with graphics or CAD applications need a greater degree of control than the average computer user, and they will need a pointing device with a high resolution. Pointing device resolutions vary from the coarse 50 dots per inch to an ultra-precise 4,200 dpi. The higher number corresponds to a finer degree of response to movement. Most mouse and trackball resolution lies between 200 dpi and 400 dpi.

Drivers are a concern with pointing devices. Specialized pointing devices need drivers to support the software you will be using. Many common pointing devices support the generic Microsoft mouse drivers. Drivers for DOS and Windows are required to make a pointing device useful. Drivers that are periodically updated often enhance the operations of the pointing device. The manufacturer of a pointing device should offer BBS driver support so you can get the newest drivers easily with a modem.

Chapter 7

Portable Computers

To best understand the full range of ideas behind buying a portable computer it is recommended that you first review the main section about the desktop computer technology because it contains some important concepts that apply to portables. The key features that differentiate portable computers on the market include size, weight, storage capabilities, communication options, screen quality, keyboard size, battery life, expandability, bundled software, and price.

The CPU

If you are going to be using Microsoft Windows it is best to get the fastest CPU you can afford. The 3.3-volt CPUs conserve power, and CPUs with power management modes also help prolong battery life. Look in the main CPU section for a description of the different chips.

Weight

A portable computer should be light enough so you are willing to lug it around town. Check the weight of the portable and the battery plus the added travel weight including the AC adapter brick and power cord.

Some portables go on a diet, saving size and weight by losing the internal floppy drive. By attaching an external floppy drive only when needed, you can shave off more than a pound of weight and a half-inch of height from the portable. The primary purpose of a floppy drive is to initially load programs onto the hard drive and to exchange data. If you intend to share data with another computer, an alternative to using the floppy drive is to utilize a parallel or serial port using a transfer cable. A cable transfer requires the computers to use additional software, but it can make the exchange of large files much easier than swapping floppy disks. The cabled transfer rate is up to 1 megabyte per second for serial cables and up to 3 megabytes per second for parallel cables. When it comes to questions of ease of use and familiarity, floppy drives are the strongest contender even though the transfer rate is closer to a slow 90 kilobytes per second. An external floppy drive can be attached to the portable computer and gives you the option to leave the drive at home or at the office when it is not needed.

A great feature found on some portables is the ability to swap out the floppy drive in exchange for a second battery or hard disk. If you just want to shed weight you can leave the slot empty.

Storage

You need enough hard disk storage space to install the programs you intend to use. Most portable computers use hard drives that are 2.5 inches in size. A minimum hard disk capacity of 200 megabytes is recommended, although a 300-megabyte or 500-megabyte hard drive allows for much more flexibility. If you plan to use the portable only when traveling, you can probably get by with a smaller hard drive, but if the portable computer is to be your dedicated computer, do not settle for less than a 300-megabyte hard drive.

Some portables are enhanced with a removable hard drive that makes sharing data easier. With a removable hard drive, you could have more than one hard drive and store different software programs on each drive. Type III PCMCIA slots are able to house a hard drive. These slots are fairly standard features on portables. An alternative to hard drive storage is flash RAM storage. PCMCIA flash RAM cards consume less energy than a hard drive does. The drawback to flash RAM is that it is expensive, so you have to pay more and end up with less storage when you choose flash RAM instead of hard drive storage.

If you have been using a computer for a while, you probably know how large a hard drive you need. If you are new to computers and do not know what size hard drive you need, first decide what software programs you want to use. Next, find out how much storage space the programs require. Take the total sum of all the programs' storage needs and double that figure for data files and future expandability. This is the minimum size hard drive you need.

Memory

Upgrading the memory in a portable computer is a possibility that needs investigation. In some portables the memory used is proprietary, which means it is probably expensive and could be hard to find. Many portable manufacturers have opted to use industry standard SIMMs (Single Inline Memory Modules) which are widely available and comparatively inexpensive.

Remember to install the minimum amount of RAM in your portable that you will require. RAM consumes energy, so the more RAM you have installed the shorter the battery life will be for the portable. On the other hand, install enough RAM to run the software programs without needing to use virtual memory. Virtual memory requires the use of the hard disk, which draws more power than does additional RAM.

Ports and Slots

Ports are connections on a computer that allow it to be plugged into accessories. These are similar to ports on a home stereo where you attach tape decks, record players, and CD players. The portable computer you choose should be equipped with a minimum of one parallel port and two serial ports. This will make attaching peripherals like printers, modems, and trackballs no problem.

Most portable computers have small screens and keyboards in comparison to desktop models. A portable computer with an external keyboard port and external monitor port allows you to attach to the portable a standard desktop-sized keyboard and bigger monitor, making the computer more comfortable to use when stationed at home or at work. Taking this route you will get most of the benefits of a desktop computer, yet this setup allows you to easily disconnect the computer and whisk it around town.

A mouse port is a convenient addition, especially if you do not like using the built-in trackball or pointing device. If you are using a high-resolution external monitor, make sure to get at least 1 megabyte of video RAM for controlling the external display. This will allow for flexibility regarding the size monitor you can connect to and increase the number of colors available.

In summary, if you are going to use the portable as your primary computer, make sure it has ports for external video, two serial ports, one parallel port, a type III PCMCIA slot, and a keyboard port.

The ports on portable computers are usually covered to prevent dirt and grime from getting inside. When the ports are located behind a hinged plastic door, make certain the door will not break off easily. Good designs use sturdy doors that are impervious to damage. Check the computer to see whether the ports are standard sizes or if they are a proprietary design. Standard ports are much better because nonstandard designs, often found in docking computers, can make finding compatible accessories nearly impossible.

Most portables come with a special slot reserved for an internal modem. This can be important for telecommunications and picking up e-mail. Computers with one or more PCMCIA type III version 2.0 or higher slots are desirable, as they let you easily add features to the computer like memory, hard drives, or network cards. A door to cover and hide the ports is a necessary feature on a portable computer to keep out dirt. Make sure the door is not flimsy or it might accidentally break off.

If you want to connect a CD-ROM to a portable computer, buy a portable with a SCSI port or an extra PCMCIA port. Do not consider a portable without SCSI if you will use the computer for multimedia presentations. There is a way to attach a SCSI device using a parallel-to-SCSI adapter, but the data transfer rate of a parallel-to-SCSI device is much slower than using a traditional SCSI port. These adapters are available from Trantor Systems and Always Technology.

What do you get with a desktop computer that you do not get in a portable computer? A portable lacks a standard sized keyboard, a big monitor, expansion slots, accelerated true color video, a bigger hard drive, a tape backup drive, a CD-ROM, and extra drive bays. You can reclaim these functions by buying a portable with a port replicator or docking station.

Some portable computers have the option of connecting to port replicators or docking stations, making connecting to keyboards and monitors an easy one-step process. Instead of attaching several cables to the ports on the computer, you just slip the computer into the docking station or snap on the port replicator. The advantage of these devices is they give the functionality of a desktop computer without having to buy a second system, plus they prevent the need to constantly swap files between two computer systems.

Port replicators or docking bars are the simpler of the two options. They are bars that permanently connect on one side to the cables that lead to the monitor, keyboard, power cord, mouse, and modem that are left at the office or home. On the other side of the port replicator are connectors that snap into the ports on the back of the portable computer. A port replicator usually does not add the availability of expansion slots to your portable computer and is used mainly for convenience. Without a port replicator, every time you get home or leave your office you need to mess with a tangle of cords, disconnecting and connecting every time you leave and arrive, a process that can damage your cables through excessive wear.

Docking stations, or **expansion chassis** provide the more advanced method of making connections. They often look like a desktop computer case with a big slot on the front panel. Inside the docking station is a connection that automatically attaches to the portable's external bus connector. The station provides connectors for serial and parallel ports, external monitors and keyboards, a power supply, and expansion slots. When you get home or to the office where the docking station awaits, just slip the portable into the slot and you're ready to compute. The docking station can be equipped with all the amenities that a normal desktop computer has, like floppy drives, additional hard drives, network cards, a printer, a big monitor, a pointing device, a modem, and extra expansion ports for other items. The main advantage of this system is the availability of expansion slots. If you need a true color display or large monitor to do page layout, a docking station could be the solution to your needs.

Some portables shed extra weight by not including a floppy drive. The floppy access is regained only when docked in a station. An alternative is to carry a portable floppy drive which connects to the portable computer via the parallel port. If you need the floppy then pack it along, but if you do not need the floppy drive you can leave it at home.

Not all docking portables can disable their internal video circuitry when you install an external video card in a docking station. This means the extra processing overhead on the CPU may not be relieved. If you plan to use an external video card, look into this matter.

One connection that is not provided by port replicators or docking stations is the standard RJ-11 modular phone line connection that you plug into the portable computer's internal fax-modem. This line must be attached and detached separately from the rest of the connections on the port replicator or docking station.

Some docking stations can support the weight of a big monitor, while other stations cannot. Check the load bearing capacity of the docking station to see if it will support your monitor. If the docking station will not support the monitor you will need extra desktop space for it to rest on. Make sure the table is sturdy enough to handle it, too. Some of the bigger monitors can be pretty heavy.

The docking station should provide all the extra amenities of a desktop station to fit your needs. Most docking stations have two expansion slots for adding cards. Check to see if they are proprietary slots or standard ISA, EISA, or VL-Bus slots. Bus mastering cards will not work with a portable in docking stations because they are too sensitive to small timing changes caused by a cable connection.

The power supply with the docking station will typically be able to deliver in the range of 25 to 120 watts. Make sure the power supply is sufficient to run all the peripherals you will be attaching to it.

The docking station should be easy to use. The portable should be inserted and ejected easily and without much preparation. An easy-to-reach system restart button and on/off switch keeps you from having to eject the portable to boot it up. The docking station should be charging the battery while the portable is docked.

A docking station that locks is a great way to secure your portable. The ease of opening the docking case can affect your ability to swiftly change adapter cards inside the unit, although this is not something you will need to do often. Most all docking stations are proprietary, meaning docking computers from different manufacturers will not fit into each other's docking stations, but many manufacturers have a line of several notebooks that will fit into the same docking station. In the event that you buy another portable made by the same manufacturer, check that it will fit into the same docking station.

Upgrading

If you want to maximize the portable's usefulness, find out if the hard disk can be replaced with a bigger one. Computers with PCMCIA Type III slots are great if you need removable hard drive storage. The maximum RAM configuration of a portable is critical to know, especially if you are going to be running a CAD program or operating systems like Windows NT and OS/2. Find out what the upgrade path is for the RAM and what type of RAM the computer needs. If the portable uses a proprietary type of RAM remember it may be hard to find when you want to add more, especially if the company goes out of business.

Keyboard

Although it will not be as comfortable as a full-size desktop computer keyboard, a portable computer keyboard needs to be comfortable enough so you can type for long stretches at a time. There are many qualities that control how good a keyboard feels. Probably the best way to decide if a keyboard is adequate is to see the computer in person and try typing with it.

The **key pitch** is a factor that controls the way the keyboard feels. Key pitch is the distance from the center of a key to the center of the next adjacent key. Most full-size desktop computer keyboards have a key pitch of 19 mm. For portable computers that will be used to type a lot, do not settle for a keyboard with a key pitch below 17.8 mm. Any shorter and you will become less productive because the keyboard will slow you down.

Keystroke length or throw is the distance the key travels to hit the bottom of the keystroke. Desktop computer keyboards usually have a keystroke length of 3 mm. Portable computers that have a keystroke throw of less than 2 mm will feel stiff and hard. The trade-off between short and long throw is if the keystroke length is too long it will cause more noise as the key reaches the bottom of the stroke, due to greater acceleration of the key.

When looking for a portable computer, ask how many keys there are on the keyboard and how many are function keys. Most portables do not have a dedicated numeric keypad on the keyboard. If you do a great deal of ten-key data entry, you may want to look for a portable that has an easily accessible numeric keypad or the ability to add an external numeric keypad to the portable.

Ideally the cursor arrows on the keyboard should be arranged in an inverted "T" formation so they feel natural. If the cursor keys are in an odd shape, like an "L" shape, it could drive you nuts. Some portables have dedicated cursor arrows keys while other portable computers' arrow keys share dual functions and are activated by simultaneously pressing a special shift key.

Portables often do without a second set of "Alt" and "Ctrl" keys found on desktop keyboards. The function keys may be double purpose keys or stand-alone function keys. The “Shift” and “Enter” keys should be oversized for maximum performance. Smaller keys may leave you fumbling around to find them.

Pointing Devices

There are four categories of pointing devices for portable computers. A *freestanding* pointer is like a mouse or penball. These are not integrated into the computer’s design and are often sold separately from the computer. A *built-in* pointing device is a permanent fixture on the computer system case. A wrist rest trackball or touch-sensitive pad usually sits in the middle-front of the portable near your thumbs and is convenient for lefties.

A *clip-on* pointing device is separate from the system case and attaches to the side of the portable. It is usually attached to the computer’s serial port with an external adapter cable. A *snap-on* pointing device is like a clip-on device except it uses a special port to attach to the computer. This means no messy cables. A *retractable* pointing device fits neatly inside the portable and pops out the side when you are ready to use it.

Many portables have built-in pointing devices like trackballs or a pointer control key. This feature will save you from having to attach a pointing device to the side of the keyboard. An external pointing device is just another thing you forget to bring with you on the road and is easy to lose. In addition, the cable that attaches a clip-on pointing device to the system can be an annoyance. Pointing devices by design can be integrated anywhere on the keyboard by the manufacturer, and this can affect the functionality of the device. A pointing device that is mounted on the area near the screen can be annoying to use.

If you are left-handed, pay extra attention to the placement of the pointing device. Lefties may be disappointed unless the pointing device is placed in a neutral position near the middle or bottom of the keyboard. A built-in trackball placed in the middle-bottom of the keyboard makes it accessible for ambidextrous use.

There are some new pointing device designs showing up on portable computers. Some portables use a tiny mouse key that acts like a little joystick for your fingertip. Surprisingly, this works excellently. A few portables use the arrow keys for the pointing device. This can be less than optimal for moving the cursor about the screen. A newer design is a snap-on front-mounted trackball. This is handy to use just like any other trackball but it also can be removed from the portable if you prefer to use another type of pointing device.

Communications

For future expansion it is best to have the option to install a fax-modem to communicate with other computers and to send e-mail. Some portables have a built-in fax-modem and others have available internal expansion slots or PCMCIA slots awaiting the addition of a fax-modem. If the portable has a built-in fax-modem, find out the maximum raw data speed and maximum fax transmission speed. Inquire as to whether the fax can both send and receive faxes. Some are send-only, an unwise limitation.

If your office is networked together, check whether you have a network card option for the portable computer. Just like a modem, a network card can be built-in or can plug into a PCMCIA or internal expansion slot. You will probably need more than one PCMCIA slot if you want to use a network card too, so the computer can have an extra hard drive and modem.

Screen

Better screens are more expensive and usually have to trade off with less battery life. The screen you choose needs to be sharp enough to read and able to work well under diverse lighting conditions. As usual, the better the screen the bigger the price.

Unlike phosphors on a cathode ray tube, LCD screens do not provide light of their own. LCD screens are composed of liquid crystals that are electrically polarized, so one end is more positive than the other. Without an electric field the liquid crystals scatter randomly, but when a charge is applied they orient themselves along the electrical charge. Light needs to be reflected off the screen to make the image readable. The portable should have a backlit (alternatively a sidelit or edgelit) screen or it may be too hard to see the screen under less-than-perfect lighting conditions. If you plan on working in airplanes, buses, or cars where the light varies, a backlit or sidelit screen is essential. If you are always on a throne immersed in fluorescent light, the backlit feature is not too important, but it is a gamble to pick a portable without it. A good feature to have is an option to turn off the backlighting to extend the portable's battery life when using it under ideal ambient lighting.

The screen size can make a big impact on the usefulness of the computer. If you are accustomed to using a 14-inch or bigger desktop computer monitor, it may take a while to become inured to the smaller portable screens. Nevertheless, a diagonal screen measurement of 8 inches can seem too compact and will display text as tiny characters. Screens that are 9 inches diagonally are a good minimum size to work with. Screens of 10 inches are even better. Once again, the trade-off here with a bigger screen is battery life.

The better screens use **active matrix** LCD panels (also known as thin-film transistors). They offer a sharper, bolder picture that displays richer color or shades of gray and faster refresh rates than passive matrix screens. The active matrix screens have a near 99:1 contrast ratio, versus the usual 13:1 contrast ratio of passive matrix screens. Dual scan passive matrix monitors divide the screen into two regions which are scanned simultaneously. This brings the contrast ratio up to near 18:1. Dual scan screens also have better tracking so the mouse cursor is easier to see when moving across the screen. The next step up in quality is active addressed passive matrix, which addresses all rows of pixels simultaneously. This offers a much sharper picture and gives a contrast ratio near 60:1.

The quality of an active matrix is close to that of a cathode ray tube monitor that desktop computers use. The speed and brightness they offer is gained by placing one or more transistor(s) at every LCD cell on the screen. There is a separate transistor controlling the red, blue, and green on each pixel. This method consumes more power than a passive matrix design. As you see, the downside to active matrix is that the screens cost more and drain the battery faster than passive matrix screens.

The viewing angle on an active matrix screen is greater than that of a passive matrix screen. An active matrix screen allows you to view the screen from the front or when sitting to the side of the screen. The viewing angle of a screen is important to consider, especially if you are going to use the computer as a sales tool for presentations. If you need to do presentations, the active matrix screen is the type to get because more than one person can view the screen at a time. Passive matrix screens can appear washed out when viewed at an angle. If you are sitting in front of the screen and have clients sitting on your left and right sides, they may not be able to see the image on the screen very clearly. Check the screen in person before you buy if this may affect your needs.

The refresh rate—the rate at which the screen is repainted—of an active matrix screen is often up to five times faster than that of a passive matrix screen. This eliminates the problem of the mouse cursor disappearing (submarining) as it is famous for doing on a passive matrix screen, although dual scan passive matrix screens are somewhat better at keeping the cursor visible.

Passive matrix screens do not offer as good a picture quality as active matrix screens. The passive matrix display offers colors that look washed-out. Their electronics address whole rows or columns of pixels at a time. The screen is divided up into rows and columns and a transistor is placed on each row or column. This makes passive matrix screens easier to manufacture, and for the end user that means they are cheaper. But this design makes the screens limited in the range of colors they can display and gives them a slow response time. These screens are unsuitable for showing motion video and can be annoying when moving the mouse pointer across the screen because of the tendency for it to disappear.

Those of you who are battery-life-conscious, take note. As a general rule, grayscale screens consume less power than color screens and passive matrix screens require less power than active matrix screens.

Some manufacturers are using enhanced passive matrix screens which come close in quality to active matrix screens. The enhanced passive matrix screens achieve this by using a double scan rate (the screen refreshing two lines at the same time). This is also known as a dual scanning screen.

A user of graphic programs should be concerned about the number of gray levels available on the screen. Most systems display 16, 64, or 256 levels of gray or color. Color screens cost more than grayscale screens. If you are only doing word processing you can probably get by without a color screen. If you sometimes use color, consider getting a grayscale screen on the portable and get a color monitor for home or office.

The alternative to buying an active matrix portable as your only computer is to buy two computers: a desktop and a passive matrix laptop with a video out port. You can leave the desktop computer at work and take the portable home where a full monitor awaits it. This setup leaves many people happy because they get the best of both worlds: portability and screen quality.

If you plan to connect the portable to an external cathode ray tube monitor, make sure it can display on both simultaneously. Otherwise you will have to switch between the two screens. The resolution available from the portable computer can vary. Some smaller portables are limited to CGA 640-by-200 or CGA 640-by-400 double scan, although most notebooks can show VGA 640-by-480 resolution. For external monitors, some portables can show SVGA 800-by-600 or even 1024-by-768 or super high 1280-by-1024 resolutions. Find out the maximum number of colors that can be displayed at each resolution and what vertical screen refresh rates are supported for external monitors.

The LCD screen on the portable should have brightness and contrast controls to adjust the screen for the best visibility. These controls should be easy to access and have a good range for adjustment. Often there is software included that allows the fine-tuning of color palettes and grayscale to create maximum visibility. If you switch from DOS to Windows often, the better screen controllers can switch to photo negative mode so the text is black on a white background when using DOS and back to the normal mode for Windows.

The design of an LCD screen is much different than that of a traditional cathode ray tube. A typical LCD screen consists of a front polarizer, rear polarizer, back glass, front glass, and liquid crystal substance. The liquid crystal is a fluid that contains little rod-shaped crystals. These rod shaped crystals twist or straighten when electrical current is applied. When the rods are twisted they bend light which is then blocked or passed on through the polarizers. If the polarizers are at 90 degrees to each other the light is then effectively blocked.

Imagine the screen as a piece of graph paper with each square representing a pixel, or picture element. A passive matrix screen is divided into rows and columns of picture elements. At the edge of the display are transistors that control the liquid crystal pixels using the grid. This is a inaccurate way to control pixels and adjacent pixels are sometimes unintentionally bent. For an active matrix screen each pixel has its own transistor. This method offers a greater amount of control over the pixels and results in a clearer picture.

A few portable computers use **gas-plasma** displays. These displays use a gas that gives off light when given an electrical charge, similar to a neon lightbulb. They consume a lot of energy and therefore need to be plugged into a wall outlet, which reduces their portability.

Some emerging screen technologies include active addressing and field-emission display. **Active addressing** can control LCD pixels to achieve a crisp display and wide viewing angle. Active addressing offers close to the same performance level as active matrix. **Field-emission display** is much like a tiny cathode-ray tube for each pixel. The screens, like desktop monitors, are coated with phosphor dots which glow when excited by electrons. Field-emission displays offer a better picture quality, are less sensitive to temperature, and consume less power than a backlit active matrix screen.

Remember, the screens on portable computers are tiny. You can strain your eyes when staring at these small screens for long periods of time. If you plan on spending a lot of time in front of the computer, give your eyes a rest and invest in a larger desktop CRT monitor to plug into the portable computer's video-out port.

If an image is left on an LCD screen too long it will temporarily remain visible after the computer is turned off. LCD screens are not as bad as old cathode-ray tubes in this respect, but if you plan on leaving your laptop computer running it is wise to get a screen saver. If the portable has an active matrix screen, use a screen saver with a white background, and if the screen is passive matrix use a black background. Even better yet, use power management software to shut the power to the screen off when the computer is not being viewed.

Batteries and Power

Batteries are of paramount importance for portable computers. The battery life of a portable computer must be enough to accomplish your needs before running out of juice. Good batteries are often coupled with extra energy conservation features to extend the battery life. There are several types of batteries used to power portable computers, including lead-acid, nickel metal-hydride, nickel cadmium, lithium polymer, and zinc-air.

Batteries Compared

Battery Type	*Nickle Cadmium*	*Nickle Metal-Hydride*	*Zinc-Air*	*Lithium Polymer*	*Lithium Ion*	*Sealed Lead-Acid*
Watt-hours per kilogram	35 to 45	50 to 60	145 to 155	75 to 85	78 to 115	45 to 50
Number of Recharge Cycles	500 to 1000	600 to 1000	70 to 400	175 to 300	500 to 1000	500 to 2000
Cost Per Watt Hour	$0.70 to $1.40	$1.50	$2.00	$0.75	$1.50	$0.70

Lead-acid batteries were used in some early portable models but are dangerous; they can explode if overcharged. Lead-acid batteries should be never be completely discharged and they should always be stored fully charged. If a lead-acid battery is stored fully discharged it will have sulfation—the lead electrodes will convert to lead sulfate, ruining the ability of the battery to hold a charge. Lead-acid batteries also carry very little charge per weight in comparison to other battery types and are not commonly used anymore.

The use of nickel metal-hydride batteries (Ni-MH), and nickel cadmium (Ni-Cad) batteries is fairly widespread. Ni-MH batteries have a few advantages over Ni-Cad batteries. Nickel metal-hydride batteries are lighter in weight than nickel cadmium batteries. **Nickel metal-hydride** (Ni-MH) batteries deliver about 25 percent more power than **nickel cadmium** (Ni-Cad) of the same weight. Ni-MH batteries are somewhat free of the problem known as Ni-Cad memory (technically known as hysteresis). This is a problem that depresses a battery's ability to be fully recharged. For example, if you use a Ni-Cad battery and run it down for only 20 minutes a few times before recharging, the battery will end up delivering only 20 minutes of power before going dead. Fixing this requires the battery to be fully drained of power before recharging, known as deep power cycling. It is recommended you deep power cycle a Ni-Cad battery once every 90 days, and once every 30 days for Ni-MH batteries. Ni-Cad and Ni-MH batteries have a lifetime recharge cycle of 100 to 500 charges, and each deep power cycling will take away one of these cycles.

Going with the better Ni-MH batteries costs more, but if you depend on a portable it is a small price to pay. In addition, Ni-MH batteries are a more green product because they readily decompose and are non-toxic. Ni-Cad has been declared a toxic substance because of the dangerous cadmium it contains.

Look for portables that can hot-swap batteries. This allows you to change the batteries without losing the work that is in progress on the computer, avoiding the need to shut down the computer before swapping. This is usually made possible by a small secondary battery on the unit that takes over when the primary battery is removed.

If you end up with Ni-Cad batteries you can prevent the unwanted memory problem from occurring by doing a deep power discharge before recharging the battery. Some portables have this function as a built-in option. If you feel the battery has succumbed to the memory effect, then run it through a series of complete discharge and recharge sessions. Technically, the discharge does not completely drain the battery, for that would also harm the battery's charging capabilities. The discharge rather eliminates power in the battery until there is very little amperage left. If the computer does not have this as a standard function, you can buy software that will do this for you. It is recommended to perform this procedure after 10 to 20 battery charge cycles. After draining the battery make sure you recharge it for several hours before using it again.

Two new and improved battery types are lithium polymer and zinc-air. **Lithium polymer batteries** weigh less because they use a solid electrolyte instead of a liquid one. This means the battery is also less prone to leakage or explosion. These batteries do not have the memory effect caused by repeated partial chargings. They reportedly deliver a charge for as long as 16 hours and lose only 1 percent of their charge over a one-month period. Ni-Cad batteries comparatively lose 15 percent of their charge over a one-month period. An added bonus is that lithium polymer batteries cost less to make than Ni-Cad batteries. Lithium polymer batteries have a lifetime recharge cycle of about 175 to 300 charges. Lithium ion batteries do not pack as much power as lithium polymer batteries, but they hold more charge than Ni-MH. Lithium ion batteries have a lifetime recharge cycle rated at 500 to 1,200 recharges.

Zinc-air batteries contain about three times as much power as Ni-MH batteries. The zinc-air battery will deliver a charge for up to a magnificent 20 hours and will not lose the charge while remaining inactive. These batteries, like lithium polymer batteries, do not suffer from the memory effect. The higher energy density of zinc-air means that portables can be either lighter or they will operate much longer than portables with Ni-Cad or Ni-MH batteries. Zinc-air batteries should be able to handle 150 deep discharge cycles and over 300 partial discharge cycles.

The computer you buy should give you at least two to three hours of power off the battery. Many of the portables today can run for four or more hours before needing a recharge or fresh battery pack. Find out the *rated battery life* for the system from the vendor. Some portables contain a bridge battery that allows you to change the battery pack without losing power. This is very convenient because you do not have to turn off the power to the unit.

Find out the battery *charge time* from the system vendor and how many hours it is rated to deliver a steady current of one ampere. Recharge times generally run from one hour to a full day. Most portables need about two hours to charge with the computer off and about 30 percent more time if the portable is in use when plugged in.

To reuse your batteries you will need a battery charger. Many batteries will discharge during periods of non-use. Often the portable has a charger built into the system and all you have to do to keep the battery charge topped off is plug the portable into the AC adapter. If you want to keep one or more charged batteries on hand you will need a battery recharger. When buying a battery recharger, make sure it is a float charger and not a trickle charger. A *trickle charger* sends a continuous current to the battery even after the battery has reached its maximum charge. Not only can this shorten the battery's life, but it also can be dangerous, as it creates the possibility of an explosion. A *float charger* charges the battery until it reaches its capacity and then reduces the current, thus preventing overcharging.

The AC power adapter that comes with your system may only be able to provide AC to DC power conversion with the 110-volt standard used in the U.S. If you plan on traveling abroad it is recommended that you purchase another dedicated 220-volt AC to DC power converter because adapters that work on both 100-volt and 220-volt currents usually are not very good. A feature to look for on an AC adapter is a status light that will let you know when the battery is charging.

For traveling it is good to know what the *battery weight* is so you will know how much extra weight you will carrying if you want to bring one or more back-up batteries on the road with you. Remember to count the extra weight of an external battery recharger if you need one of these, too.

For keeping an eye on power consumption it is best to have a gas-gauge type of display to alert you to the status of the battery. Because batteries wear out a little every time you reuse them it can be helpful to know how well they are taking a charge. This can be done by checking the battery's voltage when it is fully charged. Checking a battery's voltage is simple to do with a voltmeter, which can be found at electronic supply stores.

Here is a review of tips for prolonging battery life of your portable computer. Several things that affect the battery life include the amount of RAM installed, the screen brightness, the time the floppy drive is on for accessing data, and the power draw of peripherals. For a portable computer you want to install the minimum amount of RAM to effectively run the applications you will be using. Make sure the screen brightness is turned as low as possible while still keeping the screen legible. This is especially good to remember in brightly lit rooms.

Getting new batteries for a portable computer can be like going on an Easter egg hunt. There is hope for the future with universal battery sizes. Duracell is leading the fight for a few universally interchangeable battery sizes for powering portables. When the standards are finalized, replacement batteries will be much easier to find. Standardized batteries means battery rechargers will also be easy to find. There might even be rentals for fully charged batteries available at airports or hotels. Convenience is the key word here. Remember, if you decide to carry an extra battery and it is not in the recharger pack, keep it in an insulated carrying case. This will prevent the contacts on the battery pack from accidentally shorting out. Shorted batteries have been known to start fires from the excess heat generated.

Power Conservation

Before 1994 many portables used CPUs that ran on 5 volts. Now there are an abundance of 3-volt CPUs on the market that prolong battery power time by requiring less energy. Most of the systems built mid-1993 are hybrid systems that mix both 3-volt and 5-volt chips on the system board. In 1994 fully based 3-volt systems became available, resulting in an even greater power savings. A purely 3-volt system decreases power consumption by about 35 percent, which can tag on 15 to 30 minutes more battery life to the computer system. The 3-volt systems run cooler and can be lighter by shedding some battery weight. The only down-side is that 3.3-volt chips are more susceptible to damage by static charge. This is because the conductors are closer together, which means there is more circuitry in a smaller space and the oxide is thinner. Hybrid 3.3-volt and 5-volt systems, when the system is optimized for a 5-volt chip-set, could lose 20 to 30 percent of their speed. The 5-volt chips can run considerably hot, and without a cooling fan for the circuitry the heat can overload the system. Heat is the enemy of electronic components; if it is not controlled it can lead to system failure.

The System Management Mode (SMM), a feature of the Intel SL microprocessor line, maintains data integrity while extending battery life. AMD makes chips that replicate this mode, and they are in the SXL line. Look in the main CPU section for more information on these microprocessors.

Power-saving features keep you happily computing on the road without worrying about a battery rundown on the way to an important function like a corporate board meeting. Portable computers using Microsoft's APM (Advanced Power Management) specification integrate the operating system with the hardware and conserve energy by powering down unused components. This can extend battery life up to 25 percent. APM is best applied when combined with a CPU that integrates power management features. All this power management takes place behind the scenes, invisible to the user.

Power-saving features to look for in a portable computers include a user-definable, timed power shutdown that controls the hard drive, the backlight, and the computer sleep mode. Some systems will let you set the inactive time period, ranging from one minute to one hundred minutes or more, which triggers the power-down mode. A rest/resume button is handy because when you leave the computer you can easily activate the button and conserve power. Upon your return to the computer you just start typing and you will instantly resume to the point that you left off without having to reboot, or restart the computer.

For saving power, the CPU can slow down after a period of non-use, thereby conserving power until you resume work. This allows the user to avoid needing to turn off the computer to conserve power and then restarting it later, causing a large power drain. Look for automatic power-saving features like display dimming or blanking, CPU slowing or stopping, hard disk power down, and peripheral power down, which turns the serial port off when the communications device is not being used.

Look for a screen reversal mode which changes the screen from displaying black-on-white text to white-on-black text. The latter mode will save battery juice, especially when the brightness is turned down low.

Two low-power consumption modes are called standby and hibernation mode. In *standby* mode the computer shuts most functions down but keeps the current state in memory fresh. In *hibernation* mode the computer shuts most functions down and writes the current memory state to the hard disk. By doing this the important information is not lost in the event of a total battery power drain.

The portable computer should have some kind of power measuring device that lets you know when the battery is getting low. Some systems have an audible beep or LED light that flashes. Better yet is a power meter, similar to a gas gauge, that lets you always keep track of power drain.

Many portable computers save energy by shutting down unused parts of the computer. If you are going to print a document, make sure you first turn the printer on and then turn the portable computer on, because when the computer is powered on it searches for an active printer on the parallel port, and if it does not find an activated printer many portables disable the printer port in an effort to conserve energy. You may get an error message stating that you cannot print. If this happens simply save what you are working on and turn the computer off. Then turn the printer on and restart the computer, in that order. Now you are ready to print.

Carrying Case

Carrying cases are often overlooked when buying a portable. The case should be big enough so it at least accommodates both the computer and the AC power adapter. Remember you might need extra storage for floppies, batteries, cables, a portable printer, and paper. It is a good idea to get a low profile case to keep everyone on the street from knowing you're carrying a portable computer. There are some cases that look like a normal sack or backpack that are comfortable to carry and are very discreet.

Additional Features

The FCC regulates radio frequency emissions that are generated by computers. The FCC Class B standard is a more stringent standard than Class A. All portable computers are required to have Class B certification. When buying a portable computer, ask for the system FCC Class B identification number, which verifies that the portable computer adheres to the low radio frequency emission.

The placement of features on portable computers should be ergonomically designed. Floppy drives integrated in portable computers should be easily accessible for both right-handed and left-handed people. The floppy access should not interfere with access to the ports in case you need simultaneous access to both. Floppy drives need to be accessed with ease. If you need to transfer data from your portable to a desktop system and dread the idea of having to constantly swap floppy disks, there is another solution. There are communication software packages that include serial cables which connect your portable to another computer. Files can be managed and exchanged much faster with a serial cable than with the relatively slow floppy drive. Cable transfers also take care of transfers of files larger than 1.44 megabytes, as these files will not fit onto a floppy without splitting the file or compressing it.

Some portables are offering software applications preloaded on the computer and stored in Read Only Memory (ROM). This means you will not need hard disk space to load the programs.

The portable will also conserve energy, as gathering data from ROM takes less energy than does accessing data on a hard drive. When the new version of the application in ROM is released you might want to upgrade from the older version. If you are buying a portable with applications stored in ROM, make sure the ROM chip is in an upgradable socket and not soldered onto the motherboard. A socketed chip can be replaced with newer software, whereas a soldered chip cannot be upgraded.

A portable with a wrist rest can be easier to use than one without wrist support. If the portable you choose does not have a wrist rest built-in, you can add on wrist rests that are available as an accessory and are made of foam rubber or neoprene. Using one of these wrist rests adds to the list of things you have to take with you on the road.

Portable Varieties

The title "portable computer" is a generic name that encompasses many different types of computers. There are several classifications of portable computers commonly referred to as laptops, notebooks, subnotebooks, and handhelds.

Portable Statistics

Type	**Luggable**	**Laptop**	**Notebook**	**Subnotebook**	**Handheld**
Weight	20+ pounds	8 to 20 pounds	4 to 7.5 pounds	2.5 to 4 pounds	2 or less pounds
Size in Inches	Big	Up to 14 x 14 x 4	Up to 12 x 9 x 2.5	Up to 11 x 8 x 1.5	Up to 8 x 4 x 1
Operating Systems	DOS, UNIX, System 7, Windows, Windows NT, OS/2	DOS, Windows, UNIX, System 7	DOS, UNIX, Windows, System 7	DOS, Windows, System 7	DOS, Proprietary
Microprocessors Commonly Used	286, 386, 486, Pentium, Power PC	286, 386, 486, Pentium, Power PC, 680 x 0	286, 386, 486, Power PC, 680 x 0	386SL 486SL, NEC V30, Intel 80C88	Intel 80C88, Intel Draco, Intel Elan, Intel Polar, Motorola Dragon, NEC V20, NEC V30, NEC V820, Acorn ARM, AT&T Hobbit

The GRID Convertible features as a notebook or a pen-based tablet.

The Extras to Bring on the Road

It is always wise to be prepared for any problem you may encounter while traveling with your computer. Countries all around the world use different AC plugs and telephone jacks. The company CP+ provides a kit for world travelers that allows you connect a modem to all the various telephone adapters used in each country. To have the greatest amount of flexibility on the road, consider carrying the following in your bag of tricks:

- 20-foot AC power extension cord
- Portable AC and phone line surge suppresser
- Two-to-three prong electrical plug adapter
- Electrical tape

- Flashlight
- Extra battery
- Phone line adapters for overseas
- 20-foot telephone cord
- Male-to-male telephone adapter for hooking two cords together
- Acoustic coupler for connecting computer modem direct to phone handset
- Flat-ribbon parallel printer cable
- Serial cable for file transfer
- Backup of important data on diskettes stored separately from computer
- Boot diskette of DOS
- Minimum installation disks for Windows
- Backup copies of important software applications

If you often travel with a portable computer between two locations, like from home to the office, it is great to have two AC power adapters for the portable computer. Leaving an adapter at each location means not having to carry the adapter every day. Plus, if one adapter ever breaks you have peace of mind knowing there is a backup close at hand. Buying a new adapter usually means placing a special order at a computer store which takes ten working days or even longer. Low pressure environments can be detrimental to portable computers. If you plan on flying with your portable, make sure it is stored in a pressurized cabin. Cargo holds are usually not pressurized, and at altitudes above 10,000 feet a portable computer's screen may implode.

Security

Portable computers are especially prone to information loss. This happens primarily for two reasons: portables are damaged easily by mishandling, and they are prime targets for the ethically challenged.

If the information you carry is for-your-eyes-only, you might want to take extra security precautions. Some commercial software programs offer password protection, but this security is usually not too hard for someone who knows what he is doing to bypass. The better alternative is to use an encryption program to encrypt all important files on the hard disk. This ensures that if anyone gets hold of your computer, the contents will be entirely useless.

Insurance can ease the pain if the computer is stolen. Home insurance policies sometimes do not cover portable computers if you take them out of the house. Auto policies similarly may not cover items unless they are considered a permanent part of the car. Some insurance policies have a dollar limit on what they will cover. If you have a portable computer it is a good idea to review your insurance policies and see if it is covered. If it is not, get a rider for your policy to include the computer. Safeware and the Computer Insurance Company are companies that specialize in insuring computer equipment. It costs about $60 per year to cover $3,000 worth of computer equipment. Safeware can be reached at 1-800-848-3469, and the Computer Insurance Company can be reached at 1-800-722-0385.

Aside from keeping backups on floppy disks of new data generated on your computer while on the road, you may want to mail copies of newly backed-up data to your home or office. This way if your bags are stolen you still have those important hours of work in a safe place.

Many computers come with a security slot. This is a little hole on the side of the computer that lets you attach a lock and cable which can then be secured to furniture or the wall. These cables prevent your computer from being swiped easily but are not much of a deterrent to premeditated theft. All it takes is a $10 pair of cable cutters to free the computer from its security tether.

It is a good idea to design a custom message that will be displayed every time your computer is turned on. This can be done by putting a message in the AUTOEXEC.BAT file. Include a message offering a reward for the return of the computer and a way to contact you. If you want to go the extra step, place a picture of yourself on the computer with a message stating "(your name) is the rightful owner of the computer. If anyone else is seen using this computer notify the authorities immediately."

Alternative Energy

If you live where there is no electric service you may want to investigate alternative ways to power your laptop computer. Solar panels can provide the juice to power your computer and to charge the batteries. A great sources for photovoltaic cells are the mail order vendors Jade Mountain and Real Goods. You can request their catalogs through the contact numbers and addresses listed at the end of this book.

Odds and Ends

Remember that computers are susceptible to damage from changes in temperature. If you bring your portable in from the freezing cold, let it warm up to room temperature for a few hours before using it. Being impatient can cause the condensation to interfere with the normal operations of the computer. If you need to collect data at freezing temperatures, load the programs into RAM beforehand and then use a RAM disk instead of the hard disk. A RAM disk has no moving parts, unlike the hard disk, which is more vulnerable to the fluctuations in temperature.

At low temperatures, the LCD screen response slows way down and the battery does not last as long. In the extreme, liquid crystals can explode out of the screen, like freezing a can of soda. High temperatures will make the screen seem to swim with ripples. In extra hot situations the screen will turn dark.

Floppy disks should not be read at temperatures that approach freezing. Floppies should be able to weather below freezing storage temperatures for short periods of time. The other extreme, heat, is also the enemy of floppy disks. Floppies should not be left in an environment above 140° F. Leaving floppies in the car on a hot day can result in warped disks and lost data. Heat also is not very kind to LCD screens. At 200° F or higher temperatures the liquid crystals will start to boil and you can kiss your portable's screen good-bye.

Chapter 8

Practical Printers

Printers are the most common peripheral bought to complement the personal computer. Printers vary in their output quality and the technology used to print. The quality of a printer is dependent on the speed of the printing, the ability to print colors or grayscale, and the resolution.

Emulation

Printers use page description languages to convert computer generated images into a format that the printer can use to place ink, dye, or toner on the page. Printers vary in respect to the page description language they can understand. Printer Control Language (PCL) is a language that Hewlett-Packard developed and is a standard used by many printers. PostScript is a page description language developed by Adobe and is used at most desktop publishing businesses because of its excellent ability to handle text and complicated graphics.

PCL 5 and PostScript Level 2 are the latest releases of these two languages. Both of these standards can receive from the computer data that has been compressed. This compression speeds up printing jobs by reducing the time it takes to transmit information from the computer to the printer and is a feature that the earlier PCL 4 and PostScript Level 1 lack. Both PCL 5 and PostScript Level 2 have scaleable font technology built in. The PCL 5 standard provides a wider variety of fonts than does PCL 4. The printers with the most recent page description language utilize the latest printing technology and therefore cost more.

If you are working with desktop publishing or illustration programs, then PostScript is a necessity for your printer to include. PostScript is an actual programming language and not a set of printer control codes. Both languages use memory to store downloaded fonts from the computer, but PostScript does a finer job of handling gradients, curves, fills, and color separations than PCL 5. Because of its complexity, PostScript printers require more memory than PCL printers.

Having one page description language in a printer does not exclude the printer from using other printer control languages. There are many printers on the market that support both PostScript and PCL 5. If you are looking at one of these printers make sure it is auto-sensing or auto-switching. This means the printer can tell what kind of printing language is being sent to it. Without this feature you will have to manually switch the printer into the mode you wish to use.

Printers with auto-emulation sensing are essential to networked printers. Auto-emulation sensing determines the type of document being printed and automatically uses the correct emulation. This will prevent you from having to manually change the emulation on the printer every time you want to use a different page description language.

Most printers are flexible in their ability to download fonts from a computer. Printers that use PCL 5 or PostScript 2 are capable of downloading fonts. Some other printers require a font cartridge installed in the printer to print fonts and therefore are more limited in the font selection they have. Both Level 2 and PCL 5 allow you to choose the paper tray you wish to print from on printers with more than one paper tray.

If you are buying a printer without PostScript but think you may need it sometime in the future then make sure the printer you select has a upgrade slot that will let you add PostScript. PostScript 2 printers allow you to switch the printing resolution from the computer and allow the printer to have a SCSI hard drive attached to the printer which can store blank forms and fonts. This feature included on a networked printer enhances print performance by reducing the amount of information that needs to be sent to the printer from the computer. Blank forms stored on the hard disk can be filled in with new information by the computer using a request to use a specific form, and this cuts down on network traffic. A printer with a hard drive option can speed up a busy printer. If the printer is currently working on another print job, it can download your new print job to the printer's hard drive, which frees up your computer for the next task. Without this hard drive spooling feature, your computer will be tied up until the printer is free.

Plotters often use the HPGL plotter emulation mode. If you are purchasing a plotter, check for HPGL compatibility.

If you are going to be networking the printer to many computers look for the NPAP (Network Printing Alliance Protocol), which provides a set of printer-to-host commands that will let the printer exchange its status, configuration, and control with the computers on the network. This makes it possible for the printer and computer to relay information over the network on the printer configuration, the status of a print job, the memory allocation, and other useful information. NPAP printers can notify you of paper jams, general failure, toner status, and if the paper is low or out. This is a bi-directional protocol, meaning the computer can talk to the printer and vise-versa. This protocol works in tandem with other page description languages and communication interfaces.

Fonts

Find out how many typefaces come standard with the printer and whether they are scaleable or fixed size fonts. **Scaleable fonts**, also called outline fonts, will print at many different point sizes with no degradation of quality. Scaleable fonts achieve their dexterity by being stored as algorithms which describe the characters as curves. **Bitmapped fonts** have each character stored as a combination of individual pixels. If these fonts are enlarged they will look jagged, like type looks when printed by a dot matrix printer.

Resident fonts, fonts that are stored inside the printer, will print out quicker than fonts that need to be transferred to the printer from the computer. Fonts stored in the computer are often called screen fonts. If you are printing using only one font, you may not notice a difference in speed between screen and resident fonts, but if you use many fonts on a page the extra printing time for screen fonts will be noticeably longer. A printer that includes 35 resident fonts is a good minimum to start with.

New fonts can be added to a printer with a font cartridge. Ask whether the printer accepts font cartridges and if they are proprietary or standard cartridges. The proprietary cartridges are likely to be more expensive and harder to find than standard cartridges. Many printers are now offering flash memory or a printer hard disk, which can be used to store extra fonts. With one of these features you can permanently download fonts to the printer making for faster printing speeds. This feature is a must for big network printers. Flash memory is a faster alternative to hard drive storage, but flash memory is more expensive. The only drawback besides price is flash memory must be completely erased before you write to it and it will wear out after a number of erasures. The good news is it does not wear out unless erased about 100,000 times.

Resolution

Printers differ in their ability to print text and images clearly. The sharpness or resolution is measured in dots per inch (dpi). A printer that outputs 300 dpi does a fine job for text. This means there are 300 dots along the vertical axis and 300 dots along the horizontal axis. A 300 dpi printer should be able to print 33 possible shades of gray at 53 lines per inch.

For printing graphics the newer 600 dpi printers are able to print with more definition and can simulate 72 shades of gray at 71 lines per inch. If you are going to send out a catalog or brochure to a professional printing press to be mass produced, you will want to view a proof before committing to the layout on the page. Professional level pre-press proofs are usually printed at 1,200 dpi or at the super fine 2,400 dpi. Image setters that operate at 2,540 dpi should be able to print all 256 possible PostScript levels of gray at over 200 lines per inch.

At the heart of a printer is the printing engine. A 300-dpi printer engine can place 300 dots per inch horizontally and vertically. This yields a total possible grid of 90,000 dots per square inch. A 600-dpi printer can place 600 vertical dots and 600 horizontal dots. This yields 360,000 possible dots per square inch. This makes the total dot per square inch resolution four times greater on a 600-dpi printer than a 300-dpi printer. The 600-dpi printers are much better than 300-dpi printers for printing halftones, scanned images, graphics, illustrations, and small type.

If you want to print type that is 10 points or larger, then a 300-dpi printer will handle the job. For business graphics, text smaller than 10 point, technical illustrations, graphs, and charts, you will need a printer resolution of 600 dpi or higher. For printing publications, small typefaces, photographs, and illustrations, you need a 1,200-dpi or better printer. For the high end of the printing spectrum, like photograph reproduction, technical illustrations, color separations, or magazine quality print, you need a film-based imagesetter.

The amount of RAM a printer needs increases at higher resolutions. At 300 dpi a printer with 4 megabytes of RAM is a good amount to print just about anything. You will want at least 8 megabytes of printer RAM for 600-dpi printing and 16 megabytes of printer RAM for 1,200-dpi printing.

Many graphic images are in grayscale, and most printers can only print using a black dot or no dot at all. To make a gray image printers use special methods to convert the grayscale image into a black-and-white image. Various sized black dots printed in differing-sized clusters will trick the eye into seeing multiple levels of gray. This method of simulating grayscale is called halftoning.

To produce the gray, a matrix of black and white dots are set to simulate different levels of gray. Each matrix is divided into individual cells. In each matrix the more black cells that are added, the darker the level of gray produced. When all the cells are completely filled the image will be black. The more pixels in a halftone matrix, the greater the number of grays the printer can produce. The shape created by the pixels in the matrix is usually a dot or ellipse but sometimes can be squares, crescents, or random shapes. The number of matrix per inch is known as the screen frequency, also known as lines per inch. For example, 65 halftone dots per inch equals 65 lines per inch. In other words the number of shapes per inch equals the lines per inch. Generally printers with higher resolution can simulate a greater number of grayscales.

The lines per inch of a printer is always less than the dots per inch resolution because the halftone dot is composed of a matrix of smaller pixels. A printer with greater resolution has the potential to produce a higher number of lines per inch, but that does not necessarily mean that it definitely will print a higher lpi than a printer with a lower resolution.

Speed

Print speed is generally measured by estimating the number of **pages per minute (ppm)** that a printer engine can deliver. The ppm is a rating of the top speed that a printer engine can possibly deliver in printed pages. Some printers are rated in **characters per second (cps)**. To convert characters per second to pages per minute, divide the characters per second by 50. For example, a printer that can print 220 characters per second is printing 4.4 pages per minute.

A printer can run at its top-rated pages per minute speed when printing multiple copies of the same page. This means the **Raster Image Processor (RIP)** has already interpreted the printing codes into graphics that the printer then stores in memory. This means the printer can print the stored page without processing delays. The RIP plays an important role in real-world page per minute speed of a printer. The faster and more powerful the RIP, the quicker new pages can be interpreted into graphics to be printed. If you are printing text documents that use fonts that reside in the printer, the RIP will play a lesser role in overall printing speed. If you are printing nonresident fonts and graphics, the speed of the RIP will have a greater impact on the speed of the printing.

The page-per-minute range of printers available on the market is anywhere from 4 ppm to 95 ppm. This rating applies loosely to printing a page consisting of text. Printing graphics takes longer than the page-per-minute rating. The size of the paper used in determining these ratings is the standard letter size paper measuring 8.5 by 11 inches. Paper of different dimension will have a different maximum speed. The photosensitive drum used in laser printers is usually optimized for the standard paper size, but some printers are specialized to print on other sizes of paper.

Raster Image Processors that are controlled by RISC chips can generally process graphics much faster than RIPs using CISC chips running at the same clock speed. Printers that use RISC processors are known to out-perform printers using CISC processors by a factor of two or three times.

Picking the print speed that you will need is based on the type of work you need to accomplish. If you are budget-minded and do not plan on printing a lot of graphics, then a 4 ppm printer will do fine. If you use PostScript, print graphics, or use a wide variety of fonts on the same page, then you will probably want a printer that can handle at least 6 ppm. Networked computers that share the same printer need the higher printing speeds available; these printers are often rated at 15 pages per minute or faster. An 8-page-per-minute printer will usually drop down to 2 ppm when attempting to print graphics. Printing complex graphics can take several minutes per page on a 4 ppm printer.

Although the graphics page per minute (gppm) rating is not routinely advertised, you may want to consider the printer's gppm if you are printing lots of graphics. This rating can be a important factor if your work consists mostly of printing graphic images, because if the printer you choose does not print fast enough it can slow down your work schedule.

The amount of RAM installed in the printer is a factor that affects the printing speed. Some printers can handle dual-page printing which allows the second page to be created in memory while the first page is being printed. The amount of printer RAM also affects your ability to print text and graphics. Consider 1 megabyte as the minimum RAM needed to print a page of graphics on a 300 dpi printer. If you use lots of graphics or download lots of fonts you will want more than 1 megabyte of RAM installed in the printer.

Dumb or Smart

Printing speed is affected by the printer's on-board circuitry. A dumb buffered printer has no brain, so to speak. All the processing of the page in conjunction with a dumb buffered printer takes place in the computer. The processed print graphics are then sent from the computer to the printer, which in turn controls the printing process and other print mechanisms. This method of printing ties up your computer while the page's graphics are being calculated by the computer.

To avoid the tie-up of computer resources you will want to buy a coprocessed printer. These "smart" printers are usually controlled by a RISC (Reduced Instruction Set Chip) microprocessor. When using a smart printer the computer participates minimally when printing a document. The computer sends the document, with page-control-language commands for page formatting, to the printer where the instructions are processed. The printer takes up the processing load and converts the page control language into page graphics. This conversion is known as rasterizing and the microprocessor that performs this is called the raster image processor (RIP). After rasterization the printer then produces the hard copy. Meanwhile during processing by the printer, the computer is free for you to use for your next task.

The microprocessor that handles the raster image processing will determine the speed that the printer can print documents and graphics. Many printers are based on the Motorola's 68000 family of microprocessors or Intel's 80186 microprocessor. Both of these are Complex Instruction Set Chips (CISC chips). The clock speed of these chips affects the overall speed of the printer.

Most dot-matrix and ink-jet printers are line printers. They are fed one line of text or graphics at a time from the computer and usually have small buffers to hold the incoming data. Entry level laser printers lack their own processing power, which means they are dumb buffered printers. The second tier of laser printers are coprocessed printers; these are the printers of choice.

Color

Most printers print black or simulated levels of gray on paper or other printing media. Recently a burst of color has hit the market in the form of affordable ink-jet printers. Color printers allow presentations to really shine, can make type stand out, and are lots of fun. Many color printers use three or four colored ribbons or ink. Printers that use three colors mix them to get a range of colors. Three-color printers contain cyan, magenta, and yellow which they mix to get black. Four-color printers use black ink or dye and therefore produce output with greater contrast and richer blacks. Printers that use four-color ribbons or ink are often referred to as CMYK printers (K is for blacK). The better printers use separate ribbons or cartridges for all the colors so when you run out of a color you can replace it separately. This is especially good for people who print one color more than others.

The best professional level color printers are Pantone certified. They come with features that allow you to adjust the color output to Pantone-colored swatches. This will amend for any discrepancies between the way your printer produces colors and the way the monitor produces color tones. If you need colors on the printed page to accurately match the colors on the screen, then this is a feature to look for in a printer.

Memory

Printers use memory to store the page description before printing. If the printer does not have enough memory it will not be able to print a file with lots of data like graphics or varied fonts. For a 300-dot-per-inch printer, a regular text file with few fonts can usually be printed with 512 kilobytes of printer RAM, but having 1 megabyte or more installed is better for flexible printing. Printing a full page of graphics requires at least 1 megabyte of printer memory. A standard amount of 2 megabytes of RAM will be sufficient for most files. Three-hundred-dpi printers that use PostScript should have a minimum of 2 megabytes of printer memory installed. If you intend to print lots of graphics and images, then 4 megabytes or more is recommended. The more memory you have installed the more complex an image you can print and the better performance you will get from the printer.

Recommended Printer Memory

Resolution of Printer	*For PostScript Printers*	*For Non-PostScript Printers*
300 dpi	2 Mb	1 Mb
600 dpi	6 Mb	4 Mb
1200 dpi	18 Mb	16 Mb
2400 dpi	66 Mb	64 Mb

A 600-dot-per-inch printer needs 4 megabytes of RAM as the minimum amount of RAM installed. A 600-dpi printer with PostScript should have at least 6 megabytes of memory. A 1200-dot-per-inch printer needs a minimum of 32 megabytes of RAM to work efficiently. As you can see, the RAM needed increases dramatically when printing at higher resolutions.

Before buying a printer, find out the maximum amount of RAM that can be installed in it. Ask whether the memory is proprietary or if the printer uses standard SIMM or DIP memory chips. If the memory is proprietary it may be harder to find and will usually cost more. SIMM and DIP memory is easy to find and is competitively priced.

Duty Cycle

Printers are rated by the maximum amount of printing they can handle per month. This is known as the **monthly duty cycle**. If you intend to use the printer fairly heavily, then check for the rated monthly page duty cycle. If you regularly push the printer beyond its recommended duty cycle, the printer is likely to have paper handling problems. These problems include paper jams, incorrect paper handling, or mechanical failure.

Personal laser printers are usually rated at a monthly duty cycle of around 10,000 pages. Networked printers must stand up to heavy use and often have monthly duty cycles ratings of at least 25,000 pages. Printers with duty cycles of 50,000 pages per month can handle a good-sized network of computers.

Paper Handling

Letter, legal, envelopes, transparencies, and labels are just a few types of printing media you may want to print on. The printer you buy should be directly related to the kind of output you need.

United States Standard Paper Sizes

Paper Type	*Inches*	*Centimeters*
Legal Size	8.5 x 13 or 8.5 x 14	21.6 x 33 or 21.6 x 35.5
A	8.5 x 11	21.6 x 27.9
B (Tabloid)	11 x 17	27.9 x 43.1
C	17 x 22	43.1 x 55.8
D	22 x 34	55.8 x 86.3
E	34 x 44	86.3 x 111.7
F	28 x 40	71.1 x 101.6
G	11 x 42	27.9 x 106.6
H	28 x 48	71.1 x 121.9
J	34 x 48	86.3 x 121.9
K	40 x 48	101.6 x 121.9

Those who print on different sizes of paper often want a printer with more than one paper tray. For the most flexibility look for a printer that can accommodate more than one size of paper at the same time and with software drivers that can remotely switch to the paper tray you need to use from the computer screen. Find out how many paper trays come standard with the printer and the maximum number of trays the printer can handle. Most printers come with only one paper tray option, and a few printers come with two or more paper trays.

Most printers print on the standard 8.5-by-11-inch paper. If you need to print on odd-sized paper, this is a matter to be investigated. When shopping for a printer, request the specifications on the maximum paper size the printer will handle. A printer able to print tabloid size, 11-by-17-inch, is helpful if you are printing posters and large spreadsheets, or making presentations. Some laser and ink-jet printers handle super B-size paper, which measures 11.8 by 17.2 inches.

The paper tray's maximum capacity is an important consideration, as a smaller tray will run out of paper more often. Personal printers often have paper trays that handle a maximum of 250 sheets of paper. Network printers require large paper trays for maximum paper handling because many people will be printing from the same printer. A 500-sheet paper tray will keep you from having to constantly refill the paper tray. Some networked printers allow 1,000 or more pages. On a networked printer a combination of paper trays is especially convenient for handling more than one type of paper, like envelopes, legal, and letter sizes. Make sure the printer drivers are able to handle multiple paper trays. The paper output bin is where the paper ends up after being printed. These output bins should be able to handle large quantities of paper. A printer with an input paper tray of 500 sheets and an output tray of 100 sheets is of little help unless all the printing jobs are very small.

The paper weight handled is a quality of consideration for printers. Most printers can handle up to 24 lb. paper. This is the type of paper most people use for printing resumes. Some printers handle 31 lb., 36 lb., or even thicker paper. If you need to print card stock often, first choose the weight of the paper and then find the right printer. The paper weight is a reference to the total weight of a ream of paper consisting of 500 sheets of paper and measuring 17 by 22 inches.

If you need to print on both sides of a piece of paper, look for printers that offer **duplex** printing, a feature found mostly with networkable printers. These printers print on both sides of the paper in the right sequence, without having to feed the paper in twice. The paper train, the path through which the paper travels while printing, should be easily accessible. This makes it easier to clear the paper path in case any paper gets jammed.

What side of the paper do you print on? If you are printing on only one side of the paper, you will get the best results if you use the more appropriate side to print on. The two opposite sides of a paper are referred to as the felt side and the wire side. The wire side is rougher than the felt side. The felt side is the better side to use when printing. Look for an indicator from the manufacturer for the felt side when you open a new ream of paper. If the sides are not clearly marked and you are using watermarked bond, you can find the felt side by holding the paper up to the light. If the watermark design is not reversed you are looking at the felt side.

Recurring Costs

Toner, drums, paper, ink, and transparencies are all factors that contribute to recurring costs. Transparencies usually run about 7 cents per sheet, coated paper is about 6 cents per sheet, and laser printer plain white paper is about 1 to 2 cents per sheet.

Printer ink and toner cartridges are rated at the estimated number of pages that they will print. This is an estimated figure and your mileage will vary with real use because the actual number depends on how much ink you use on the page. The manufacturer usually bases the recurring cost on optimal conditions such as pages printed with double-spaced text and without graphics. Nevertheless it will still give you a hint to how long you can expect the ink or toner to last. Part of the recurring cost can be minimized by using refilled cartridges instead of buying new ink or toner cartridges. To save cost, check the documents on the computer screen in print preview mode before you print the page and you can eliminate unnecessary waste. Some printers allow for draft mode printing to print a document using half the amount of ink or toner on the page. The output will look gray instead of a full black, but you will see what the page layout will look like.

Part of the overall cost to operate a printer is attributed to its engine life. When the printer engine wears out, it is time to get a new printer. Check how many printing copies the engine is rated to produce so you can budget for a new printer at the end of the life cycle. Printer engines are usually rated to print in the range of 200,000 to 500,000 copies.

Since most printers do not have a "fuel gauge" that lets the operator know when the ink or toner is almost completely consumed, it is smart to always have a backup cartridge available. This ensures that when the printer does run out of ink or toner it will not interrupt important printing jobs. New cartridges may have to be special-ordered from a computer store if they are not in stock, and that can take several days. Having an extra cartridge allows one to be recharged while the other is in use. Store the extra cartridge in a dark, cool environment to prolong its shelf life. Most toner cartridges will last for two years if stored properly.

Ports

Most printers attach with a cable to the parallel port of the computer. Some printers, like plotters, attach via cable to a serial port on the computer. The serial port is much slower at transferring data than the parallel port. If you are running a network make sure the printer can interface with the type of network you have, like Ethernet or Token Ring. If there are Macs on the network you may need an AppleTalk interface on the printer. A printer that accepts a SCSI attachment to the computer can be daisy-chained with up to seven other devices like scanners and CD-ROMs.

When you order your printer make sure it is supplied with the proper cabling to link it with your computer. This will save you a second trip to the store when you realize that the printer came without a cable. Find out how long the printer cable needs to be to reach from the printer to the computer. Parallel cables work best at less than fifteen feet. It is not recommended that you run the cable more than fifteen feet, but if you do, make sure the cable is high-quality and shielded. At fifty feet or longer the parallel signal degrades and the printer may not operate correctly. If you need to have the printer more than fifty feet away, consider getting a buffered printing system that will boost the parallel signal so it will travel the long distance.

Bi-directional printer ports allow the printer to communicate with the computer with greater interactive control. With a bi-directional port, the printer can send "Out of paper," "Paper jam," or other messages to the computer screen to let you know the document is not printing.

For network printing look for a printer with an "all ports active" feature, which means all the printer's ports are constantly ready and listening for input. This allows for automatic switching when printing. A printer lacking this feature would require you to manually flip a switch to activate the proper printing port.

When one printer port receives data, the other ports are temporarily disabled from receiving. Having a network connection allows users to transfer data to the printer faster than via the parallel port and also eliminates the need for a dedicated printer server on the network. A print server is a computer that is used only to handle printing. Common choices for networking printers include Token Ring, Ethernet, and AppleTalk. The appropriate standard choice is best left to a networking expert.

Portable Printers

The primary concern of portable printers besides the quality of the print is the weight of the printer and the number of pages the printer will print. Portable printers commonly use ink-jet or thermal-fusion to print on paper because it is energy efficient and allows the printer to be lightweight. There are not any portable laser printers because laser printers consume too much energy and weigh too much. Thermal-fusion portable printers usually print about 25 pages with a single-strike ribbon and up to 75 pages with multistrike ribbons. These ribbons cost about $5 US. Ink-jet printers usually print 300 to 500 pages with a single cartridge. These cost around $30 US to replace. Portable printers usually compromise on their speed because they are designed to run on batteries and therefore must conserve energy.

The AC adapters that portable printers use average at near half a pound. To fully recharge the printer's battery usually takes about six hours. The number of pages a printer can deliver before the battery runs out of charge is an important consideration. Most portable printers print around 50 pages before the battery needs to be recharged or swapped.

Most portable printers take single fed paper. You have to load paper one page at a time, and to get the paper properly positioned can take a steady hand. Optional cut-sheet feeders are available for most portable printers and generally handle thirty to fifty sheets of paper at a time. This can make bigger print jobs less of a hassle because you can request a printout and leave the printer unattended while it prints the document for you. If you want to shed weight on the road, just leave the sheet feeder behind.

Chapter 9

Printer Technologies

Dot-Matrix Printers

Dot-matrix printers are popular because of their speed and low cost. They are not best suited for high quality and fancy printing jobs like graphics or halftones, but they can deliver fairly good print and operate at a fraction of the cost of most other printers.

Similar to the way the computer screen displays an image, a printer's **resolution** is dependent upon how small and close together small dots of pigment can be printed. The resolution on a dot-matrix printer varies depending on whether it is a 9-pin or 24-pin model. The 9-pin produces a poorer image quality but is less expensive than the 24-pin, and the 24-pin printer produces near-letter quality. The best dot-matrix resolution available is near 72 dpi (dots per inch), making it legible for text but insufficient for printing graphics or photo images.

Dot-matrix printers use an impact technology which tends to make them quite noisy. The pins strike against an inked ribbon to produce an image on the page, and when the pins strike they create noise. Some printers have a noise reduction feature that can make them nearly as quiet as laser printers, but this feature usually slows down the printing speed by 50 percent.

The speed of a dot-matrix printer is often measured in the number of characters per second (cps) it can print. Most dot-matrix printers can print about two to four pages per minute depending on the printer buffer size and the speed of the print head. Speed is also affected by the print mode. Many dot-matrix printers can print in draft mode which is a reduced quality. The normal printing mode, which is a near-letter quality mode, approaches ink-jet printing quality. Printing documents in near-letter quality mode takes about three times as long as printing in draft mode, and printing in graphics mode takes longer than near-letter quality mode.

The print buffer size can affect the speed of the printing. The print buffer is the place where the printing information is temporarily stored after being sent from the computer. Printing text using resident fonts usually requires about 3 kilobytes per page. If you do not use resident fonts each page can take 8 kilobytes or more. Most dot-matrix printers have an 8-kilobyte or larger buffer, and most printers can upgrade the buffer size as an option.

Many dot-matrix printers can use tractor-feed continuous paper, a special paper that has holes along both sides. Some dot-matrix printers use friction feed to print on single loose sheets of paper. Some can print on both loose sheets and continuous-feed paper. Many of these printers feature auto-parking, allowing you to print envelopes, letterheads, or single sheets without having to remove the continuous-feed paper. This avoids wasting continuous-feed paper and alleviates the hassle of having to reload the paper when switching paper types. Many printers have several paper feed paths that can each handle a different size and type of paper. These paper paths can be top loading, bottom loading, front loading, or rear loading.

In general, the more resident fonts a printer comes with the better. Resident fonts print much faster than fonts that need to be downloaded from the computer to the printer. The more resident fonts available, the more flexible the print jobs the printer can handle.

The control panel on the printer should be easy to use. This is especially true because the most common adjustments you will make use the control panel. Cryptic control panels can consume lots of your time when you need to make a simple change.

Dot-matrix printers usually connect to the computer's parallel port, but some offer the option to connect to the slower serial port.

If you plan to print multipart forms make sure the printer can strike hard enough to pass the image through the number of forms you will be using. Most dot-matrix printers are able to strike through five-layer forms, but some can only strike through two-layer forms.

Color is a feature found on a few dot-matrix printers. Dot-matrix printers that handle color have a coarse and limited range of hues, making them unable to handle detailed work. Dot-matrix color printing is prone to *banding*, meaning there are visible marks made from the multiple passes the print head must make. Another drawback is the printed colors tend to fade as the print ribbon wears out. If you need to do very limited color with little detail, a dot-matrix printer may accomplish the task.

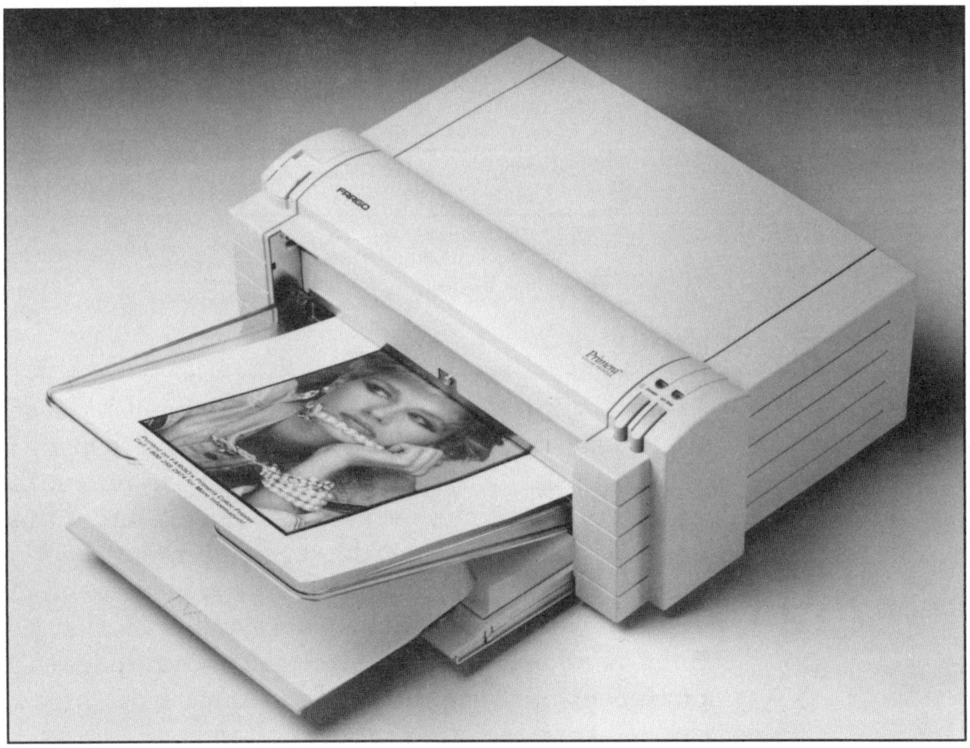

Fargo Printer

Printer Technologies Compared

Printer	24-Pin Dot-Matrix	Ink-Jet	PCL 5 Laser	High-Res Laser	Thermal Wax Transfer
Application	Multipart forms, wide paper	Memos and letters	Documents	Graphics and documents	Presentations and full page proofs
Average Pages Per Minute	1 to 2 ppm	1 to 2 ppm	4 to 10 ppm	8 to 16 ppm	0.5 to 2 ppm
Average Dots Per Inch	160 to 360 dpi	300 to 360 dpi	300 dpi	600 to 800 dpi	300 dpi
Paper Handling	Tractor-feed, cut sheet, and forms	Cut sheet paper and transparencies, labels, envelopes	Cut sheet and transparencies, labels, envelopes	Cut sheet paper and transparencies, labels, envelopes	Glossy paper and transparencies
Pros	Paper paths for different media, low cost, energy efficient	Inexpensive, quiet printing, near laser quality, some do large format	Business quality output	Business graphics, networkable	Brilliant full page color, great transparencies, less expensive than dye-sublimation
Cons	Noisy, marginal output quality, poor graphics	Slow printing, ink can smear if wet, dithered halftones	Marginal graphic output, slow when lacking RISC processor	More expensive, memory hungry	Needs special paper, colors are dithered, slow printing
Average Cost Per Page	Less than 1 cent	3 to 8 cents	3 cents	1 to 3 cents	50 cents to $1

Liquid Ink-Jet Printers

Liquid ink-jet printers have small printing heads or valves that shoot liquid ink onto print media akin to using rows of tiny squirt guns. The ink is stored in an ink reservoir. Ink-jet printers use different methods to push the ink out of the nozzle and onto the page. Thermal ink-jet printers use heat to push the minute drops of ink onto the page. Some high-end ink-jet printers use crystal-stimulated glass capillaries that are more refined in their ability to place ink on the page. The size and placement of the ink droplets is much more precise with this method than the other ink-jet methods.

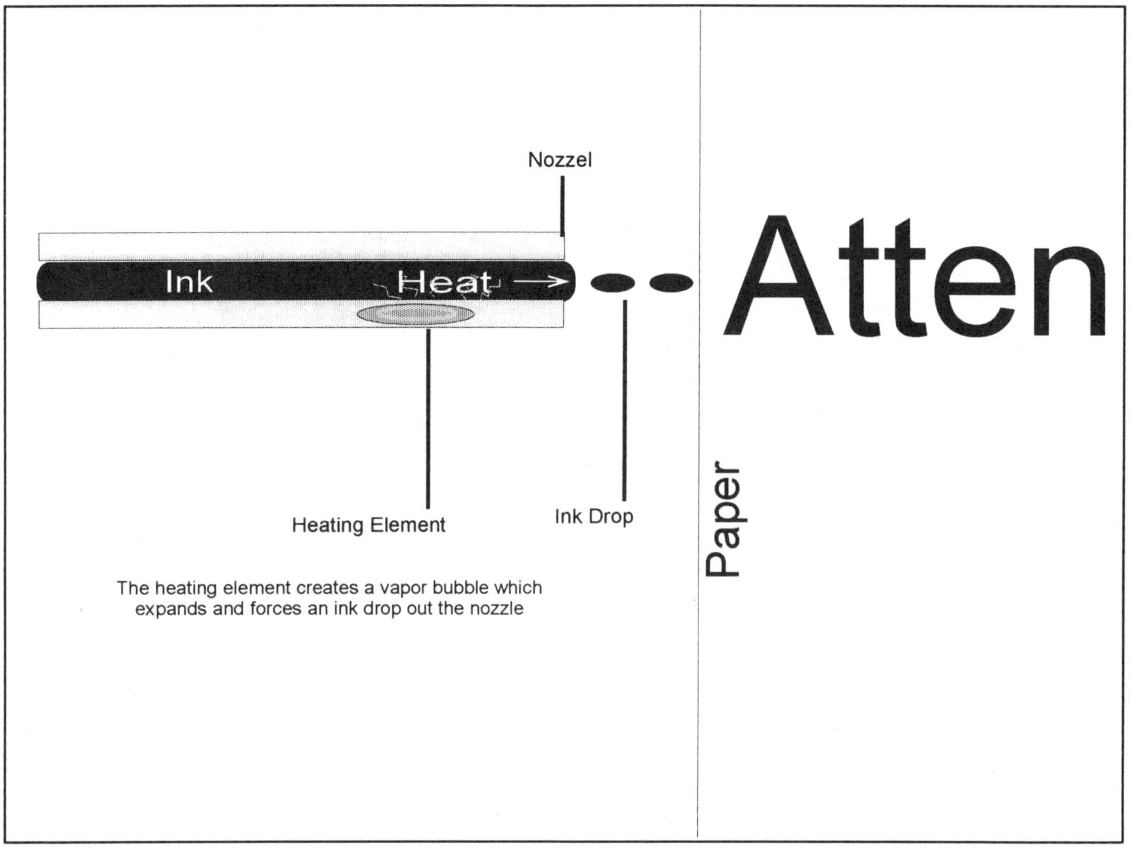

Look at Thermal Ink-jet Printing

Ink-jet printers can print black, color, or both. *Color* ink-jet printers have four ink reservoirs containing colors cyan, magenta, yellow, and black. These four pigments mixed together in varying degrees can create or simulate a wide spectrum of colors. The color ink-jets place dots of colors on the page and when viewed appear as halftones. A process commonly used to create colors or shades of gray is called dithering. Dithered printing places small dots of primary colors close together that fool the eye into seeing shades other than the cyan, magenta, yellow, and black inks used. Output can appear muddy and splotchy with banding when one color blends into another color.

Many people use ink-jet printers to do overhead projections. When printed on a transparency and projected on a screen, dithered colors appear less brilliant. For best results when printing color, use specially coated paper or transparencies.

Noisy printers can be disruptive in a business environment. Ink-jet printers can be *noisy* but usually are not nearly as loud as dot-matrix printers, and some ink-jets are as quiet as laser printers.

The resolution of printing affects the quality of the image. Most of these printers place 180 to 360 dots per inch on the page. A 300-dpi ink-jet printer does not produce as crisp and clean a print as a 300-dpi laser printer. This is because the ink bleeds into the page leaving a blurred edge. The laser printer's toner gives a fuller and richer black than ink-jet ink.

Some ink-jet printers use *continuous-feed* paper, but most use *loose sheets* of paper. If you need to do printing on 11-by-17-inch paper, look for printers that can fit that tabloid size paper. The ink can still be wet as it leaves the printer, so if the paper is handled too soon the ink will smear. Most ink-jet printers use water-soluble ink, and if the paper gets wet, it too will smear. If you are printing mailing labels and the labels get wet, the post office may not be able to read the address. The quality of the printing done by an ink-jet is considered letter quality for text.

In general ink-jet printers are not too great for graphics and images because too much ink on the page may over-saturate the paper and cause bleeding of the image. This happens because the inks are suspended in a water-based medium and the result is a blurry image. Printed images can smear if wet and will run if contacted with water.

If you have ever tried writing with a fountain pen on a napkin you know the problems of using ink on an absorbent surface. To optimize the print output you will want to use specialized paper made for ink-jet printers. The paper must be absorbent enough to let the ink dry, but if it is too absorbent the print will not look smooth and crisp. For someone doing pie charts and graphs, an ink-jet should do a fine job. If you do plan to print graphics, some of the higher-end ink-jet printers come with PostScript.

Ink-jet printers use relatively little energy and can be compact in design which makes them a good choice for people looking for a portable printer. Portable ink-jets usually lack the paper handling for large print jobs. Most come as single feed printers with paper trays as an option. Most ink-jet printers are utilized for basic business graphics and charts or for home use.

Ink-jet printers in general are slow, averaging under two pages per minute and 100 characters per second (cps) for text. Color ink-jet printers take a couple of minutes per page. Ink-jet printers are the least expensive color printers. Black ink-jet printing for text is about 4 cents per page. The cost per page for color ink-jet printing with about 15 percent page coverage is about 14 cents per page; for 75 percent coverage the cost is about 30 cents per page. Color ink-jets start around $500; black printers are much more affordable starting near $250.

Solid Ink-Jet

Solid ink-jet printers use a waxy solid ink that looks like a fat crayon. The ink stick is heated to make it melt and the ink is then sprayed onto the page. The solid inks are not water soluble and therefore do not smear on the page. This process creates much better coloring than liquid ink-jet printers, but it takes up to 20 minutes for the printers to warm up before they are ready to print.

The solid ink-jet printers are versatile because they are able to print on most media types. They are not as finicky as liquid ink-jets in this respect. The one area in which they are weak is their ability to print on transparencies. The solid ink tends to bead and disperses light differently than the transparency film. Some transparencies have an extra layer of lamination added to the surface so they have the same optical density as the ink. Transparencies made from this media look more impressive. For projection on transparencies, the solid ink does not transmit light as clearly as thermal wax transfer or liquid ink-jet. The images will look dimmer than the other methods, but these units are generally more expensive than liquid ink-jet printers.

Solid ink-jet printers can produce more color variations than liquid ink-jets. The ink solidifies on the page before it has a chance to blend with the fiber of the paper, which gives it a raised print feel. When the ink solidifies on the page it is prone to cracking if the media is bent or folded. As you see, solid ink-jet printing has its benefits and also its drawbacks.

Continuous-tone Ink-Jet

Continuous-tone ink-jet printers send out a continuous stream of tiny droplets of ink and the unwanted droplets are reflected by an electrical field. The drops of ink are so small they can create halftone dots. The size of the dots can also vary. These printers output a wonderful near-photographic quality image. Continuous-tone ink-jet printers are expensive and are used mainly for proofs in commercial printing.

Thermal-Fusion

Thermal-fusion printers are a type of printing technology used often by portable printers. Many people are familiar with this type of printing, as it is commonly used with fax machines. Unlike fax machines, instead of printing onto flimsy thermal paper, the thermal fusion printers use a special printing ribbon and print onto normal cut-sheet paper.

Laser Printers

The quality of **laser printers** is better than that of dot-matrix and ink-jet printers. The consistent output of laser printers is superior to ink-jet printing. Laser printers are capable of printing higher resolutions and are faster and quieter than dot-matrix and ink-jet printers. Laser printers also are more expensive than dot-matrix and ink-jet printers.

Laser Printers Compared

Printer's Use	Network Printer	Small Office	Home Use
Recommended Emulations	PCL 5, PostScript Level 2, Automatic Switching	PLC 5, PostScript Option	PCL 5
Recommended Resolution	300, 400, 600, 800 dpi software controlled	600 dpi	300 dpi
Recommended Speed	20+ ppm	8+ ppm	4+ ppm
Recommended Interfaces	Parallel, 10Base-T, 10Base-2, Ethernet, Token Ring, Local Talk	Parallel, Ethernet	Parallel
Paper Capacity	1,000 sheets	500 sheets	250 sheets
Recommended RAM	8 Mb or more	6 Mb	2 Mb

The resolution that a laser printer is capable of printing has an effect on the quality of images and graphics. The resolution that the least expensive laser printers produce is 300 dots per inch. This resolution is too coarse for graphics but is acceptable for typed text. Six-hundred-dpi laser printers are becoming more popular and can print raw proofs for pre-published material. 1,200-dpi laser printing is even better for prepress proofs and a 1,200-dpi printer handles graphics pretty well. High-end 2,450-dots-per-inch imagesetters are necessary for the high-quality images used in publishing.

Some laser printers are capable of resolution enhancement, producing an output that appears better than the print engine specifies. The resulting enhancement is made along the horizontal rows and the number of dots per inch along the vertical columns is left unchanged. The vertical printing resolution is set by the number of scan lines per inch on the drum. This can only be changed by replacing the printing engine. The horizontal resolution of the printer is controlled by the pulses of laser light. Along the horizontal rows the laser beam is usually varied in intensity to five different levels. The intensity is directly related to the resulting toner dot size. The enhanced mode printers control the laser beam with greater accuracy and timing, which leads to better output on the paper.

If you see an advertisement for a enhanced resolution printer that claims resolution of 1,200 by 600 or 600 by 300, the smaller number gives the true resolution capability of the printer engine and the bigger number is the enhanced resolution.

The technology used in a laser printer is the same type as used in photocopiers. A laser draws images onto the electrostatic drum, giving it a charge that attracts toner. The toner is then transferred to the paper and is heated and bonded to the paper.

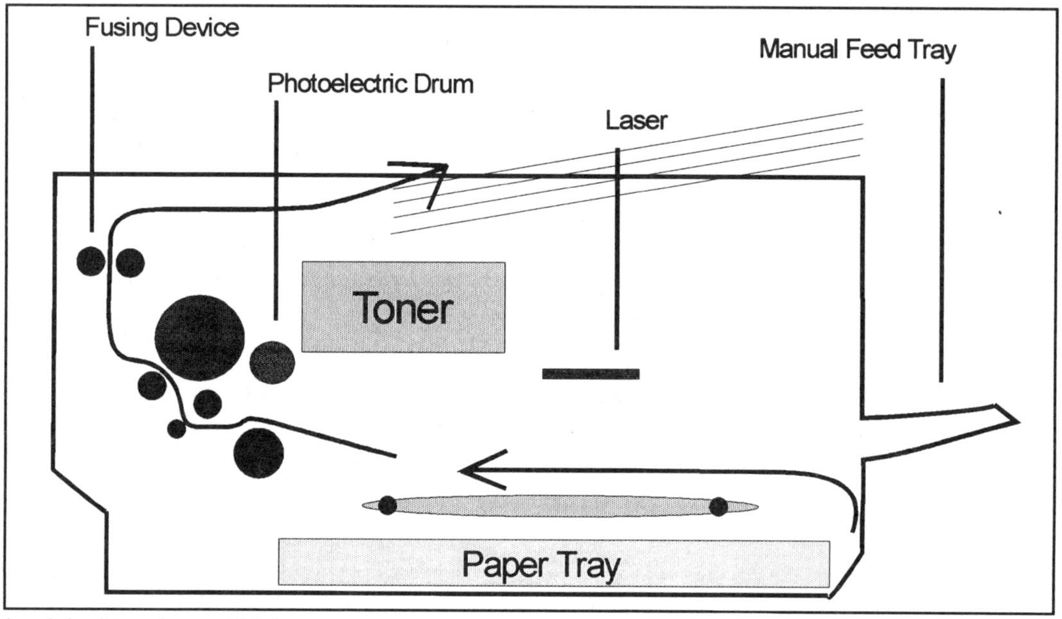

Look Inside a Laser Printer

Make sure you get a laser printer that has paper trays that will hold the size of paper you intend to use. Some printers have more than one paper tray and most are capable of having paper manually fed into the printer. Some laser printers can accept B-sized paper (11-by-17). A few laser printers can handle continuous-feed paper, but this is not common. It is great to have a printer that can handle three paper trays which can be selected from the computer at the time of printing: one paper tray for 8.5-by-11-inch, another tray for letterhead, and a third paper tray for envelopes.

Look for a printer that has easily changeable toner-drum cartridges. Avoid buying a printer that has a lot of exposed plastic pieces that can break off easily. When you buy toner replacements for the printer make sure the toner is the right size for the resolution you want to print. For higher resolution printing the toner is finer than the coarse toner used for lower resolution printing. Using a coarse toner with a high resolution printer means the advantage of having a higher resolution printer is lost.

Some toner cartridges contain both the toner and the photosensitive print drum. In these packages the two are replaced together when you buy new toner. A better and cheaper alternative is a printer designed with a separate toner cartridge and photoelectric drum because the drum will usually last three times as long as the toner cartridge.

Laser printers that contain RISC or CISC microprocessors are known as smart printers. They are much better than dumb buffered printers because dumb buffered printer image processing is done completely by the computer. This ties up your computer while the graphics are being processed. With a microprocessor-based printer, the graphic commands are downloaded to the printer to be processed. This frees up your computer's CPU to do whatever you wish to accomplish next.

Laser printing technology is similar to that used in photocopy machines, so paper designed to be used in photocopy machines will also work well with a laser printer.

Many people are wondering why they need to buy a separate laser printer, scanner, copy machine, and fax machine. Soon there will be more integrated printers available that also work as scanners, photocopiers, and fax machines. Four machines combined into one unit will cost less and take less space than four separate machines.

Laser printers cost about 2.5 to 3.5 cents per page to operate. The laser printers designed for personal use or home office use cost about $500 and up. Most small business laser printers start at $1,500 or more.

Thermal Wax Transfer Printers

Thermal wax transfer printers, also called thermal transfer printers, are good high resolution color printers that can produce great color proofs for prepress publishing and excellent transparencies. Thermal printers generally use four colored waxes that are wrapped on a roll like cellophane, and the wax ribbon is melted with heated elements onto the nearby paper or other printing media. The image is a result of many overlapping tiny dots that when viewed from a distance give the illusion of many different colors. This process is known as dithering. Thermal wax transfer printing produces rich, brilliant, glossy colors, and each page takes several minutes to print.

Because the waxy film does not diffuse light as much as ink-jet printers the thermal wax transparencies come out looking much better. Aside from the normal uses there are some specialized printing tasks you can do with thermal wax printers, like printing onto static cling plastic, the kind that sticks to windows without glue. Graphic artists appreciate the ability to print an image to the edge of the page.

Depending on the type of wax used, thermal prints are often prone to cracking. All color printers can print to transparency, but thermal wax transfer printers produce the best quality and work well for prepress proofs. Most thermal wax printers are available with a PostScript option, which is important for professional printing. Printed areas that have gradual color changes can be problematic with thermal wax printing because of banding or rough transitions between shades of colors. Thermal wax printers cost anywhere from $3,000 to $16,000.

Although most thermal wax printers require a specially coated paper to print on, some companies have designed thermal wax printers that will print on plain paper. They have an extra roll that lays a foundation for the colors. Inside thermal printers are rolls of plastic film that are coated with wax-based pigment, one for each color used in the printing process. Four separate panels are consumed in printing just one page (cyan, magenta, yellow, and black). Some printers use only three ribbons, cyan, magenta, and yellow. In order to print black, the colors are a mixed composite. This method usually produces muddy-looking blacks that are more of a gray color. To put all this ink on the page the media makes several rotations past the print head, once for each color. The paper is handled with a great degree of precision so the registration of adjacent colors lines up perfectly.

For those of you concerned with data security, you will want to know that after printing documents the ribbons that are used are wound on a take-up spool. Somebody could take the used ribbon and unwind it to read the documents that were printed. To prevent this you will want to destroy the thermal wax on the take-up spools after you finish printing.

Thermal wax printers usually provide a resolution of up to 300 dots per inch. Most thermal wax printers output fixed dot sizes of color onto the page. The VT2 (variable dot thermal transfer) technology lets the print head vary the size of the printed dots on the page. Printers using VT2 can produce a higher quality output than traditional fixed dot thermal wax printers. The recurring cost on average is 50 cents for printing coated paper and 65 cents to print on plain paper. The reason plain paper printing costs more is because the printer uses an extra clear base coat first and then lays the colors down on the page. The cost per page for thermal wax printers is the same whether you cover a little of the page or the entire page. This is because an entire ribbon is used to print each page and is discarded even if only a tiny section was printed using the colored ribbon. Doing full page printing using a thermal wax printer can be less costly than using an ink-jet printer, but doing partial page printing is usually cheaper with ink-jet printing. The special transparencies used for thermal wax printing cost about $1 per page, and thermal paper costs 3 to 6 cents per sheet in bulk. These printers are slow, generally not much faster than two pages per minute.

Electrophotographic

These printers work quite the same way as laser printers or black-and-white photocopiers. They use charged areas of paper to attract dry powdered toner which is then fused to the page. The result is a excellent color print, but due to the opaque quality of the toner they do not make good transparencies. Electrophotographic printers are expensive at $50,000 and up and therefore are found mostly in commercial printing shops.

Dye Sublimation Printers

Dye sublimation printers, also referred to as dye transfer, dye diffusion thermal transfer, or D2T2, offer even better graphic color results than thermal printers. A dye sublimation printer uses four solid dyes which, similar to thermal wax machines, come on ribbons. During printing the dye pigment is vaporized by heated print heads and the vapor impregnates the paper adjacent to it with color which then cools and solidifies on the paper. The heated print head controls how much color is actually transferred by varying the intensity and duration of the heat. During this process the colors are mixed to produce continuous-tone print. When the ribbon is heated the dye sublimates, which means it turns from a solid to a gas without a liquid phase in between. The gaseous dyes are absorbed by the printing paper. Like liquid ink-jet printers, when the ink is absorbed by the paper it tends to diffuse, leaving the edges of images a bit blurry. This diffusion helps the printer create continuous tones of color because the dots of ink blend together. The ink tends to diffuse better in relation to the axis that the paper is traveling because as the paper moves it enlarges the area that the ink is applied to—kind of like spraying paint on a canvas while moving the canvas up or down.

The dye sublimation process usually gives a resolution of 300 dpi, but the print appears much clearer due to the color mixing. The dye on the paper is transparent and can be layered to create a wide array of colors. Although the graphic images it produces are extremely good, this technology is not a good choice for text. Printed text appears fuzzy—an anomaly which is especially apparent when printing smaller point sizes. For printing text you will want to stick with a laser, ink-jet, or thermal transfer printer.

Dye-sublimation printers create brilliant photographic quality print images. For high-end proofing this is the best route to take. The only drawback is if you show clients graphics printed on a dye sublimation printer as a proof it may look better than when it is finally mass produced on a printing press. Since the ink is mixed together the color transitions from one shade to another do not show banding. Dye sublimation printers are capable of producing 16.7 million colors. Dye-sublimation printers with PostScript are available and offer an excellent print quality for graphic artists.

The speed of these printers is mighty slow. If you desire to print on plain paper, forget about dye sublimation, as these printers require a special and expensive paper to accept the printing dye. The paper used resembles photographic stock and costs about $3 to $4 per page. The total printing cost per page of these printers can be fairly expensive, ranging from $3 to $11. These printers require deep pockets, as they tend to cost $10,000 and up.

Imagesetters

Imagesetters produce extremely high printing resolutions. Imagesetters print either to film or photographic paper that has been covered with light-sensitive emulsion. This emulsion is burned off by a guided laser that draws the image, then the film or paper is processed in the same manner as photographic film. Imagesetters are capable of making both positive or negative images. They are able to produce color separations of computer generated artwork that will be camera-ready for commercial publishing.

Most imagesetting is done at a resolution of 2,540 dots per inch or higher. Color illustrations in magazines are usually set at 2,540 dots per inch or better. Imagesetters reproduce both graphic images and text, halftones, color separations, grayscale pictures, and illustrations.

The two types of imagesetters are known as capstan printers and drum printers. **Capstan imagesetters** use roll-fed media that is transported across an imaging head. Inside the capstan printer are a supply roll and a take-up spool. Because the printing media in these devices is in motion, capstan imagesetters are thought to take second place to drum imagesetters. If you are purchasing a capstan imagesetter, check to see if it incorporates a page buffer which can store all the page data until the entire print job is ready to be printed in one pass. Some extra-large images cannot be stored in a buffer, which means the image will have to be processed part of the way and then printed in stages, or alternatively the data can be spooled to a hard disk where it will be retrieved for printing after the whole image has been processed. Using a one-stage printing process will minimize the movement of the film and leave less room for error. Other capstan imagesetters use an extremely fast raster image processor (RIP) instead of temporary storage to achieve the same effect. There are two functions of an RIP: it is the interpreter which gathers the page description data, and it also is the renderer which uses the processed data to control the print head.

Drum imagesetters feed film onto a drum, where it remains while the imaging occurs. This keeps the margin for error low but also limits the total size of the image to the capacity of the drum. Internal drum and external drum are the two main types of drum-based imagesetters. An internal drum device has film that is registered on the inside of the drum and the film emulsion is placed side-in. The imaging beam travels through the drum while the film remains stationary. External drum devices have the film attached to the outside of the drum. The drum then spins with the imaging beam moving alongside the film.

The light source for the imaging beam is commonly a HeNe laser, argon laser, light-emitting diode, or laser diode. Each of the different light types requires a specific type of media. HeNe lasers emit a red light and use a red-sensitive media that cannot be used in traditional red light darkrooms. The argon lasers emit a blue-green light that can be used in red-lit darkrooms. The two laser diode imagesetters are infrared and red. Infrared light is an invisible light just like the remote control for a TV uses. A red light diode is in the visible light spectrum. Light-emitting-diode imaging beams do not put out as much light as the other beams and they need a more sensitive media for printing.

Plotters

Plotters are large scale printers that are very accurate at reproducing line drawings. They are commonly used for technical drawings such as engineering drawings or architectural blueprints. The two basic types of plotters are called flatbed plotters and drum plotters.

Flatbed plotters are horizontally aligned with a flat surface to which a piece of paper is attached. The paper remains stationary and the printer moves pens across the paper to draw the image. **Drum plotters**, also called upright plotters, are vertically positioned. They have a drum that the paper rolls on. Drum plotters usually make more noise and are more compact than flatbed plotters.

Film Recorder

Film recorders do the opposite job that slide scanners do—they print computer-generated images to film. A film recorder consists of a small cathode ray tube, a color wheel with red, blue, and green filters, a camera, and control circuitry. An image from the computer is sent to the CRT which is photographed once through each of the color filters resulting in a full color image on film. Some film recorders are PostScript capable. Different film formats used on film recorders include 35-mm film, 4-by-5, and 8-by-10 film. Some film recorders can output directly to Polaroid film.

Imaging speed is a reference to the timed opening and closing of the shutter. Film recorders can usually image one slide per minute, but the rasterization process of putting the image on the CRT may take much longer. The faster the raster image processor, the less time it takes to display a new image on the CRT.

The resolution of a film recorder is dependent on the number of pixels on the CRT. Most film recorders offer 2,000 or 4,000 resolution. With this kind of resolution you could take a 35-mm slide and enlarge it four or five times and still have a high enough resolution to make a high-quality print.

Many film recorders offer 24-bit resolution or even 32-bit or a whopping 36-bit color depth. The higher the color depth, the less likely unwanted banding will occur in the image, and higher sampling bit depth allows you to make gamma color corrections with greater accuracy. Film recorder quality can be affected by distortions that can occur on a CRT. See the main section on monitors to review CRT distortions.

Chapter 10

Magic Modems

The modem is a way to connect your computer with other computers and share information over vast distances. A modem is a device that allows the computer to send information over the normal phone line. The word modem stands for **mo**dulator **dem**odulator. By modulating a signal, two modems are able to communicate and thereby link two or more computers together.

Modems can connect your computer with a national Bulletin Board System (BBS) like CompuServe, Internet, and America Online. They can also connect to any local BBS in your area. A BBS is a computer that is set up to take incoming calls from other computers. The BBS usually has message areas where you leave messages for others with similar interests in topics ranging from skiing to Nordic bellydancing to quantum mechanics.

Bulletin board systems also have chat areas where you can meet and communicate with others in the chat area. BBSs usually contain files like text files or shareware programs. Many national BBSs have services such as booking travel flights, stock market information, and online encyclopedias. Databases online can get you the latest information from services like Nexus, Dun and Bradstreet, and countless other information banks.

BBSs are an important source of information in this digital age and are sometimes replacing the printed page for information. Services like America Online have late-breaking news sections where you can find the latest in business, sports, and entertainment news. The estimated number of bookstores today in the

United States is 26,787, and the estimated number of BBSs is 50,000. To stay on top, you'd better get online.

What Type Do I Need?

The modem makes the connection from the phone line to the computer. Some modems are categorized as **fax-modems** and can send or receive faxes directly from the computer, a great feature if you need to send out the same fax to many people. This is called broadcast faxing. Using a fax-modem you can store the faxes sent and received inside the computer, or print them, or both print them and save them on the computer.

To be able to fax a non-computer-generated document, like a newspaper clipping, you need a scanner to capture the image for the computer. After the document is scanned into the computer, you can fax it to one destination or to a whole list of people. This is a chief advantage of faxing from the computer. Not only can you easily fax to hundreds of people, you also can do it during a specified time. You can schedule the faxes to be sent after hours so as not to tie up the computer when you need it most, and by taking advantage of reduced phone charges at night you will save money on your phone bill.

One drawback when using a fax-modem to receive faxes is that the computer must remain powered on 24 hours a day in case you receive an incoming fax. If you are not actively using your computer but still need to leave it on to receive a fax, push the turbo button, which slows down the clock speed of the computer. This means the CPU will be producing less heat. Remember, heat is the enemy of electronic circuitry.

Some fax-modems also provide a voice mail feature. This is great for a small business that does not have a private answering service or secretary to take calls.

Some fax-modems on the market are *send only*, meaning they cannot receive incoming faxes. These fax-modems are disappearing and are being replaced by modems that are *send and receive fax* capable so they can both send out and receive faxes. If you plan on receiving faxes to the computer on a phone line that also receives voice calls, then look for a fax board that has

automatic call detection. This feature will route voice calls to the phone and intercept fax calls to the computer. If the fax-modem you want does not have automatic call detection you can add an external call detector later. These boxes are used often with fax machines that do not have a handset.

Most modems connect one computer to one phone line, but a few modems called **net-modems** can connect to many computers and will allow them to share the modem and phone line. The computers use the net-modem in the same way that they use a printer on a network.

Some modems do not connect to a phone line at all. These are called **cellular-modems** and operate on the same principles as a cellular phone. Using a cellular-modem allows the user to connect with distant computers wherever they travel as long as there is cellular support in the area. This is a great feature for portable computers. An alternative to getting a cellular-modem is to instead use a normal portable modem and couple it with a cellular phone that has an auxiliary jack that is used to connect with a modem. This is becoming a more standard feature on cellular phones.

Packet radio modems transmit data via radio using a communications protocol called AX.25. Packet radio modems run faster, are less expensive, and are more secure than cellular modems. The packet radio modems run at 9,600 bps using data compression. You are charged by the message sent instead of the connect time. The downside to packet radio modems for now is their coverage, but they now are active in about 100 cities. The two existing networks are called Ardis and Mobitex.

Another alternative for portable modems is a built-in modem or a **PCMCIA modem**. These modems should have a little sliding door that allows you to plug in a standard RJ-11 phone jack or have a cord that attaches with a RJ-11 phone jack on the other end. There are portable battery powered modems, called **pocket modems** available for portables without internal modem options. The external modem requires an available serial port and cables to hook up with the portable. Having an external modem is great if you do not always need a modem. If you use the modem a lot is can be a hassle because it is another thing you have to remember to bring along. Modems are a big drain on a portable computer's battery, so look for power management features on the modem to enhance the battery life. When you finish using a communications program on a portable computer, make sure you exit the program to deactivate the port. Doing so will conserve battery power.

Additional features that are offered with some modems include built-in voice mail and scanner ports. The voice mail feature could replace your answering machine or answering service. They can be helpful to a growing business. The scanner port is a great option. Just plug in a scanner and you can fax documents that are not computer-generated. Another feature is the ability of the modem to turn the system on when it receives a call on the phone line. This is a nifty energy-saving feature that may be an option on all modems in the future but now usually requires an additional piece of hardware.

Some modems incorporate into the package a telephone for making voice calls. This allows simultaneous voice and data transmission over a single phone line and can eliminate the need for multiple phone lines.

Internal or External

Modems can be internal, inside the computer case, or external to the case. Most external modems connect to the computer's serial port. For high-speed serial transmission make sure the input/output port on the computer has a 16550A UART chip or better controller, otherwise the computer may not be able to handle the speedy inflow of data that the high-speed modems are capable of transmitting.

A few external modems are using the parallel port instead of the serial port. The parallel port can transmit data faster than serial ports that do not use a 16550A UART. A parallel modem can bypass the limitation of a slower serial port. Parallel modems can be great for portable computers whose serial port may already be occupied by a mouse or other pointing device.

External modems usually have lights that indicate the status of the modem. The lights indicate modem ready, terminal, ready, auto answer, receive data, send data, carrier detect, off hook, high speed, request to send, clear to send, and error control detection. The better alternative is to have an LCD display on an external modem because it can provide more in-depth and readable information. Internal modems lack the ability to show these status lights because they reside inside the computer case where you do not see them; however, some software programs compensate for this limitation by incorporating a similar feature on the computer screen.

External modems are easy to share among more than one computer. Switching the computer to the modem is as simple as pulling out one serial cable and plugging in another serial cable. This is handy, especially when sharing one modem with both a Macintosh and a PC. An internal modem for the PC cannot be shared with a Macintosh.

Internal modems are good because they generally cost less, don't clutter up your desk, and do not require an additional power converter. External modems have the advantage of being easily unplugged and connected to another computer. With external modems, any phone line power surge will stay outside the computer case, allowing an extra protection buffer.

If the modem is internal it will include a serial port on the board. For the best uninterrupted signal transmission make sure it has a 16550A UART or other type of specialized memory buffer. Some internal modems have a coprocessor to make fax receiving operate smoothly in the background. Because it operates in the background, you can be working on a spreadsheet or other program without disruption while the computer is receiving a fax. Because a coprocessed modem takes the task load off the system CPU, it is the much-preferred choice. The coprocessor does all the compression and error correction and frees the CPU to perform other tasks.

Jacks

Fax-modems are usually supplied with at least one phone jack to plug in the phone line. The exception is with cellular models which, like cellular phones, do not require a physical phone line.

For fax-modems that use phone lines, the better option is two phone jacks. The first jack is where you connect the unit to the wall, and the second jack allows you to plug in a telephone. This way you do not have to reach around to the back of the computer to unplug the phone and plug in the computer every time you want to use the fax-modem.

Some fax-modems have automatic phone, data, and fax switching that will recognize whether the incoming call is intended for the phone or for the fax-modem. The better units will shut down the voice jack if a fax or data is being transmitted. This prevents the communication from being disrupted.

Phone lines are susceptible to high-voltage surges, which can damage the circuitry inside a modem and the computer. If you plan on using a modem, do yourself a favor and get a good surge suppresser with extra jacks to suppress phone line surges.

Portable Fax-Modems

There are three major types of portable fax-modems to choose from. These include a PCMCIA 2.0 card with a fax-modem in it, an external battery-powered unit, and an internal proprietary fax-modem.

The proprietary models are specifically designed to fit into the odd-shaped expansion slots inside portable computers. These are usually pretty expensive and are usually unable to work in any other portables unless the computers are designed by the same manufacturer. If you use an internal modem you will not have to tangle with extra interface cords, power packs, batteries, or the external modem package which you normally have when using a portable pocket modem.

The more expensive modem route to choose is a PCMCIA fax-modem. These tiny credit card-shaped units have the advantage of being compatible with any computer with a matching PCMCIA slot. A PCMCIA modem will run off your portable's batteries, shortening the portable's battery life. Pocket modems usually run off their own batteries or an AC adapter. A few pocket modems run off the power on the telephone lines or off the small amount of current in the portable's serial port. Pocket modems can have status lights, but PCMCIA modems do not because they fit inside the computer.

The LCD screens on portable computers take up a lot of CPU time and therefore can limit the speed at which you can use the modem. For the best situation look for a coprocessed modem so the processing time is relieved from the portable's CPU. Faster modems also use more battery power, which means less transmission time is available, but since you also transfer more data in less time this is kind of a neutral trade-off.

Software

Make sure the modem you select comes with software for Windows and DOS or the operating system you use. The software should include both data and fax capabilities. Extra bonus points are given for software with Optical Character Recognition (OCR). When you receive a fax, it is in a graphic format. To edit the fax as text you need to use OCR to turn the graphics into text you can use in a word processor.

Most modems are bundled with second-rate software. If you plan to use your fax-modem extensively, you should look into buying a high-end software communications package. Look in magazines for the latest communication software reviews, and you will be able make a wise choice regarding which software to buy.

Speed

Modems are rated at the speed they can transmit data. The speed of a modem affects your phone bills because you accrue the same telephone charges as you would with a voice call. If you make a data call around the world for a couple hours you are bound to feel faint when the phone bill arrives. The best way to reduce your phone charges is to buy a fast modem. Modems are commonly measured by their speed, called the **bits per second** (bps) transfer rate. The earlier models transferred data at **300 bps** or **1,200 bps**. These speeds are very slow by today's standards, and some BBS system operators will not even allow you to use their BBS with such a slow modem. A sysop is the systems operator, the person who takes care of the computer you are calling.

The **2,400 bps** modems are still pretty slow, as it takes about 70+ minutes to download a 1 megabyte file, roughly the amount of information stored on a floppy disk. The 2,400 bps modems are fine if you do not intend to send or receive data files, but you will notice a difference between a 2,400 bps modem and faster modems even if you are just browsing through the message base or chatting in chat areas.

The next step up in speed is a **9,600 bit per second** modem, which is much better than the 2,400 bps for file transferring but still is not the fastest. For those who really want to save on their phone bills the **14,400 bps** or **28,880 bps** modems are recommended. These have dropped in price considerably to a street price range of $200 to $800.

Do not confuse bps with baud. When modems send information over the phone lines they use sound signals that fluctuate and represent digital information. The baud rate is the number of times the signal fluctuates in a second. A modem using the Bell 103 standard connects at 300 bits per second and the signal frequency also changes 300 times a second, meaning the rate is at 300 baud. In this case each fluctuation carries only one bit of information. With other communication standards a signal fluctuation could indicate a transfer of more than one bit. A 14,000 bps connection sends 6 bits per signal fluctuation and runs at only 2,400 baud. When buying a modem, the important performance factor to look for is the maximum amount of uncompressed bits per second that the modem is capable of transferring.

Look for modems that use a general purpose Digital Signal Processor (DSP) which can be upgraded to faster speeds with a new set of software instructions loaded into flash memory. Other upgrade paths allow you to replace the old ROM chips with more advanced versions. These methods keep you at the cutting edge of technology without having to completely replace antiquated hardware.

Modem Speed Comparison Chart

Transfer Speed (bits per second)	*Estimated time to transfer a 1 megabyte file uncompressed*
300 bps	7.72 hours
1200 bps	1.94 hours
2400 bps	58.25 minutes
9600 bps	14.5 minutes
14,400 bps	9.7 minutes
28,800 bps	4.8 minutes

These transfer times are in reference to ideal line conditions.
Your mileage may vary.

Fast Modems vs. Slow Modems
If you need a fax-modem mostly for faxes, you can get by with a slower modem.
If you are doing file transfers that are very small, you can get by with a slower modem.
If you make mostly local calls and have a dedicated data line, you can get by with a slower modem.
If you are making large file transfers, you need a fast modem.
If you are making long distance calls, you need a fast modem.
If you have one line for voice and fax, you need a fast modem.
If you do not want your modem to be obsolete soon, get a fast modem.
If you don't want to regret your purchase, get a fast modem.

Read the section that describes the UART (Universal Asynchronous Receiver/Transmitter) which is critically important for modems using speedy transmission rates. The original UART is fair at speeds below 9,600 bits per second, but at higher data transmission rates you need a better UART with more buffering capabilities. A buffer is a little room, actually memory, where information is held temporarily. Kind of like your short-term memory. You put information there you will need soon but do not want to cloud your brain by remembering it permanently. With external modems the UART is positioned in the serial port circuitry on the computer but internal modems have the UART placed on the modem itself.

If you are using several high-speed external modems, you should be using a special serial port board that has an additional RAM buffer and a coprocessor to manage the data stream. Data transmission rates of modems are split into two primary categories. The data speed over the phone line is called the Data Communications Equipment (DCE) rate. The data speed between the modem and the computer is called the Data Terminal Equipment (DTE) rate. The DCE rate is often less than the DTE rate if the modem uses a compression method.

To make your modem investment pay off in the long run, look for upgradability features. Some modems that use flash ROM or a DSP will allow you to upgrade to faster data transmission standards as they become available.

Standards

There are many different standards that modems use to communicate, compress, and error-correct data. In order to communicate, the modems on both ends of the transmission need to share the same data transfer protocols. Watch out below, for the world of communication is overflowing with mumbo-jumbo. The following paragraphs explain the most common standards.

Hayes-Compatible

Modems that are described as Hayes-compatible refer to the commands issued by the computer to the modem. Hayes is a manufacturer who has lead the modem industry. Most modems use the Hayes command set, but some modems run on a totally

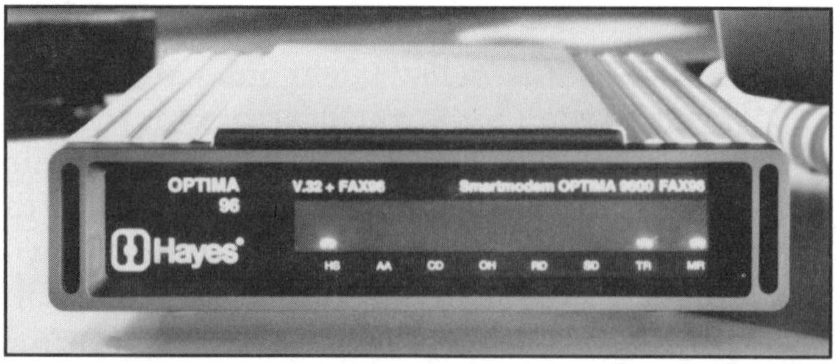

Hayes Modem

different standard. When considering a modem make sure it is Hayes-compatible to ensure you can link with the majority of modems in use.

CCITT

An acronym for Consultative Committee on International Telephone and Telegraph. This standards group changed its name in 1993 to the *International Telecommunications Union-TSS* which is sometimes abbreviated to ITU-TSS. This is a branch of the United Nations and is an organization of technical experts who design the standards that modems use. Most modems manufactured conform to ITU-TSS (CCITT) standards. These standards that are created by the CCITT are named by numbers that are preceded by a "V dot," for example V.32.

MNP

Short for Microcom Networking Protocol. A protocol is an agreed form of communication. These standards generally do not perform as well as the ITU-TSS standards.

Modulation

Modems use the same modulation standards to connect with each other. The standards of communication allow for different speeds of information exchange. To be able to communicate, both connected modems must adhere to the same standard. When modems with more advanced standards connect with older modems, they will fall back to the slower protocol. This is called backward compatibility. The following are widely used modulation standards.

Bell 103	Bell 212A
CCITT V.21	CCITT V.22bis
CCITT V.29	CCITT V.32
CCITT V.32bis	HST
PEP	DIS
CCITT V.32fast	CCITT V.17

Error Correction

Allows the modems to scan the data being transmitted to identify errors; when errors are found the modem requests the damaged data to be resent. Errors can occur due to line noise which can be as tame as a low hiss or as overwhelming as an opera performance coming from radio interference that is broadcast by a nearby radio station. For error correction to work, both the sending and receiving modems must be able to recognize the same error correction standard, just like for two people to play cards they both must know the rules of the same game. The following are error correction standards:

CCITT V.42
MNP Class 1 through 4
Hayes V-series

Data Compression

Some modems have the ability to reduce the amount of data they send by compressing the data before it is sent. This can reduce the time spent sending information on the phone line, and by using compression you will save money by reducing long distance charges. The compression ratio depends on the type of file being sent. Some information is like a sponge; it can be compressed easily into a little space. Other information is more like steel, it does not easily compress. The average compression ratio for computer data is 2:1 or a 50 percent amount of shrinkage. Some modem advertisements claim an "effective data transfer rate" that is based on a best case scenario using data compression. If the files being sent are already compressed there is no further gain in transmission speed. Many files on BBSs and online services are already compressed with programs like PKZIP, ARJ, LZH, and ARC.

MNP Class 5
CCITT V.42bis
CSP

Description of the Standards

The following are the major standards used in the land of the modem. You will probably need to know this information to decipher modem advertisements.

Bell 103

Bell 103 is a modulation standard used in the United States and Canada. It transfers at 300 bps and uses a frequency fluctuation at 300 baud that transmits one bit per baud. This full-duplex standard is very slow by today's standards.

Bell 212A

Bell 212A is also a U.S. and Canadian modulation standard. It allows a transfer of 1,200 bps. It uses differential phase shift keying (DPSK) at 600 baud and transmits two bits per baud.

V.17 This is a half-duplex method of transmitting faxes and is an extension of Group 3 fax. The standard of V.17 is capable of transmitting speeds of 14,400, 12,000, 9,600, 7,200, or 4,800 bits per second.

V.21 V.21 is similar to Bell 103 in that it also transmits 300 bps. This is a full-duplex international standard that is used mostly outside the U.S.

V.22 V.22 is a 1,200 bps, full-duplex international standard. It also is used primarily outside the U.S.

V.22bis "bis" is Latin for second and therefore follows and improves V.22. V.22bis is a full-duplex data transmission standard that sends at 1,200 bps. This is an international standard that uses quadrature amplitude modulation (QAM) at a rate of 600 baud. It transmits 4 bits per baud.

V.23 V.23 is a dual standard that sends 1,200 bps in one direction and 75 bps in the opposite direction. This is referred to as "pseudo-full-duplex" because it is able to transmit simultaneously in both directions but not at the maximum data rate. This standard is used primarily in Europe.

V.26ter This allows data transmission at 4,800 bps and is obsolete except for compatibility with older modems. It is sometimes used for faxing.

V.27ter Fax communication protocol for speeds of 4,800 bits per second.

V.29 V.29 transmits data at 9,600 bps. This is a "half-duplex" transmission standard, meaning it only transmits data one way at a time. Group III faxes often use this standard. Modems seldom run this standard because it is not too well defined.

V.32 V.32 transmits 9,600 bps at "full duplex", which means both directions simultaneously. V.32 uses trellis coded quadrature amplitude modulation (TCQUAM) that transmits 4 bits per baud at 2,400 baud. This standard includes error correction to ensure the data is not corrupted. If the telephone connection will not support the high speed of 14,400 bits per second, then V.32bis modems will slow down to 1,200, 9,600, 7,200 or 4,800 bits per second, whichever works best at the time.

V.32bis

V.32bis is a 14,400 data transmission standard. V.32bis uses TCQAM modulation to send 6 bits per baud at 2,400 baud. This is a full duplex modulation and is a very good standard which supports use of V.42 error correction and V.42bis data compression.

V.32Terbo

This is not a real CCITT standard but is used by some modems based on an AT&T Microelectronics chipset. It allows speeds up to 19,200 kbps; with V.42bis compression, 76.8 kilobytes.

V.FC

V.Fast Class is another nonstandard speed that transmits data at 24,000 bits per second. As it is not a real CCITT standard, this class will probably disappear when V.32Fast is finalized.

V.34

V.34, also known as V.Fast, allows for a rapid 28,800 bps data transfer rate. This is a full duplex standard. This rate is the theoretical maximum data transfer rate possible given the current signal-to-noise ratio on U.S. phone lines. This is known as Shannon's theory.

V.42

V.42 is an error correcting standard that includes MNP Class 4, which is also an error correcting standard. MNP is an abbreviation for Microcom Networking Protocol. V.42 is a better standard than MNP 4 because it allows a 20 percent greater transfer rate because of its better transmission algorithms. When data is corrupted by phone line impairments V.42 uses Link Access Procedure for Modems (LAPM) to automatically request a retransmission of the corrupted data.

V.42bis

This is a data compression standard that has 35 percent better compression than MNP Class 5. V.42bis is more advanced because it first analyzes the data to be transmitted and then determines if compression would be helpful. If the file is already compressed, trying to compress it again will make it larger in size and defeats the purpose of compression. MNP Class 5 will always compress data whether is compressed already or not. This can lead to slower transmission times. These two standards are not compatible but most V.42bis modems also include MNP Class 5 data compression. To use V.42bis a modem must also include V.42, so a advertisement stating a modem uses V.42bis has both standards. V.42bis has the best compression, followed by MPN Class 7 and then MPN Class 5. V.42bis allows for a theoretical 4:1 data compression ratio. When used with a V.32bis modem it can send data at a maximum rate of 57,600 bps.

CODEX V.Fast A standard that may hit raw data speeds of up to 56,000 bps.

HST HST is a half-duplex allowing 14,400 bps and 9,600 bps in one direction and 450 bps or 300 bps in the other direction. This communication protocol was designed by US Robotics.

DIS DIS is a 9,600 bps proprietary standard made by CompuCom. It uses dynamic impedance stabilization (DIS) to control phone line noise.

CSP CSP is an acronym for CompuCom Speed Protocol. This is a data compression and error correction protocol used on CompuCom DIS modems.

MNP Class 1 MNP Class 1 referred to as block mode, is a half-duplex (one way), asynchronous, byte-oriented error correction that is only about 70 percent efficient. MNP 1 is a half-duplex protocol. It is not commonly used.

MNP Class 2 MNP Class 2, called stream mode, is a full-duplex (two way) error correction. MNP 2 is a full-duplex protocol. It only offers a 16 percent speed increase and is rarely used.

MNP Class 3 MNP Class 3 incorporates MNP Class 2 and is an improvement. MNP 3 is a full-duplex protocol. Its throughput is about 108 percent of that of a modem without MNP. It is not as good as V.42.

MNP Class 4 MNP Class 4 uses Optimized Data Phase and Adaptive Packet Assembly. This increases performance by 5 percent but can be as high as 50 percent depending on the line conditions. This is also not as good as V.42.

MNP Class 5 MNP Class 5 uses a real time adaptive data compression algorithm. This can increase performance by 50 percent depending on the type of data being sent. Files that have already been compressed can be enlarged by MNP Class 5 and doing so effectively decreases performance. MNP 5 allows for compression rates up to 2:1. To use MNP 5 your modem must have MNP 2, 3, or 4 error control.

MNP Class 6 MNP Class 6 is an enhancement to the previous standard. It uses Universal Link Negotiation that allows modems to start at a slow data transfer rate and work up to faster transmission rates. When the high speed carrier uses half duplex modulation, MNP Class 6 uses Statistical Duplexing which monitors and manipulates the half-duplex to deliver full-duplex service.

MNP Class 7 MNP Class 7 is combined with MNP Class 4 to obtain up to a 300 percent increase in performance. This is made to be used primarily with V.22bis modems. This standard is not as good as V.42bis. MNP 7 allows for a compression ratio up to 3:1.

MNP Class 9 This is a data compression standard that when combined with V.32 can deliver up to a 300 percent higher data transmission rate than V.32 would alone. The Class 9 also uses Enhanced Universal Link Negotiation to ensure the highest possible level of performance.

MNP Class 10 If you are planning on sending data over a cellular phone, look for support of this standard. This standard allows for data transmission over channels with poor quality lines. When two modems connect they first perform a handshake, which decides several factors. With CCITT standards the fastest connection is tried first and it stepped down until both the modems agree on the fastest speed available. With MNP 10 the opposite occurs. The modems start at the slowest speed and work their way to the fastest possible speed. Another feature used by MNP 10 is called aggressive adaptive packet assembly. With a CCITT standard, the modems decide the best data packet size by starting with the biggest packet and working smaller until the best common transfer occurs. With MNP 10 the smallest data packet is tried first and then progressively larger data packets are tried. The MNP 5 dynamic speed shift allows the data rate to increase or decrease depending on the quality of the line. This is also common of a V.32bis modem.

V-Series

V-Series is an error correction made by Hayes and used in some of their modems. This is not used widely due to the competing V.32 and V.32bis standards.

Fax Board Standards

Group 1

This specifies the CCITT T.2 recommendation from 1968. This standard will transmit an A4 (8.5 x 11 inch) page in about six minutes. The page is sent in 1,144 scan lines at a rate of 180 lines per minute. This is an older standard and is not widely used now.

Group 2

This is the CCITT T.3 standard recommendation issued in 1976. Under Group 2 an A4 page will be transmitted in about three minutes. This process can send gray levels as well as black and white at a resolution of 200 dots per inch. The document is sent as 1,145 scan lines at a rate of 300 lines per minute, or up to 4,800 bits per second. This is an older standard and is not widely used now.

Group 3

This is the CCITT T.4 recommendation of 1980. It specifies a transmission rate of up to 9,600 bits per second and adds data compression that complies with CCITT V.27 or V.29 modulation. Under Group 3 an A4 page can be transmitted at about one minute or as fast as twenty seconds. Resolution can be as good as 400 dots per inch.

Group 4

This standard requires an ISDN connection, which is a special digital wire connection rented from the phone company. Group 4, which arrived in 1984, is capable of sending an A4 page in 5 to 10 seconds with a resolution of 400 dpi. These machines operate at 64,000 bps.

Fax Board and Software Compatibility

Fax-modems have been standardized so they will be compatible with a variety of software packages available on the market. The following are the standards that are widely used. These classes are set by the Electronic Industries Association (EIA).

Class 1

This was the first try at creating a fax-modem and software standard. Because it was very loosely implemented, there are still some problems with some Class 1 modems trying to communicate with each other. While using a Class 1 fax-modem most of the faxing burden is placed on the computer's CPU and therefore ties up the computer while attempting to fax. A Class 1 modem cannot distinguish whether an incoming call is a fax or a data call and has to be set to receive one or the other. Most manufacturers offer one or more of the following standards with their fax-modems. For an extra measure of safety find out if the fax software and hardware you plan to use are compatible by asking your vendor or by calling the manufacturer.

Class 2 and 2.0

This standard is more efficient that Class 1. It puts the fax processing power onto the modem instead of the CPU. This frees the CPU for other tasks. Class 2 provides extra features like station ID and flow control. Many software and hardware creators have altered this specification to meet their own agendas and therefore the standard is not as widely compatible as it should be. Earlier use of this standard is called Class 2. The more updated and solidified standard is referred to as Class 2.0. In November of 1992 the Class 2.0 standard became more defined, and that results in greater compatibility between hardware and software. These modems can distinguish whether an incoming call is a fax or data.

CAS

This is a specification put out by Intel and is an abbreviation for Communications Application Specification. CA, like Class II, shifts much of the faxing burden to the fax-modem, leaving the CPU free to accomplish other tasks. Many hardware and software creators have adopted this standard. If you want to multitask, choose CAS or Class II standard fax-modems.

T.611 A standard that has the backing of Intel and will probably take the place of CAS.

T.4 A specification for encoding data to a compression algorithm used in faxing.

T.30 This standard is used with Group 3 fax machines and controls the handshake between the modems. It facilitates the negotiations for speed and data encoding. T.30 is sent via a 1,100 Hz tone between two faxes.

On the Road

If you plan to use a fax-modem around the world, be prepared, as there are many different phone connectors on the far side of the globe. Unlimited Systems Corp. in San Diego, CA makes the Konexx Kit, which provides all the tools you need to connect your modem to any telephone in the world at speeds up to 9,600 bps. The Konexx coupler also lets you connect to a digital PBX system with a phone coupler. If interested give them a call at 1-800-275-6354.

Synchrotech in Los Angeles offers a package of 35 cable adapters connecting to any phone system around the world and another set of 10 adapters that work for all of Europe. Synchrotech can be contacted at 29A Bridge St., Pinner, Middlesex, HA5 3HR, England. The telephone number is 44(0)81-429-0479. Another option for international travelers is Synchrotech's Phone Kit. If you do not need a worldwide phone connection kit you can opt to buy individual connectors for specific countries. Synchrotech can be reached at 318 South Detroit Street Suite 303, Los Angeles, CA 90036 USA, or call (213) 937-4428 or 1-800-793-9207.

If the phone connection you encounter is not modular and has no phone jack, you may be able to disassemble the phone or wall box and connect directly to the phone wires. Radio Shack sells cable #279-391 that has a normal RJ-11 phone jack and on one end and clips at the other to attach to the phone wires. The wires generally used for the telephone line are the red and green wires. Alternatively, you can undo the telephone mouthpiece and connect the clips to the wires inside. When using this method, take the phone off the hook before making the call and hang it up after the transmission is finished.

Other items you should bring on the road include:

- A small flathead and Phillips screw driver
- Needlenose pliers
- A small flashlight
- A phone coupler to connect two phone cords together
- A Y-connector to give you two phone jacks on one line so you can have the telephone and modem both connected to the phone line
- A three-prong-to-two-prong AC adapter
- Surge suppresser for phone line and AC power

Tips

Call waiting can be a great feature for voice calls, but when making data or fax transmissions it can really mess things up by knocking your modem out of whack. Make sure you turn the call waiting feature off before you start your data or fax call. To do this add *70 to the beginning of your dialing string; for example *70-415-555-1212. Sometimes #70 is used instead of *70.

UART Chips

The UART is a Universal Asynchronous Receiver/Transmitter. What does that mean? The computer works with information in parallel with eight or more bits at a time. One of the connections to the outside world for the computer is the serial port. This port only allows information to file in or out in a single file line. The UART is at the core of translating information from serial to parallel or vice versa.

If you plan to use a serial connection, the UART used can have an impact on how fast the data can flow, an important consideration especially if you plan to use a high-speed external modem. The UART is disappearing these days and is being replaced by an ASIC (Application Specific Integrated Chip). These chips often integrate a UART or microprocessor to perform the translation duties.

The following is a brief description of commonly used UARTS. If you are using a high speed modem make sure the serial port uses a 16550 UART chip or better.

8250 This is a very old UART that has a couple of bugs. Some old BIOSs are written to expect the bugs, but this chip is best avoided.

8250A The 8250A chip fixes some of the bugs in the 8250 UART. One of the bugs fixed has to do with the interrupt enable register, and because some BIOSs expect this bug they will be incompatible. It does not operate well at transmission speeds of 9,600 bps or faster.

8250B This is an updated version of the 8250 and 8250A. It fixes some of their bugs and adds the interrupt enable register bug in order to gain compatibility with BIOSs that expect the bug. Although this chip is better it still does not offer sufficient performance for data transmission speeds of 9,600 bps or faster.

16450 The 16450 chip fixes the interrupt enable bug and is incompatible with some BIOSs that expect the bug. This chip increases the allowable data transfer throughput over that of the 8250B.

16550 This is an improvement over 16450. It allows multiple DAM channels but cannot use FIFO (first in, first out) buffering, and that limits its performance.

16550A This chip is recommended over the 16550. It has two 16-bit FIFO buffers, one for transmission and the other for reception. This chip also allows multiple DMA channel access. This chip is necessary for data transmission of 9,600 bps or faster unless the serial device is in an expansion slot and is coprocessed.

Future Watch

All the modem information discussed so far has been regarding analog type modems. These modems take digital information and translate it into analog signals to send over analog phone lines. The next step is pure digital communication on digital phone lines. These phone lines allow faster rates of transmission and are less susceptible to line noise. Digital phone lines can transmit up to 128,000 bps, which is much faster than the analog maximum of about 64,000 bps.

Integrated Services Digital Network (ISDN) service is available in many metropolitan areas. It can transmit information six times faster than normal phone lines. In 1992, the ISDN-1 standard was issued making coast-to-coast ISDN transmission possible. This standard made specifications on interfacing local phone carriers and interexchange carriers.

The big competition to the phone companies is cable. Cable modems are able to transfer much greater amounts of information than standard phone modems. Claims of being 50 times faster than 9,600 bps modems are surfacing in this race for speed.

Chapter 11

Perfect Power Control

To run properly, a computer needs a steady power supply that is free of voltage variations or spikes. Voltage surges are power irregularities that are above the normal voltage an outlet is meant to supply. To prevent damage to the sensitive electrical components inside the computer it is essential to have power protection between the wall and the computer. There are three main types of power protectors. These are known as surge protector, power conditioners, and UPSs (uninterruptable power supplies). Computers are vulnerable to surges that range from 800 to 6,000 volts. The power supply in the computer can usually handle power spikes below 800 volts, and surges above 6,000 volts will ground themselves out before getting to your computer.

Surge Protectors

Surge protectors are the simplest way to protect your computer from harmful fluctuations in the power supply. Fluctuations can occur when lightning strikes a power line or when the power company switches power sources. During the day the power demand in your area will change. At times of increased or decreased power demand the power company will reroute its power to match demand, and power surges are known to occur when the power company makes the switch. A power fluctuation could harm the computer's components, so to prevent this you place a surge protector between the wall outlet and the computer. The power surges are usually released in the form of heat. Good surge suppressers absorb a surge emanating from any of the three wires; hot, neutral, and ground.

The four types of devices used to handle power surges are metal-oxide varistors, gas tubes, reactive circuits, and silicon avalanche diodes. Most surge suppressers use *metal-oxide varistors* (MOVs) and divert any power above 200 volts to ground. MOVs are not able to handle very high level power surges and destruct when diverting a large surge but are popular because they are inexpensive. The unfavorable side to MOVs is they degrade over time as a result of being hit by surges. Sooner or later an MOV stops working, but if properly made it should last over ten years.

Gas tubes are tubes filled with special gases that conduct electricity at predicted voltages. The problem with gas tubes is they do not absorb surges but instead short out. This means your wiring must absorb the surges, and that can be a fire hazard. With gas tubes, when the power arcs over the gas it often takes longer to get the normal flow of power back to the computer, and this may cause the computer to shut down if the power is not supplied back soon enough.

Reactive circuit surge suppressers spread a power surge out over a longer period of time but may not be able to handle all types of power surges. *Silicon avalanche diodes* allow voltage to flow unimpeded until it reaches the overload point and then the diodes switch on to remove excess voltage. These devices operate quickly but have limited ability to handle large power fluctuations.

Most surge suppressers have MOV surge suppression, and the better surge suppressers use a combination of surge suppression technologies in a series of stages. All good surge protectors should have a light that indicates the surge protector has not been hit by a large power surge and is still operating correctly. If the light is off, then a power surge has occurred, and when that happens you need to flip a circuit breaker or replace the fuse on the surge protector. Circuit breakers are easier to reset than fuses because you just flip a switch.

To clean the voltage that comes into the computer look for surge suppressers that include choke coils which act to slow down surges and reduce electromagnetic interference and radio frequency interference. Capacitors are sometimes coupled with choke coils to further reduce electromagnetic and radio frequency interference.

When shopping for a surge protector, look for one with a United Laboratories UL 1449 TVSS 330 volts protection standard. This is a good standard for protection. Make certain that surges are suppressed on all three lines of the AC outlet. This covers the hot wire, the neutral wire, and the ground wire, which all are susceptible to power surges. A surge suppresser should have at least six outlets to plug into. Surge suppressers ideally should be able to protect against lighting surges. To do this they must provide a 2,000-to-1 spike attenuation, which means a 6,000 volt surge will be reduced to 3 volts. Surge protectors are sold for $20 to $200.

If your computer has a modem in it, protect the computer from power surges that travel through the telephone wire. Surge protectors are available from computer supply stores and guard against surges that travel along the telephone wires.

Power Conditioners

The power that travels in the electrical wires into homes and offices ideally should be a clean signal, but most often the power received is "dirty." Electrical noise affects the power supply, which is supposed to be a perfect sine wave. You have probably noticed electrical noise when watching television while someone is trying to vacuum the house. The picture on the television becomes fuzzy. Noise can be induced by radio-frequency interference, telephones, light fixtures, or other devices. Essentially the wiring in your building acts like an antenna that picks up all kinds of electrical noise.

Perfect power is supplied in a nice, constant wave form, like the waves on a lake on a pleasant day, and a noisy power supply is more like choppy waves on a windy day. A power conditioner converts power from an AC outlet into a perfect sine wave pattern that is inherent in a clean power supply. The power conditioner smoothes out dips or spikes in the power. The better conditioners can fare through worse power conditions. Power conditioners usually include some form of surge protection. Top-quality power conditioners usually cost about $100 or more.

Standby Power Supplies

What happens when the power fails while you are working on that last-minute proposal? Everything that has not been saved to the hard disk is lost. Standby power supplies or uninterruptable power supplies can help if the AC power supply is ever disrupted. A standby power supply is an off-line device that constantly monitors the AC power supply for power fluctuations. If the line power dips below normal, the standby power supply unit switches on and delivers power for 5 to 30 minutes. A standby power supply contains a power inverter that converts its DC battery power to the 110-volt current AC power that is supplied to your computer system.

The problem with standby power supplies is that they wait until the power fluctuates before switching to the alternative backup power supply. If the switching time is not fast enough, the computer will shut off and then reboot (turn on) after the backup power is supplied. This means the computer loses any information that is in RAM and has not been saved to disk, which is contrary to the reason for using a backup power supply. When buying a standby power supply look for a fast power transfer time of 4 milliseconds or less.

Some standby power supplies have an interface port for Local Area Networks. This helps computer systems make an unattended software shutdown. This is an essential feature for big computer systems. During a long blackout a standby power supply should have some type of warning signal to alert users that the battery power is running low. This will allow time to save data and shut down the computers in an orderly fashion.

Some standby power supplies have line conditioning included; those that do not need an additional line conditioner. The best standby power supplies use a ferroresonant transformer, which supplies power to the computer during the brief power switching period. Be aware that some companies misrepresent their standby power supplies as uninterruptable power supplies. The latter are superior for continuous power supply.

Uninterruptable Power Supply

A UPS usually protects electrical equipment from power surges and conditions the power, and if the AC power is dropped the backup battery will run the computer long enough for you to save whatever you are working on and shut down the system.

APC Uninterruptable Power Supply

A UPS supplies the AC power from the backup battery at all times. It uses a voltage inverter to convert the battery power to regular 110-volt AC power. The best UPSs use better power inverters that produce a pure sine wave output, not an inferior square or stepped wave. The UPS battery is being constantly charged from the wall socket AC power. When the power goes out there is no power switch because the battery is already the outgoing power source. When the power is disrupted the UPS is no longer being charged. This means the computer never loses power, even for a split second, until the battery is drained.

This allows enough time to save your open documents to disk and perform an orderly system shutdown.

UPSs are rated by the amount of power they can supply and the amount of time they can supply that power. A UPS with a capacity of 250 to 300 volt-amps is sufficient to run a PC, although a 400 volt-amp UPS supplies power for nearly twice as long as a 250 volt-amp UPS. A well-designed UPS has spike protection and voltage regulation included. Electrical current coming through the wall outlet often fluctuates, and if there is a power spike the innards of the computer could fry. An especially dangerous time for power spikes is during electrical storms, because lightning is prone to hitting the electrical wires that carry electrical current. A UPS with ferroresonant transformers is recommended because it has the best type of line conditioning and power protection. A good UPS includes a battery tester that helps determine when the batteries wear down and need replacement.

A power conditioner that has too small a power supply will cause circuit problems. A surge protector that has too large a supply costs more than you need to spend. To determine what capacity UPS is needed, consider the parts of the computer system that need backup power protection, such as monitors, internal drives, modems, and the computer itself. Leave printers off the list because they drain a large quantity of power and you will not lose valuable data if the printer loses line power. Remember to still use surge protection for the printer.

To determine the amps of the items you wish to protect, look for a sticker on the device that has an Underwriters Laboratory logo on it. If the ratings are not there then check the technical documentation that came with the equipment. Typical amperage ratings for PCs are close to 3 amps, for monitors between 1.5 to 2.8 amps, and for modems a couple of milliamps.

After tallying the combined amps needed, multiply that number by the voltage. In the United States it is usually 110 volts. Since amperage multiplied by voltage equals wattage, you now know the total number of watts the computer system requires. Take this final number of watts and add extra wattage to allow for upgrades you might make to the computer system in the future.

Other Power Tips

Ideally a computer should have its own dedicated electrical socket to plug into. Printers and other appliances such as heaters or microwaves can cause fluctuations in the power if plugged into the same outlet, so use different outlets if possible. Extension cords should be avoided, but if necessary use high-quality cords that have three-prong plugs and sockets to ensure a proper ground for the computer.

Chapter 12

Super Sound Boards

When motion picture films were developed they did not always have sound. Silent movies were made which were interwoven with titles to convey the subject matter. Today a film released without sound is extremely rare, because so much is conveyed through the use of sound. Like film, computers were first developed without sound. They are now experiencing the sound revolution with the advent of multimedia. Users can bring a symphony of music to your presentations or make computer games boom to life with a sound card. Educational programs

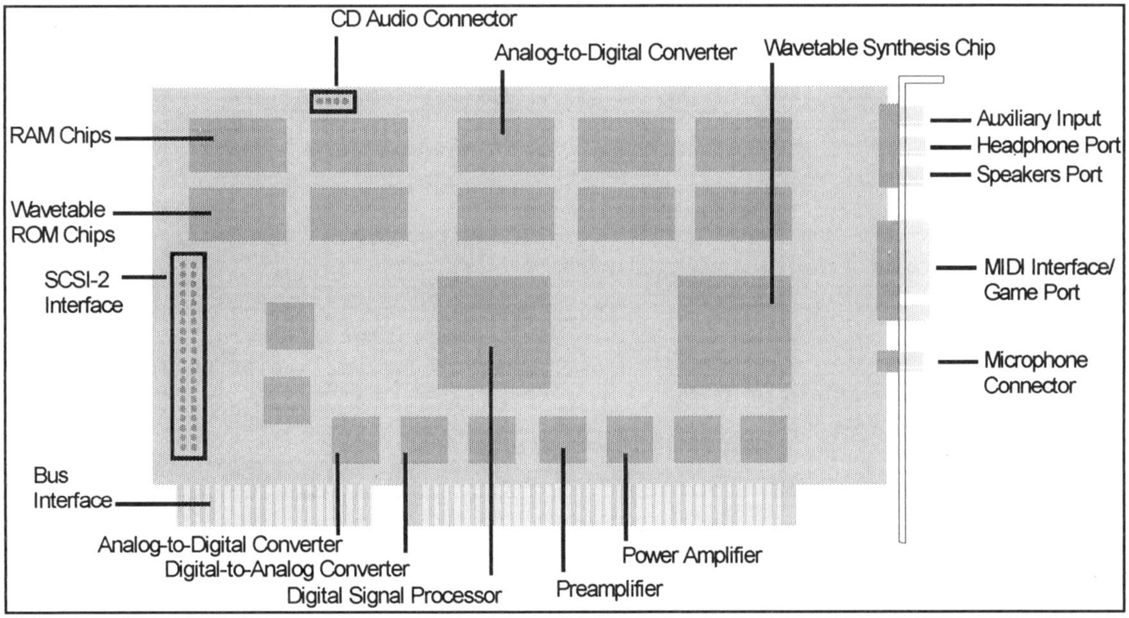

A Look at Sound Cards

can teach you Japanese and sound out characters on the screen. When you buy a sound card you can hook it up to powered speakers or to a stereo for excellent sound, or for private matters use headphones.

Sound Digitizing

Many sound boards allow both playing and recording music that you create. The physics of sound is an interesting phenomena. Essentially, sound waves ripple the air like water ripples when you throw a rock in it. The waves in sound can be slow or fast, and this is measured in waves or cycles per second. The human ear can hear sounds that are 20 Hz to 20,000 Hz. Hertz is equivalent to a wave or revolution. Ideally we want to capture all the waves of sound when we record them.

Audio CDs play back sound samples at 44.1 kHz (44,110) samples per second. This is the **sampling rate or sampling frequency** needed for high-quality sound. Some sound boards sample stereo sounds at 44.1 kHz or higher, while other sound boards' sampling rates are limited to monophonic sound at 22.05 kHz or 11.025 kHz. There are a few sound cards that record using 48 kHz sampling, but unless you are a real serious audiophile you will not be able to discern a difference between 48 kHz and 44.1 kHz sampling rates.

Sound Wave Frequencies Compared

Sound Quality	*Frequency to Record in kHz*	*Range of Audio Frequency Captured in kHz*	*Uses for Recording*
CD-A	44.1 or 48.10	0-22.05	Music, high quality
FM Radio	22.05	0-11.025	Multipurpose audio
AM Radio	11.03	0-5.513	Voice, low-fidelity sound
Telephone	8	0-4.0	Narration

The **sampling rate** of sound is twice the rate of the highest sound recorded. The Nyquest theorem states that if a given signal's highest frequencies are less than a certain frequency, which we will call f, then that signal can be effectively reconstructed if samples are taken at the rate of at least 2 times f per second.

For example, the highest pitched sound you can record at a 44.1 kHz sampling rate is a 22.05 kHz sound. 22.05 kHz is at the high end of human hearing, so recording at this rate is good enough for most applications. At a sampled rate of 22.05 kHz the highest recordable sound is 11.025 kHz. Recording at this rate cuts off a lot of the high pitches that give sound its timbre or richness.

The **sample resolution** also affects the sound quality. This is the number of bits used to represent each sample. Compare this with the number of bits that represent each pixel on a display screen. The more bits per pixel, the better the color depth, the more bits per sample, the better the sound. Sound boards digitize sound into 8-bit or 16-bit data resolution; this is known as the bit depth. Sound cards that use an 8-bit sampling rate sound kind of scratchy like a telephone conversation, while 16-bit sound is much better, like an audio CD. A 8-bit sample at 22 kHz sounds like AM radio, so it is fine for speech but not good enough for music. An 8-bit sample can hold 256 possible digital values, whereas a 16-bit sample allows over 65,000 sound values. A 16-bit sample contains enough information so that the sampled sound can be reconstructed with close resemblance to the original sound.

Sound Sample Bit Depth

Sample Size	*Common Use*	*Observations*
4-bits	Low-fidelity, suitable for voice commentary only	Audio can be compressed to this rate using ADPCM
8-bits	Better for voice than music	Often paired with a 22.05 kHz sample rate
12-bits	Intermediate level quality	Sounds similar to sound used in telephone system
16-bits	High-fidelity	Often used with 44.1 kHz sample rate and stereo sound

Stereo sound is better than mono, as you probably know—it gives a greater depth to the recorded sound. It is wise to avoid sound cards that can play 16-bit sound but are unable to record 16-bit sound.

In general, the better the quality of a sound recording, the more storage space the sample will consume. One second of 8-bit 22 kHz sound takes up 22 kilobytes of hard disk space, and at this rate a five-minute speech will take 6.45 megabytes of disk space. This is about equal to four and a half high-density floppy disks. A 16-bit sound sample recorded at 44.1 kHz, a rate considered good for music, takes up 88 kilobytes of disk space. Five minutes of music will take up nearly 25 megabytes of space.

Sound digitizing is the process of converting analog sounds into a digital format. This is like taking sound on a record and putting it on a CD. Sound cards can also convert digitized sound into analog sound which can be played over headphones or stereo speakers. This process requires a DAC, or digital-to-analog converter, and for capturing the sound an ADC, or analog-to-digital converter. Some sound cards use a special digital signal processor (DSP) to convert sounds from digital to analog and vise versa. DSP chips are usually found on the better sound cards. They can handle some of the audio processing and can speed overall performance by taking part of the burden off the CPU.

Check out potential sound cards for their rated Total Harmonic Distortion (THD). This gives an idea of how much distortion is generated by the sound card's circuitry. Distortion causes listening fatigue, making listening to the sounds a chore. Most sound cards have THD ratings ranging from 3 percent to .003 percent. Lower numbers represent better quality.

Sound Flavors

A sound board is an electronic circuitboard that fits into an expansion slot inside a computer. Expansion slots are covered in the motherboard section and come in several flavors known as ISA, EISA, PCI, and VL-Bus. The sound boards range in quality from high-fidelity to grainy, mushy sound. Most multimedia sound cards have the ability to connect joysticks, MIDI, and a CD-ROM. Since there are a variety of sound cards to choose from you can easily find one that best fits your needs and budget. The drawback to sound cards is they can be difficult to install, so if you do not feel comfortable opening your computer case, hire an expert to do the job.

Sound Features

Many of the better sound cards allow recording in a compressed format and are able to mix several soundtracks in real time. Some sound boards use Adaptive Differential Pulse Code Modulation (ADPCM), a lossy compression method that is sometimes used for speech. Some of the data is lost when using ADPCM, and that is why it would not be used for high-fidelity sound, as some of the sound quality is lost. ADPCM compression can squeeze sound at up to a 10:1 compression ratio. ADPCM methods review every sampled sound, storing only the differences from one sample to another. An 8-bit sound using ADPCM can approach the quality of a 12-bit sound. The problem is that since it is not completely standardized, if you record a compressed sound with ADPCM using your sound card, it is not guaranteed to play back with other sound cards.

Ports

Many sound boards come equipped with a SCSI interface which allows you to plug in a SCSI controlled CD-ROM without needing to use another controller card. If you get a sound board with SCSI, make sure it offers the SCSI-2 standard so it will be compatible with most other SCSI devices. Look for a four-pin or five-pin connector on a sound card for audio input from a CD-ROM. These connectors allow the sound board to control the sound mixing from the CD player.

Some sound cards are capable of handling digital input and output direct from an audio CD, DAT, or other digital source. This means that unlike analog recording, there is no generation loss when recording the sounds. The most popular digital formats are known as AES/EBU (Audio Engineer Society and

European Broadcasters Union) and S/PDIF (Sony/Philips Digital Interface Format).

Portable computers usually do not contain expansion slots unless they can be attached to a docking station, in which case they do not have an expansion slot when on the road. An **audio port** is a sound device that attaches to the parallel port of a computer. These are advantageous to people with portable computers because portables usually cannot otherwise handle an internal sound card. Audio ports are easy to install and configure. You don't have to be a rocket scientist to get one to work. The disadvantage to using an audio port is that some do not let you print without first disengaging them or using an AB switchbox. The quality of sound generated by an audio port is not as good as most internal cards, and although most audio ports do not include MIDI capabilities, there are a few MIDI devices available that will hook to an external serial port.

To connect to external synthesizers a sound card must be equipped with MIDI ports. Usually there is at least one MIDI input and one MIDI output for controlling 16 channels of sound. The MIDI connectors attach using a three-conductor DIN cable. **MIDI** (Musical Instrument Digital Interface) was developed to create a common interface for electronic musical instruments. MIDI sound files take only about one percent of the space that would be taken for a comparable digital recorded sound. This is because instead of storing sounds MIDI stores commands that trigger sounds stored in MIDI instruments. With MIDI you can also enhance sound using chorus, reverb, delay, pitch bend, and other musical effects. With MIDI control, the tempo of a song can be adjusted without affecting the pitch of the song.

Look for a sound jack for headphones and a line out for connecting self-powered speakers. If you do not have self-powered speakers, try regular speakers on the headphone jack. These are usually between 2 and 4 watts at 8 ohms and can power efficient speakers. Another port needed on sound cards is a microphone port. This port is important if the sound card is to be used for voice recognition, a feature that lets the computer be controlled using voice commands.

Synthesis

Most sound cards have a synthesis chip included on the card that can produce musical sounds. The two basic types of synthesis are FM (frequency modulation) and waveform samplers. **FM** chips produce completely computer-generated sounds. The quality of the sound relies heavily on the number of operators on the chip. Operators are wave forms that combine to form a singular sound. The greater the number of operators, the more complex the quality of the sound can be, making for greater harmonic complexity. Generally the chips on sound boards come with two or four operators resulting in a relatively simple and raw sound.

Waveform synthesis chips have digital recordings of actual instruments, like trumpets or guitars, stored on ROM chips or loaded into RAM. To record new sounds, additional equipment needs to be integrated with the system. Waveform samplers make FM synthesis sound very weak in comparison. Some high-end products combine the two synthesis styles to create complex textured sound.

Synthesizers vary in their polyphonic capabilities from 4-note to 32-note polyphony. A synthesizer that has 8-note **polyphony** can play eight notes at the same time, kind of like being able to hit eight keys on a piano simultaneously, but no more. A 24-note polyphonic synthesizer would let you play 24 notes simultaneously.

Multitimbral is the ability to play more than one type of sound at the same time. For example a 4-channel multitimbral synthesizer could play the sounds of a guitar, trombone, drum, and piano simultaneously. Sound boards generally offer 8-, 10-, or 16-channel multitimbrality.

Synthesizers create sound that can fill even the biggest hard disks pretty quickly. Instead of storing the sound of songs you create you can store MIDI files that are much smaller and essentially tell the synthesizer what to play. This is a very popular format and is used by professional musicians. MIDI is essentially a programming language that lets your computer store information on how to control MIDI instruments like keyboards. To assure your instrument will work with the sound card make sure the MIDI is compatible with Roland's MPU-401.

If you need MIDI on a portable computer there is a way to avoid needing an expansion slot. Yamaha's Tone Generator (CBX-T3) is an external MIDI device that plugs into the computer's serial port and it is compatible with both Macs and PC computers. This sound module contains 192 instrument sounds and accepts audio-in for sound mixing.

Considerations

A good sound board must have a microphone input jack to record sound. Most sound boards contain small amplifiers so they can drive self-powered speakers or connect to a stereo system.

To use your sound card with games make sure the card will emulate game sound standards made by Creative Labs Sound Blaster or the Ad Lib Music Synthesizer card. Without these compatibilities your games may not be able to blast off using your sound card. The new **VESA BIOS Extension/Audio Interface** (VBE/AI) may soon become the universal standard used by sound cards. This standard will eliminate some sound card incompatibilities and should make it easier for game developers to create sounds for their programs.

Some sound cards come equipped with a microphone and speech recognition software. It can be fun to take control of your computer using voice commands. If you are susceptible to repetitive stress injury, voice recognition software is a lifesaver. Give your hands a rest and let your mouth take over.

Make sure the speakers used with your sound card are shielded if you want to use them near your monitor or hard drive. Shielded speakers have had their magnetic interference minimized. Unshielded speakers placed near the monitor will distort the picture by causing the electron beam to stray from its path. Unshielded speakers can cause data loss on floppy disks and hard drives.

Speakers should have controls for volume, bass, treble, stereo separation, and balance. An on/off button is also a good feature.

Make sure the speakers have a headphone jack because many sound cards only have one output jack. Without an extra jack you will constantly have to be fumbling with the connections on the back of the sound card when using headphones. It is best to have speakers with more than one sound input jack so you can plug in a sound card, MIDI instrument, CD player, or other device at the same time.

The power output of speakers can range from a wimpy 1.5 watts to an full 35 watts. A 10-watt system can deliver a pretty good sound range. Some speakers have simulated stereo circuits that will make monaural sound seem to be in stereo.

Some self-powered speakers are battery powered, allowing you to make portable presentations without worrying about finding an AC adapter. Several speakers come with subwoofers that give an increased bass response. Under-the-monitor console designs keep the speakers out of the way on the desktop.

Some speakers come with one full-range speaker but the better speakers usually contain two or three speaker cones to handle different frequencies. The hearing range of the human ear is about 20 Hz to 20 kHz, and an ideal speaker system should be able to cover this full range.

Microphones

Some multimedia kits include a microphone. If yours does not and you want to record voice, there are many varieties of microphones to choose from. For recording with a stationary mic while you move around the room you will want an omnidirectional microphone. If you are in a noisy environment where you cannot control the background noise you need a unidirectional microphone. A unidirectional mic will cut out the extra unwanted noise but will also limit the recording range, meaning you will need to remain near the mic. A metal or plastic mesh on the mic prevents spurious pops. If you are in a windy area you will want a wind shield for the mic.

Sound cards use 1/8-inch mini phono plugs, so make sure the mic has a male 1/8-inch phono plug or comes with an adapter. Most professional sound equipment uses 1/4-inch phono plugs, and adapters for these are easily found at music and electronic stores. The cord that attaches the mic to the sound card must be able to reach around to the back of the computer. A cord of at least 6 feet in length is recommended. To properly match the mic with your sound card the impedance, which is rated in ohms, must lie within the proper range. Impedance is often rated at 4 ohms or 8 ohms. Check the manual for the proper specification.

If you plan to make voice annotations make sure the sound board can mute its output or you are likely to get feedback from the speakers. If the sound board you buy does not have a mute option, you can avoid feedback by turning down the volume on the speakers or by plugging the headphones into the sound jacks of the speakers.

Chapter 13

Amazing CD-ROMs

CD-ROMs are growing popular among the wired generation. The actual CD-ROM disk looks just like the audio CD that is used with a stereo system. Data is recorded onto a CD in a single spiral track, like a record. The CD-ROM disk is 12cm (4.75 inches) wide and can store nearly 670 megabytes of information. That is roughly equivalent to 300,000 pages of text. A smaller 3.5-inch version stores roughly 128 megabytes of data. The data stability of a CD-ROM is somewhere near 100 years, and the cost per megabyte is only about 6 cents.

Information stored on CD-ROM is read-only, meaning it cannot be changed once it is written. This also means it cannot be accidentally erased. The quality of not being erasable coupled with the fact that the stored data is not susceptible to magnetic fields makes CD-ROM disks a great way to store large amounts of reference information.

Titles offered on CD-ROM include encyclopedias, yellow pages for the whole United States, huge libraries of clip art, how to learn Japanese, interactive games, and multimedia presentations. One of my favorite CD-ROMs is a encyclopedia of musical instruments that gives a history of each instrument, shows pictures of the instruments, and will even play a sample sound to familiarize you with how the instrument sounds.

Every day there are new CD-ROM packages being produced and brought to market. Many new software application releases like CorelDraw and Microsoft Word are now available on CD-ROM. As an extra bonus, CorelDraw comes with a CD library of clip art that is extremely large and rated as the best clip art collection available.

Installing programs from CD-ROM is much easier than installing from floppies because you do not have to do the floppy disk shuffle and there is no fear of erasing the data on the CD. This is especially handy with programs like Windows NT, which comes on more than 20 floppy disks. To install the floppy disk version you have to sit at the computer a very long time and feed in the next disk when the computer prompts you. For the CD version all you have to do is start the installation and then take a break for an hour or so and voila, the program is ready to be used. CD-ROMs are also less vulnerable to dirt and dust than magnetic media like floppy disks.

How does a CD-ROM drive work? A laser scans tracks on the CD and can decode information that is stored in binary (a bunch of zeros and ones). The CD has small regions that contain recessed and filled reflective areas. A lens in the CD-ROM player decodes the CD by detecting whether the laser light is reflected back from the surface or not. Most CD-ROMs connect to the computer using a SCSI interface. If you already have a SCSI interface with other devices attached, you can chain the CD-ROM drive to the rest of the devices.

CD-ROMs are slow compared to hard drives. The CD-ROM access time is roughly 280 ms; that is nearly ten times slower than most hard drives. Fast hard drives have access times that hover around 8 ms. The transfer rate of a CD-ROM drive is usually 150 kilobytes per second for a single speed drive or 300 kilobytes per second for a double speed drive. The better transfer rates are found in double, triple, or quad-speed multispin drives. On these drives the CD-ROM is spun at different speeds: faster for images and data and slower for audio.

For maximum compatibility with your computer system, look for a CD-ROM that is MPC (Multimedia Personal Computer) compatible. A disk player with this standard will be able to play about 95 percent of the CD-ROMs available for Windows and DOS. These drives are often sold as a package deal with a sound card and speakers. Package deals usually come bundled with one or more CD-ROMs. The price on these packages is usually better than buying each of the components separately. If you have to compromise for quality on one of these deals, make sure the compromise is for the speakers; most packages do not come with the best speakers anyway, and the speakers are easily replaced.

Performance

Previous to the release of CD-ROMs, the drives that played audio CDs did not have to be very fast. The audio CD spins just fast enough to play the music back at the right speed, and there is no need to quickly random-access the information stored on an audio CD.

The fastest CD-ROM has nearly a 200 ms access time, while the slower CD-ROMs can have as long as a full second access time. Compare this with hard drives, which are usually in the 10 ms to 28 ms range. One of the quickest CD-ROMs currently available is the XM-3401 made by Toshiba. It is a good choice for its performance. Do not plan to buy a CD-ROM with an access time slower than 300 ms. Any multimedia tracks played on such a drive will appear jerky, which can take away from the enjoyment of the medium.

A built-in disc cache of 64 kilobytes or more will enhance performance of a CD drive. The largest caches are about 512 kilobytes in size. A cache will hold the information that the drive will probably need to access next, thereby speeding up the transfer of information. Often the cache will hold the most recently used information in anticipation that the user will want to use that information again. A read-ahead cache buffer puts the next block of information on the CD into the cache, speeding retrieval. This type of cache is good for scrolling through text because the cache can get ahead of where the user is reading and scroll new information quickly and smoothly.

Both the access time and transfer rate are affected by the speed the CD-ROM player spins the disc. **Multispin** players will spin the disk at more than one speed. Slower speeds approaching 200 rpm to 530 rpm are used so that the audio on the CD will sound right. This speed setting will maintain a 150-kilobyte-per-second transfer rate used for Red Book audio. Some multispin players can double or quadruple the speed the CD is spinning for enhanced data transfer of images and text. The top transfer speed of double speed CD-ROMs is near 330 kilobytes per second, and a quad speed CD-ROM can transfer up to 600 kilobytes per second. A CD must be written to be read at the faster speed to get this performance gain; not all CDs can be read this fast. Most CDs on the market before January of 1994 were written for single speed transfer, which means they are read at the slower rate.

Formats

There are a few types of CD standards that have been formed to ensure that CDs can be exchanged easily. The more standards a CD conforms to, the more likely it is that a CD drive will be able to read it. The following is a description of widely used standards. Many of the standards were released in books with colored jackets, and that is how they came to be named.

CD Drives and Standards

CD Type	***Audio CD***	***Single Session CD-ROM***	***Multisession CD-ROM***	***Photo CD***	***CD-R***	***CD-I***	***CD-MO***
ISO 9660		Yes	Yes	Yes	Yes	Yes	Yes
Red Book	Yes	Yes	Yes	Yes	Yes	Yes	
Yellow Book		Yes	Yes		Yes		
CD-ROM XA			Yes	Yes	Yes	Yes	
White Book			Yes			Yes	
Green Book				Yes		Yes	
Orange Book				Yes	Yes		Yes

High Sierra

A widely used standard for storage is called High Sierra. This is named in honor of the Nevada hotel where the standards committee met in 1985. A more formal version of this standard is known as ISO 9660. A High Sierra drive will work with a Mac or PC with the proper adapter. This format is a type of substandard used for CD-ROM file organization.

ISO 9660

This is a more formal version of High Sierra. ISO is an acronym for Industry Standards Organization. Just like High Sierra, ISO 9660 can be played back on a variety of computing platforms. The ISO 9660 allows for up to 72 minutes of storage on a CD. The ISO 9600 file names follow the DOS standard of eight characters with a three-character extension separated by a period (i.e., pumpkins.exe). If the data on an ISO 9660 CD-ROM is written in a cross-platform format, the file will be able to be used on both a Mac or PC.

HFS

HFS, the Hierarchical File System, is the bottom line format used for the Macintosh. HFS is used to manage files and folders and allows for long file names, color icons, and the graphical user interface. This format is used exclusively with Macintosh systems and does not comply with ISO 9660. An HFS-formatted CD is not meant to be read on a PC. This is the preferred format for a Mac-based CD.

Mixed Mode CD-ROM

This disk format allows for a mix of video and audio on the same disk. The sound files need to be strategically placed so they are easily accessed while accompanying a visual presentation. Mixed mode slows the CD to single speed for reading audio tracks and can increase the disc spinning rate when accessing graphics.

Multisession Photo CD

After you use your camera to shoot a roll of film you can have the images transferred to a photo CD. In addition to having the pictures developed on photographic stock, the images are compressed and stored on a CD. To read a photo CD your drive needs to be **Mode 2** capable. When you have pictures stored on a CD they often do not fill up the whole CD. A single session CD has one roll of images stored on it. To have the option of adding more images to a half-filled photo CD, the CD drive needs to be multisession-capable or the added images will not be able to be retrievable.

Photo CD images are stored in resolutions as high as 2,048 by 3,072 pixels. The typical storage space on a CD is 100 photos at 24-bit color depth. To view the images you need a VGA or higher resolution monitor attached to your computer. To display the image your computer must have RAM and disk cache that are larger than the image you want to display. A 24-bit image at

2,048 by 3,072 would need at least 30 megabytes of combined RAM and hard disk cache.

For information on photo CD facilities that can scan pictures onto CD for you, call Eastman Kodak at 1-800-242-2424, extension 36. There are over 20,000 locations that can transfer film onto CD. Scanning a whole roll of 24-exposure film costs about $20. Scanning slides and older negatives costs about $1.50 per image. A benefit of using photo CDs is that your pictures will not fade or become worn with age like photos, and the rated lifespan of a CD is 100 years.

Red Book

This is the first CD format, also known as CD-DA, and it was spawned in 1980. CD-DA (Digital Audio) describes the encoding and decoding of digital information for the audio format. If you own an audio CD it is in the Red Book format, and that is why your stereo CD player is able read it. A Red Book CD can hold up to 74 minutes of stereo music using pulse code modulation (PCM), a sequence of individually stored sound values. CD-G (Graphics) is an extension of the Red Book standard and is commonly known as Karaoke.

Yellow Book

This format was introduced in 1983 and forms the foundation for computer-related CD-ROM. There are two subcategorizes for this standard: Mode 1, which includes ISO 9660 and HFS, and Mode 2, which is **CD-ROM XA** (eXtended Architecture). Mode 2 allows for variable sound compression and varying levels of quality and is better than Mode 1 because it can store more data in each sector; 178 Kilobytes per sector compared with 150 kilobytes per sector. The reason Mode 1 stores less data is because it uses a portion of the area for error correction.

For smoother and better operating multimedia movies and soundtracks, the drive of choice needs to be **CD-ROM/XA** compliant. This format allows for up to a 19-hour audio capacity using audio compression known as ADPCM (Adaptive Differential Pulse Code Modulation). ADPCM stores the amplitude difference between successive digital samples instead of storing the actual digital samples of the sounds and therefore can store four to eight times more audio on a CD than the Red Book standard allows. ADPCM does not store all the data from the original sound and permits for some data loss, which is also known as lossy compression. CD-ROM/XA can interleave audio, which means sound can be divided and intermixed with other types of data.

If you buy a CD-ROM/XA, it will also be Mode 2 capable. Yellow Book applications can be PC- or Macintosh-compatible or both, depending on the software engine used to run the CD-ROM. Most CD-ROMs available on the market are Yellow Book-compatible.

The two levels of sound recording quality used in the CD-ROM/XA standard are referred to as Level C and Level B. Level C recording is 4-bit recording at a sampling rate of 18.9 kHz in mono, and Level B is better with 4-bit sampling and a 37.8 kHz sampling rate.

Green Book

This standard was developed in 1986 by Philips for its CD-I (Interactive) format as an addition to Yellow Book Mode 2. A CD-I disk can contain Red Book audio, video, and text that can all be interwoven. The CD-I specification calls for a system with an integrated computer and NTSC output. The processor used to run a CD-I is a Motorola 68000 microprocessor. CD-I uses MPEG (Moving Pictures Experts Group) video compression. This is a compression standard used with a sequence of still frames often used in desktop video.

Orange Book

This standard was introduced in 1990 and specifies writing to CD. This includes CD-R (Recordable), magneto-optical, and the Kodak Photo CD. Under the Orange Book standard, magneto-optical is referred to as Part 1 and CD-R is referred to as Part 2. **CD-R** or **CD-WO** (Write Once) is a device that will record and play CDs. This is great for archiving data or making training and reference CD titles. It provides an excellent way to review your CD before you bring it to a service bureau to get it mass-produced. Mass production service bureaus usually charge about $1,000 for mastering and $1 to $2 per disk with a 100-disk minimum. CD-R costs about $20 to $40 per disk plus the cost of the drive and software. If you need to do a run of 20 or less it is a good idea to stick with CD-R, but if you need 500 or more duplications, a service bureau is more economical.

White Book

This standard established in 1993 is known as CD-Bridge or FMV (full motion video). White Book is referred to as CD-Bridge because it bridges between computing platforms. This standard was put together by Philips, Sony, JVC, and Matsushita. White Book allows for up to 74 minutes of video to be encoded in MPEG 1 format on a 5-inch CD. Two CDs are required to store a feature-length movie. White Book is compatible with NTSC, PAL, and SECAM. It also can perform freeze frame, slow motion, and fast forward scanning. Kodak Photo CDs conform to the CD-Bridge format and can be read by a CD-I player.

AVI

Microsoft's AVI (Audio Video Interleave) standard, also called Video 1, allows CD-ROM playback of an image 160 x 120 pixels in 256 color at 15 frames per second. This is half the number of frames per second shown on television, so the movement will appear jerky.

DVI

IBM has teamed with Intel to produce DVI (Digital Video Interactive) which needs extra hardware to decompress and compress full motion video. Intel developed a special 750 video chip that performs all the compression and decompression on an IBM controller board. DVI supports full motion video at 512 by 482 pixels per frame. With compression DVI can fit 72 minutes of full motion video on one CD.

Commodore CDTV

The CDTV is related to the ISO 9660 standard but allows for longer file names that can be up to 32 characters long. These disks are intended for use on the Commodore systems and are not readable by other systems. The basic CDTV player contains the Motorola 68000 microprocessor. It can be augmented to be used by an Amiga computer.

3DO

This is a 32-bit RISC-based system that uses a double speed CD-ROM. It can show video at 30 frames per second. It is intended for mass market to the high-end game package consumer and has yet to gain acceptance.

Video Information Systems (VIS)

This is a joint venture of Tandy and Microsoft and is a consumer-level product. It is based on the ISO 9660 format and allows true color video and three levels of audio playback including MIDI, waveform, and CD-Audio. VIS players hook directly to the television similarly to a VCR.

Connections

The interface that the CD-ROM uses for your computer is either parallel, serial, proprietary, or SCSI. Most drives will require an exposed drive bay in your computer. The controller cards are usually ISA boards, but you can also find EISA, MCA, VL-Bus, or PCI cards. Proprietary devices usually accompany low-end CD-ROM models and have a disadvantage because they are not standardized. Proprietary controllers might have compatibility problems with your computer system. If you do get a proprietary CD kit make sure it is returnable if you cannot get it to work with your computer. The proprietary interfaces are usually based on variations of the IDE interface. The IDE interface is commonly used with hard drives that have a capacity of 500 megabytes or less.

The advantage of getting a drive controller that uses a SCSI interface is that it can also be used to link other devices, like a scanner or hard disk, to your computer. Another advantage is that SCSI has a faster data transfer rate than the other methods so there is a performance benefit of choosing a SCSI interface. The disadvantage of picking SCSI is that installation can be a bit more difficult than simply slipping on a parallel adapter, which is quite simple. The proprietary cards available from Sony and Philips are not compatible with SCSI. Make certain if you choose a SCSI interface that it is a full SCSI-II interface so you will get the best performance. If your computer does not have a SCSI port or if you are using a portable computer without a SCSI option, then parallel ports are the only choice for external CD drives. Using a serial connection is far too slow for CD use. Parallel port CD drives are comparatively slow and are not advised for multimedia use. The drives are fine for text retrieval but are recommended only as a last solution.

If possible, be sure to get a CD player that is bundled with a SCSI adapter. This way you ensure that the CD-ROM is compatible with the adapter card. Also look for a pass-through SCSI port on the drive so you can link other equipment, like a scanner, to the drive.

Prime Location

The CD-ROM drive can be an internal or external unit in relation to the computer case. If you are connecting it to a laptop you need an external unit because laptops do not have extra exposed drive bays that would allow them to house a CD-ROM. A company named Trantor makes a SCSI-to-parallel-cable interface that allows you to connect an external SCSI CD drive to your printer port on the computer. The advantage of external units is they can interface with the parallel port, which makes them easy to connect to more than one machine. They can be uncoupled and shared by another computer fairly easily. The external CD drives are easier to control and to attach output wires to for speakers. The drawback is a parallel port connection cannot handle as fast a speed of data transfer as can a SCSI connection. If you plan on using a CD drive often with a portable computer, make sure you get one with a real SCSI port.

If you have an extra exposed drive bay on the front of the computer case you have room to install an internal CD drive. You will need a 5.25-inch drive bay, and the drive for most units will fit into a half-height bay. Internal units will draw power from the power supply inside the computer case, unlike external units which require an extra AC plug to draw power. If you are getting an external drive, make sure the cable connecting the unit to the computer case is long enough. An 18-inch or shorter cable might not make the stretch to the place that you want the drive to rest on your desktop.

Bundled for Fun

CD-ROM players are sometimes bundled with CD-ROMs to entice you to buy the package. Evaluate the software to see if you actually need it; if you do make sure the player can perform well. Often the CD-ROM drive is of inferior quality and is offered with the software so the vendor can sell it easier. The same goes for MPC upgrade kits, which combine CD-ROM drives, sound boards, and sometimes CD-ROMs. These kits sometimes have a weak link in terms of quality. Look them over carefully so you know what you are getting. Check out the software that comes with the sound card. Sound editing software is usually included, and some even come with a microphone and voice recognition software. The benefit to getting one of these kits is you are assured the drive, sound card, and speakers will be compatible with each other.

Odds and Ends

Look for headphone jacks and volume controls for playing audio CDs. There can also be line-outs for connecting the CD drive to your stereo system or amplified speakers. There should be a connection for hooking up to your sound card which allows you to record and play sounds using the sound card.

The CD-ROM drive should have a dust door or one that can close to prevent dust from contaminating the drive mechanisms. Some drives require a caddy that encases the CD and look similar to the jewel boxes that audio CDs come in. This prevents damage to the CD because the user does not come in direct contact with the CD. When using a caddy there is no worry about scratching or leaving fingerprints on the CD because you never touch the CD. The CD drive should have an eject button for manual ejection of the CD-ROM in case the software-based eject does not work. Many of the drives come with an automatic lens cleaning feature. This will ensure your CDs will play better because the laser will not be obstructed by dust or dirt.

The drive mechanism, the part of the drive that actually does the reading of the CD-ROM, is made by one of about a dozen companies. The chassis and rest of the drive are made by individual manufacturers who assemble the drives. This means many drives on the market will perform similarly because they often contain the same drive mechanism. The one key difference can be attributed to the quality of the software drivers included with the drive.

If you plan to use your external CD on your travels around the world, make sure it contains an autoswitching power supply; that way you will not have to carry an extra step-down power converter in your travel pack. Remember to bring a power surge protector, as many countries have unstable power that can damage delicate electronic circuitry. A drive with a built-in fuse is a good feature for extra power protection, as the fuse will blow before the drive can be damaged.

There are several things that can make hooking up the drive easier. A built-in SCSI terminator is a good feature, as it is an easy-to-switch SCSI ID selector. Lights that indicate the drive is on and is being accessed are a necessity. A case made of metal is usually more impact-resistant than one made of plastic, which is an important consideration especially if you move the drive around often.

Manufacturer driver support is important for CD drives. The drivers let your computer know what kind of CD drive you are using. A good manufacturer will release new, improved software drivers often. If the manufacturer has a forum on CompuServe or another online service, that makes it easy to get the new drivers when they are released. An alternative is for the manufacturer to have a bulletin board system that contains updated drivers or mail-out updates.

CD-R

CD recorders are a valuable asset for people who want to produce their own CDs. If you need to send blueprints, large documents, or other vital information around the globe by overnight shipping, a CD is a great and inexpensive format because it is both lightweight and relatively indestructible. Recording a CD-R takes about 30 to 60 minutes depending on whether you are using a single speed or double speed drive. If you are planning on recording your own CD-ROM, make sure you get a hard drive that can handle the job. The CD-R counts on having a steady stream of data fed to it, and if that stream is broken, the CD being burned may be corrupted.

As hard disks heat up, the physical dimensions of the disks change, making the position of a track change slightly during use. Many big hard drives use thermal recalibration to fine-tune themselves while in operation. If a drive decides to recalibrate itself while you are writing a CD, the data stream may be disrupted. If you are recording to CD or making transfers to videotape there are special hard drives available that prevent data loss from thermal recalibration. These disks usually forbid recalibration while the hard drive is reading or writing to a track.

After producing your own CD, you can read these CD-R discs from any CD-ROM drive just like a commercially mass-produced disk. A CD-R disk comes in two capacities; a 63-minute disk that can store 550 megabytes and a 74-minute disk that can store 650 megabytes. To make sure a CD will work correctly before you record it, you can test the files with a software simulation utility. Using this method, problems and performance are checked before committing the data to CD.

You can use a CD-R drive to make backups of data. This method offers fast performance compared to backups using a tape drive.

Some CD-R drives allow incremental and multisession recording. An incremental recorder lets you add more information to a partially recorded CD. With this method, until the recording session is completed by adding a leadout and a table of contents, the CD will only be readable by the CD-R drive; a regular CD-ROM drive will not recognize the contents. A multisession CD-R allows more than one complete session to be recorded on a CD. This is great for utilizing unrecorded areas if the first recording only fills part of the CD. If you wish to use multisession recording, make sure the format used on the CD-R is also readable by the CD-ROM drive which will read the CDs.

After you have tested and pressed a CD-R and everything works just as planned, you may want to get the CD mass-produced. When you send the CD data to the mastering plant, they first test the ISO file structure and then write the information to a glass master disk which is coated with a special photosensitive lamination. The lamination is exposed by laser light, which creates write pits. The glass master is then electroplated with nickle, which is separated from the glass master. This nickel negative is called the father. If the father did not wear out too quickly it could be used to make CDs. From the father, a positive image is made using electroplating. This master is called the mother and is tested for defects. If the disk checks out without any problems, several images are made from the mother which are known as stampers. These stampers are used to actually replicate CDs. Mass-produced CDs are then molded from the stamper disk and are coated with reflective aluminum and sealed in plastic.

If you need to make more than one CD at a time, look for CD-R drives that can be chained together for mass duplication. If you need several hundred CDs, get them mass-produced. Many companies offer this service.

More Info

If you have a yearning to learn more about CD-ROM titles available to the public, there are some great resources available in the urban jungles. The Bureau of Electronic Publishing offers CD-ROMs for sale and offers a catalog that describes them. Call 1-800-828-4766 for more information. They also have a BBS that you can access for 10 minutes at a time with a modem. For more about the BBS and to receive a password, call (201) 808-2700.

The *CD-ROM directory* is available in hard copy or on CD-ROM from UniDisc for $160 to $199. They can be reached at 3941 Cherryvale Avenue, #1, Soquel, CA 95073.

The *CD-ROM Directory* is available from TFPL Publishing and is updated twice yearly. The directory is available on CD or in a 1,000-page printed catalog and contains about 3,500 titles. The one-year subscription is about $220. Phone: (202) 296-6009.

CD-ROMs In Print 1993: An International Guide to CD-ROM, CDI, CDTV, and Electronic Book Products is available from Meckler, 11 Ferry Lane West, Westport, CT 06880. Tel: 1-800-635-5537. It costs about $100.

For the general consumer a good way to find CD titles is to browse magazines for mail order outfits that sell CDs. If you request a catalog from these companies they will often send beautiful full color catalogs that describe numerous CDs with a great selection of titles. Magazines with a multimedia slant, like *New Media*, *CD-ROM World*, and *Electronic Entertainment Magazine*, have CD-ROM reviews in every issue. CompuServe has a CD-ROM Forum, which is a great place to find the latest CD-ROM titles.

Chapter 14

Storage Devices

The information used on a computer needs to be stored somewhere, just as a library stores books. Floppy drives and hard drives are the most common storage devices. They are often complemented by other storage devices to offer additional capabilities.

When considering other types of storage first try to estimate the amount of storage capacity you will need. For just a few hundred megabytes of storage a removable disk such as a SyQuest or Bernoulli drive is suitable. For mass storage an optical disk is the best choice. When considering different storage types there are several factors that will determine the best medium for your needs. These considerations include transfer speed, access speed, data capacity, cost of drive, cost per megabyte, media life, and exchangeability of information.

Comparison of Media and Chips

Storage Type	*Cost per Mb*	*Years of Media Stability*	*Size of Media*	*Capacity of Media*	*Access Time*	*Transfer Rate*	*Rewritable*
Chips							
CPU	Varies		N/A	N/A	10 - 60 ns	40 - 200 Mb/sec	Yes
CPU on chip Cache	N/A		N/A	1 kb - 16 kb	15 - 60 ns	40 - 200 Mb/sec	Yes
SRAM	$100		N/A	16 - 512 kb	20 - 100 ns	20 - 80 Mb/sec	Yes
DRAM	$40 - $70		N/A	128 kb - 16 Mb	60 - 200 ns	20 - 80 Mb/sec	Yes
Flash Memory/ RAM Disc	$100		N/A	1 Mb-128 Mb	50 - 100 ns		Yes

Storage Type	*Cost per Mb*	*Years of Media Stability*	*Size of Media*	*Capacity of Media*	*Access Time*	*Transfer Rate*	*Rewritable*
Magnetic Media							
Hard Drive	$1.5 - $3	5	1 to 5.24"	20 Mb - 2 Gb	12 - 30 ms	1 - 10 Mbps	Yes
ED Floppy Disk	$2.50	5	3.5"	2.88 Mb	100 ms	250 - 500 kbs	Yes
HD Floppy Disk	$0.50 - $1.00	5	3.5"	1.44 Mb	100 ms	250 - 500 kbs	Yes
Floptical	$0.95	5	3.5"	21 Mb	100 ms	250 - 500 kbs	Yes
QIC Cartridge	$1.80	5	5.25"	44 Mb - 150 Mb	10 minutes	5 Mb/minute	Yes
DAT	$0.01	5	3" x 2"	750 Mb - 2.3 Gb	25 seconds	10 Mb/minute	Yes
Bernoulli	$0.67	5	5.25"	150 Mb	35 ms	2 Mbps	Yes
SyQuest	$0.25	5	5.25"	270 Mb	22 ms	2 Mbps	Yes
Optical Media							
WORM	$0.23	100	5.25"	200 Mb - 1000 Mb	40 - 100 ms	0.2 - 1 Mb/sec	No
CD-ROM	$0.06 - $0.10	100	5.25"	660 Mb - 1024 Mb	1,000 - 250 ms	1 - 5 Mb/sec	No
3.5" Optical	$0.77	10	3.5"	128 Mb	40 - 100 ms	0.2 - 1 Mb/sec	Yes
Optical	$0.28	10	5.25"	400 Mb - 650 Mb	40 - 100 ms	0.2 - 1 Mb/sec	Yes

Removable Cartridge Hard Drives

Cartridge hard drives (also called removable hard drives) are hard drives that allow you to remove the hard disk and replace it with another. The disk is encased in a plastic shell and usually holds either 44, 88, or 105 megabytes. The disk is written to on both sides by the drive. When removing the disk the read and write heads are moved away from the surface of the disk, preventing the two from touching. Only the disk and the cartridges leave the drive; the rest of the components remain behind. The cost per megabyte hovers near $1.80 and the magnetic media is stable for about 5 years.

An advantage of these removable disks is they have the ability to store large files that would not fit on a floppy disk. This storage medium comes in handy when the need arises to send files to service bureaus for printing or storage. Most commercial printers have cartridge drives that can handle the various capacity cartridges on the market. If you already use a service bureau you might check what type of cartridge system they use so you can exchange data easily.

A great feature of removable hard drives is that if a disk fills up you can just pull it out and swap in another disk. Voila! You have more disk space to store those big CAD files or spreadsheets. If you travel extensively between offices, all you have to do to transport data is grab the disk and go. When you get to the other office just pop it in and it is ready to go. The disks can be organized to reflect different projects, different data, or different users. You can also boot the computer from a removable hard disk, making custom system configurations easy.

For data security, removable disks can be used when at the computer and locked up when not using the system. This is probably the best way to keep information away from unwanted eyes.

SyQuest and Bernoulli are well-known types of removable drives. SyQuest drives are used at about 99 percent of all printing service bureaus and are handy for transferring large files. The access times for these devices is around 20 ms.

Iomega's Bernoulli has a cartridge drive capable of storing 150 megabytes that is compatible with disks with capacities of 35 Mb, 65 Mb, 105 Mb, and 150 Mb. It will also read and write to Bernoulli 44-megabyte and 88-megabyte disks. The Bernoulli is about 20 percent slower than a SyQuest drive. Bernoullis use a flexible disk, similar to a big floppy, and are thought to be more reliable than SyQuest because they are less susceptible to head crashes. The prices for removable cartridge drives range from about $550 for 44-megabyte drives to $700 for 88-megabyte drives.

SyQuest drives are faster than Bernoulli. Both formats are susceptible to data corruption from dust. SyQuest comes in a 5.25-inch format in both 44-megabyte and 88-megabyte capacity. There is also a 3.5-inch SyQuest that stores 105 megabytes of information. SyQuest drives are also available in a 3.5-inch drive with a 270-megabyte capacity and a 5.25-inch drive with a 200-megabyte capacity.

Removable drives can be used for backing up data. They are relatively quick especially if compared with tape backup systems and can access the stored information much faster. This is because disks are random access storage devices. An 88-megabyte backup can be performed in only 8.5 minutes. That is pretty fast and painless. The average cost for these drives ranges from $600 to $1,200.

Storage Systems Compared

Storage System	Bernoulli	SyQuest	Floptical	Magneto-Optical
Cost of Drive	Moderate	Moderate	Low	Expensive
Cost per Mb	High	High	Medium	Medium-low
Pros	Moderate speed, reliable	Used in desktop publishing bureaus, fast drives, widely used	Cheap drives, drives read conventional floppies faster	Low cost for media, durable medium, impervious to stray magnetic fields
Cons	Medium vulnerable to stray magnetic fields and dust, noisy	Medium vulnerable to stray magnetic fields and dust, expensive cartridge, less than great reliability	Low capacity medium, slow access time, vulnerable to stray magnetic fields	Expensive drives, slower than hard drives
Ideal Use	Backup of moderate to larger files	Transport of data to service bureaus	Backup of small files	Mass storage, secondary storage
Access Speed	40 ms	22 ms	1,000 ms	25 to 100 ms
Max Capacity	150 Mb	270 Mb	21 Mb	1.2 Gb
Used as Primary Storage	Very Good	Very Good	Poor	Fair
Used as Secondary Storage	Excellent	Excellent	Good	Good to excellent
Used for Backup	Excellent	Excellent	Excellent	Excellent

Storage System	Removable Hard Drive	WORM	Tape Backup	Solid State Drive
Cost of Drive	Expensive	Expensive	Cheap	Very expensive
Cost per Mb	Super high	Low	Extremely low	Very expensive
Pros	Fast access, wide range of capacities	Inexpensive disks, durable medium, impervious to stray magnetic fields	Low cost, many drives available	Extremely fast
Cons	Expensive drives, not as easily transported, vulnerable to stray magnetic fields and shock	Expensive drives, slower than hard drives	Extremely slow access, unsuitable for primary or secondary storage	High cost, volatile memory

Storage System	Removable Hard Drive	WORM	Tape Backup	Solid State Drive
Ideal Use	Fast access to files, primary storage	Mass storage, backup, archive	Backup data	Super fast access to data
Access Speed	7-20 ms	1,200 ms	30 seconds to 5 minutes	Less than 1 ms
Max Capacity	1 Gb	3 Gb	4+ Gb	60+ Mb
Used as Primary Storage	Great	Poor	Very poor	Very poor
Used as Secondary Storage	Excellent	Good to excellent	Poor	Excellent
Used for Backup	Poor	Poor	Excellent	Not an option

Tape Drives

It is important to have a backup system to ensure your data is safe from being corrupted or destroyed. The key is redundancy; if one copy of data is destroyed, you will want other copies of the data that can be retrieved and restored. If it takes too much time to back up your data from your hard drive to floppy disks, then it is time to get a tape backup unit. You need a tape backup if you have more than 50 megabytes of files on your hard drive to back up. If it takes longer than an hour to do a backup, it is time to get a tape drive. Tape drives are not used for everyday information access, as they are far too slow. Tape drives are all slow but are convenient and very cost-effective for storing large amounts of information.

For the best setup, buy a tape drive that can fit your entire backup onto one tape. This way you can start the backup process and then leave the rest of the backup unattended. With some Windows software you can arrange for an automated backup schedule to occur once a week and an incremental backup every day. This can happen in the background while you use other programs, or the alternatively the backup can occur unattended. When you return later, the backup is done—no hassle, no floppy swapping. Take note that you will not have to back up all the data on your hard drive, just the files you create while using your programs. The programs themselves can be restored the same way you originally installed them onto the hard drive, but for convenience it would be easier to restore all the programs from a backup on tape.

Many backup programs supply the option of compressing your backup files. Using compression will allow you to store more information on the same capacity media. Often the data compression can double the storage capacity. For example, a 250-megabyte backup tape can store 500 megabytes of compressed data.

When you choose to actually perform a backup is a subjective matter for you to decide. The more often you back up, the less data you will probably lose in the event of a hard disk crash. When you feel that you had better not lose the data you have created, then it is time for a backup. This could be hourly, daily, weekly, or even monthly.

Make sure the tape backup you choose has an adequate data buffer. These buffers temporarily hold data and keep it transferring in an uninterrupted stream. This prevents the data from overflowing in the event the drive processes information slower or faster than it is receiving or sending data.

When restoring data from a tape, make sure the tapes equalize in temperature to the environment you are going to use them in. If the tape is not at room temperature, some condensation can occur which can cause the drive to damage to the tape.

Many backup drives have LED status lights and tape wear indicators. If you plan to use the tape drive in different countries be sure it has a universal power supply. A universal power supply will let the drive run on 110 or 220 volt electricity. Some tape drives come standard with self-cleaning heads. If your model does not, the tape heads should be cleaned with special a kit. Cleaning is usually done once a month or less if the drive is not used often.

There are four major types of backup tape formats: DC-2000, DC-600, 4mm DAT, 8mm, and DAT-DDS cartridges. The formats that can store more data and are faster are also more expensive.

DC-2000 Tape Drives

The smallest capacity of the formats is the DC2000. The **DC2000**, also called a mini-cartridge, is half an inch thick and will hold about 40 to 120 megabytes. The tape looks like an extra-wide audio cassette tape. If you use compression it can store up to 240 megabytes of data. These tape drives cost between $200 and $500. The internal drives are less costly than the external drives. The external drives require a free expansion slot for a controller and the internal units can run off a normal floppy drive controller, but the drives that use an expansion card are usually faster. For convenience there are drives that can plug into a parallel port. These are easily connected for use and easily removed after use.

These drives use QIC-40, QIC-80, or another proprietary backup format. *QIC* is an abbreviation for Quarter-Inch Committee and QIC sets standards for tape drives. QIC-40 drives can format 40 megabyte and 60 megabyte tapes. QIC-80 drives can format 80 megabyte and 120 megabyte drives and are backwardly compatible with the earlier QIC-40 format. The QIC-525 tapes can store about 500 megabytes of data and the QIC-1350 can handle about 1,300 megabytes of data.

If you plan to share the information stored on a tape with other computers, make sure the other tape drives use the same format. You can buy these tapes blank, but you may want to get them preformatted because otherwise you will have to format the tapes yourself, and this process can take about 1.5 to 3 hours. When a buying preformatted tape, make sure it is specified to the type of tape drive you have.

QIC Tape Backup Drives

QIC Drive	QIC-40	QIC-80	QIC-525	QIC-500	QIC-555
Cost	$135 to $300	$170 to $600	$500 to $1,200	$500 to $1,000	$550 to $1,000
Data Capacity	40 Mb	120 Mb	500 Mb	500 Mb	550 Mb
Compressed Data Capacity	120 Mb	250 Mb	1,000 Mb	1,000 Mb	1,100 Mb
Compatibility	DC2000	DC2120	DC6525	QIC-minicartridge	QIC-143 minicartridge
Transfer Rate Per Minute	2 Mb to 3 Mb	2.5 Mb to 4 Mb	7 Mb to 12 Mb	8 Mb to 18 Mb	8 Mb to 18 Mb

QIC Drive	QIC-40	QIC-80	QIC-525	QIC-500	QIC-555
Computer Interface	Floppy drive controller	Floppy drive controller, parallel port	SCSI controller	Floppy drive controller, parallel port	SCSI controller
Pros	Affordable	Inexpensive	High capacity, good transfer rate	High capacity, good transfer rate	High capacity, good transfer rate, comparatively less cost than similar drives
Cons	Slow transfer rate, low capacity	Slow transfer rate, low capacity	Expensive, consider DAT as alternative	Expensive, consider DAT as alternative	Expensive, consider DAT as alternative

DC-600 Tape Drives

The **DC600** is a tape cartridge that can store from 60 megabytes to 1.35 gigabytes. The cartridges labeled DC6000 are the same size but contain a longer tape. The price range for a DC600 drive is $1,000 to $2,000. Since these units cannot run off a floppy drive controller they will require another controller card to operate. The smaller capacity drives often use a QIC controller, while the larger units tend to use a SCSI controller. If you buy a SCSI controlled tape unit, make sure the backup software can support backup to a SCSI controlled unit, as not all software can do it. The DC600 drives often use the QIC-80 format. Tape drives compatible with QIC-40 and QIC-80 interfaces are supported by a multitude of backup software. A format that is authorized by Windows NT is Maynard's Maynstream. This standard may be the best choice if you plan on using Windows NT, and it may become the standard format used by most drives.

4-mm DAT Tape Drives

DAT is the cheapest storage option, costing only 1 cent per megabyte. The **4mm DAT** (Digital Audio Tape) cartridge is smaller than the DC2000 but it can store up to 4 gigabytes of data. A DAT tape used with stereo systems is the same size, but do not be tempted use them interchangeably for computer backup. The stereo system tapes are not as sturdy and the constant winding and rewinding can stretch the tape, which means endangering your data. Two widely used recording formats are DDS (Digital Data Storage) and DataDAT. To record the data a Helical-Scan technology is used where the tape head does not remain stationary but rather floats up and down in a wave pattern.

DAT Storage Comparison

DAT Format	**DDS**	**DDS-2**	**DDS-3**	**DDS-4**
Tape Capacity	2 Gb	4 Gb	8 Gb	16 Gb
Year of Introduction	1991	1993	1995	1997
Transfer Rate	183 kbps	366 kbps	700 kbps	1500 kbps

8mm Cartridge Tape Drives

An **8mm** cartridge looks like a 8mm video tape cartridge and can hold up to 10 gigabytes of data. The transfer rate ranges from 246 kilobytes per second up to 500 kilobytes per second. This is the highest capacity backup system available and is ideal for networked systems. DAT tape drives cost from $2,000 to $4,000. They are invariably SCSI-controlled. The recording format is Helical-Scan just like in video recorders.

DAT DDS

DDS (Digital Data Storage) has a capacity of 1.3 gigabytes to 2 gigabytes. It has a transfer rate from 183 kilobytes per second to 366 kilobytes per second. These drives are in a 3.5-inch design. The tape used measures 2 by 3 by 3/8-inches. The tape lengths are available in 60 meters, 90 meters, and 120 meters.

DAT DDS-2

This digital storage format can handle up to 4 gigabytes of data and has a transfer rate of 366 kilobytes per second to 510 kilobytes per second.

DDS-3 and DDS-4

DDS-3 will hold 8 gigabytes of data. DDS-4 will hold 16 gigabytes of data and will be released in 1997.

Computer Interface

Most tape backups use a SCSI or QIC-02 interface to connect with the computer. Some of the lower-end models use a Shugart Associates 400 (SA-400) interface, the same type as a floppy controller. The interface used will affect the transfer rate and reliability of the backup. The connection will also determine whether an adapter card will be needed. The adapter card will take up an expansion slot inside the computer.

Using a floppy controller eliminates the need for a spare expansion slot. Using a floppy controller makes the data transfer slow with a maximum transfer rate of 2 megabytes per minute. The maximum tape capacity is 40 megabytes, and there is no error-detection nor error-correction to ensure the data is not corrupted. This route is suitable for personal use but is not recommended for business use.

QIC-02 can transfer data at 5 megabytes per minute. It requires an extra expansion slot in the computer to accept an adapter card. This type of interface is supplied with most available tape drives.

SCSI can transfer data at a faster rate than the tape backup drives can handle the data. This limits the transfer rate to 5 megabytes per minute. SCSI requires an expansion slot on the computer for a SCSI adapter board. The problem with SCSI is it is not a very firm standard, and not all backup software will support it. The advantage of SCSI is that one interface can control seven devices. For example, you could hook up a tape drive, a scanner, a CD-ROM, and four hard disks to one SCSI controller card.

For portable computers, unless you have a SCSI port built into the computer you will want to get a tape drive that has a parallel port interface. This will be an external tape drive because there is no room inside a portable for a tape drive unit. Units that connect to parallel ports are also are a great choice for those whose computers lack extra expansion slots or drive bays.

External or Internal

The tape drives can be mounted in a free bay inside your computer case, or the drive can be housed in its own chassis external to the computer case and connected to the computer by a cable.

The advantage of having an internal unit is there will not be another box crowding the desktop. If you already have an external CD-ROM and modem you may not have the space for a tape drive on your desk. If you only need to back up data from one computer this internal drive may be the solution, but if all the drive bays in your computer are taken you will have to get a bigger case to install an internal tape drive.

External units are usually a little more expensive than internal units but they also have advantages. The computer case does not need a free drive bay to use an external tape drive. It can be connected to the computer when needed and disconnected after the backup is completed. This allows you to use the same drive to connect to more than one computer and back up the data they contain. All that is needed is a SCSI or QIC adapter card for each computer. These usually cost as little as $100.

MTBF, A Four-Letter Word

Tape drives are rated for MTBF (mean time between failure). This is a rough gauge of how dependable the drive will be. Sometimes a duty cycle accompanies this rating. A drive with a 7 percent duty cycle rates the tape drive's lifespan as one that is used 7 percent of the time while it is powered on. The magnetic media on the tape backup cassettes have a stability of about five years. After five years the data tends to deteriorate. If you are archiving data it is recommended to refresh the data on the tape every five years.

Magneto-Optical Discs

Optical discs are a combined technology media of both magnetic and optical. MO drives are fairly expensive, but the media used for storing data is low in cost. Magneto-optical drives come in two flavors: a 5.25-inch which can hold up to 1.3 gigabytes, and a smaller 3.5-inch version which can hold up to 128 megabytes. The newer 3.5-inch discs can handle 230 megabytes and 256 megabytes. MO disks average about 28 cents per megabyte and have a rated 35-year stability. The capacity of optical discs range from 400 megabytes to 1.3 gigabytes. With an average 35 ms access time, they are slower than hard disks but share properties of allowing them to be erased and rewritten. Magneto-optical disks are enclosed in a cartridge and are easily transported.

Magneto-optical drives store the data on a disk composed of a terbium-iron-colbalt alloy that is enclosed in a wrap of clear polycarbonate. This mix of alloys can have its polarity altered when heated to 200° C, which is its Curie point. The trick is done with a laser beam and magnetic head. The shift in polarity affects the way light reflects from the disk. For writing data the drive makes an extra pass to ensure data integrity, so writing data is slower than reading.

MO disks use a combined technology of both magnetic and laser. A laser heats the optical disc coating so a magnetic head can write tracks to the disc. The tracks are then read by the laser at lower intensity. These discs cannot be altered by a magnetic field which makes them less prone to accidental erasure than other magnetic media. Most MO drives require two passes to write data, the first pass to erase the tracks by writing all zeros and a second pass to write the new data. Often a third pass is used to ensure data integrity. A faster design called phase change writes data in just one pass using only a laser; no magnet is used. A second pass is then made to verify the data, slowing down the whole process.

The higher capacity drives use a format called Zoned Constant Angular Velocity (ZCAV) to store data more efficiently. In traditional storage the disk is divided into sectors like slices from a pie with each sector storing an equal amount of data. The larger areas near the outer rim contain the same amount data as the smaller inner edge. Since the outer edge has more room than the inner edge, ZCAV makes use of this extra space by storing more data on the outer tracks.

Magneto-optical disks, like hard drives, need to be low-level formatted before writing data to the disk. There is no standard for doing a low-level format so disks written on two different drives may not be interchangeable. If you need to use disks on two computers it is wise to buy the same type of MO drive for each computer.

The 3.5-inch MO drives are about 60 to 90 percent slower than SyQuest or Bernoulli drives but are much faster than tape backup. The 5.25-inch MOs are about the same speed as SyQuest and Bernoulli.

If you need to access lots of large data files, an MO would be a good choice. Individual drive features to look for include a front panel power switch and lights that let you know the drive is on or when it is writing information to the disk. An SCSI ID selector is needed as well as an SCSI through port allowing other SCSI devices to be chained to the drive. Without an SCSI through connector the drive will have to be the last device on the SCSI chain. Connecting a drive using a SCSI interface is tremendously faster than using a parallel port.

MO discs are moderately priced. The cartridges are durable and are not influenced by magnetic fields when in storage. The MO drives are expensive for entry level but are a good choice for high capacity storage because the per-megabyte cost runs only about 30 cents. That is much cheaper than the average $1.60 per megabyte of SyQuest storage. MO drives cost from $1,200 to $5,000.

If you need to store vast amounts of data, a magneto-optical jukebox may be the answer. Like a jukebox you find at the local 1950s diner, optical jukeboxes store many disks. The MO jukebox can automatically play the disk you need to access.

Video Discs

A video disc stores information in analog form, not digital. To be displayed on the computer the information must be translated to a digital form. This translation can be microprocessor- and time-intensive.

Video discs are usually implemented when giving presentations. The computer controls which image from the video disc are being displayed on a television monitor or projector instead of a computer screen. Using this technique the computer does not have to translate the analog signal to a digital signal but can still tell the video disk what to play and when to play it.

WORM Drives

WORM is an acronym for Write Once Read Many. This removable disc measures 5.25 inches and has slow access time. It is an optical storage device that can be written to only once but read many times. The primary use of a WORM drive is for archiving files. The media stability of a WORM disk is approximately 100 years, much longer than magnetic media lifespan, which averages 5 years.

To record data a high-power laser heats a new WORM disk, burning pits into the coating. The same laser at a lower power setting is able to read the information it wrote. The reading process is similar to the way the CD-ROM reads data.

A WORM disk can typically store 200 megabytes to 1 gigabyte of information at an average cost of 28 cents per megabyte. Optical jukeboxes are available for WORM disks and allow fast access to multiple disks. These machines can store anywhere from 10 to 1,000 disks. Having this much information available is cost-effective and eliminates labor-intensive searches.

RAM Disks

RAM discs are comprised of a set of solid state RAM chips on a board that is usually inside a box external or internal to the computer case. RAM disk capacities start around 80 megabytes and are also offered in much larger sizes. A RAM disk acts similarly to the DRAM located on the motherboard and is used primarily for manipulating big files. An example of a large file that could use a RAM disk is a CAD drawing, graphic file, or complex scientific experimentation. These files can be stored in the RAM disk and accessed much faster than if they reside on a hard drive. A RAM disk is well-suited to applications that do not operate effectively with caching or for use with read-intensive files. A RAM disk is ideal for applications that demand heavy use of a small number of files. The cost per megabyte at $120 is the highest of the storage options.

When the power goes off the information stored in a RAM disc is lost. This is because RAM is volatile memory and constantly needs to be electronically refreshed to keep the data in its memory. To avoid loss of stored information users of RAM disks often acquire a UPS (uninterruptable power supply) which offers an alternate power source if the power is suddenly cut off. The UPS provides enough power to transfer the RAM information to a magnetic disk drive for more permanent and nonvolatile storage. SCSI solid state disks can have data mirrored or disk striped just like in a traditional magnetic disk.

Floptical Drives

Floptical drives look like floppy drives, and the floptical disk looks like a 3.5-inch floppy disk. Floptical drives offer much better performance and more storage capacity than a normal floppy drive. The spin rate of a floptical drive is 720 rpms, which is more than twice the floppy drive 300 rpm rate. This means you get lower latency and faster access rates with a floptical drive. The random access time of a floptical is about 80 ms, which is far faster than that of a floppy drive. A extra bonus with floptical drives is they will also read conventional floppies at a faster rate because of the faster spin rate.

The great advantage to floptical drives is that they can store up to 20.8 megabytes on one formatted diskette, more data than you could fit on 14 high-density floppy disks. The technology that allows this great storage is due to a combination of laser and magnetic heads. The floptical disk has 755 concentric servo tracks that are just a little over 5 microns wide. The tracks are positioned 20.4 microns apart. The total servo markings add up to about 1.5 million. The optical heads on the floptical drive can sense up to eight different tracks at once and can position the magnetic read/write head with pinpoint accuracy. This makes it possible to record 1,510 data tracks on both sides of the floptical disc. These drives will connect to your system with a SCSI card, allowing you to daisy chain it to other devices like a CD-ROM or hard drive.

Because of the low cost of this medium it may be a dream come true for storage of graphic files or for backing up data. Watch for drives that can store 44 megabytes or 88 megabytes. Floptical storage costs about $1 per megabyte, which is about the same as for floppy disks. Floptical drives cost about $500.

Chapter 15

Motion Video Capture Boards and Multimedia Projection

A whole new industry has arrived with the advent of multimedia. Desktop video is an exciting area of the computer domain that is becoming more affordable to enter. Television images and computer images are two related but still distant technologies, and they are joining together to form powerful desktop editing suites. Video capture boards convert the analog video signals into digital signals that the computer can then manipulate. Many also convert computer-generated images back to video so the images can be transferred to videotape or displayed on television.

This basis for exchanging computer graphics and video is called *scan conversion*, which is also called frame grabbing, video digitizing, or video capture. Scan conversion is essentially a translation of different information formats. To be able to integrate images from television to computers or vice versa, the computer needs a video capture card with a codec (encoder-decoder). The computer stores images in a digital format which can precisely control the color information for each pixel on the screen.

Doing It in Real Time

Television standards use analog signals for broadcast video, which is a much less precise method of disseminating information than digital signals. The National Television Standards

Committee in 1954 set the standard for broadcast video in North America. There are 60 (technically 59.94) fields per second and 525 horizontal lines of resolution for NTSC images. NTSC uses interlaced scanning, meaning that two electron beam scans of the monitor make up one video frame. These scans are done so quickly that the eye perceives the image to be stable, a phenomena known as Persistence of Vision. Phase Alternate Line (PAL) is another video standard used in the United Kingdom, Australia, Europe, and South Africa. PAL paints 50 fields per second (each field is 262.5 lines). There are a total of 625 horizontal lines and 25 frames per second for PAL images. The Sequential Color and Memory (SECAM) format is used in France and the Commonwealth of Independent States. SECAM also uses 625-line, 50-Hz scanning but is different from PAL and NTSC.

Two fields comprise what is referred to as a frame in the motion picture industry. Video uses interlaced scanning of the video monitor. To completely refresh a full image, the screen is scanned twice. The first scan refreshes the odd lines, and the second pass scans the even lines. If you read a book in an interlaced method you would read all the odd lines on the page first, and then read all the even lines. It would effectively take two scans to read one whole page. In contrast to the television standards for scanning a monitor, with computers there are a varying number of video refreshes per second and a different number of lines of resolution.

To convert full screen motion video, a video capture board must be capable of converting 30 frames per second for the NTSC standard (25 frames per second for the European PAL and SECAM standards). Some video cards cannot handle this tremendous flow of information and instead handle only 24, 20, or even 15 frames per second. The fewer captured frames will deteriorate the picture quality, making the moving images appear jerky. A converter that can translate 30 frames per second is called a video digitizer. A **digitizer** is capable of capturing a sequence of complete frames and usually uses compression techniques to accomplish the conversion in real time.

A video converter that scans less than 25 frames per second is called a frame grabber. The **frame grabber** can capture one frame at a time, which can then be manipulated or converted to a computer graphic format. Some scan converters are frame grabbers, and the better scan converters are digitizers.

The best scan converters handle component video as opposed to composite video. **Component video** splits the video information into different channels; the chrominance and luminance and sync information are separate signals carried on independent wires. Component video does not reduce bandwidth or degrade the color components; it preserves a higher picture quality than composite video. Component video is sometimes referred to as Component Analog Video (CAV) and the three signals are designated as luminance (Y) and color (R-Y and B-Y). A **composite video** signal carries all the video information in one combined signal on a single wire using a coding standard like NTSC, PAL, or SECAM.

There are a couple of different ways of implementing scan conversion. The most basic method utilizes special software that controls the computer's video card to emulate the same refresh rate as the video format. The problem with this is that not all graphics cards operate the same or are able to be changed by this software approach. To properly show the software augmented images, the computer display must be a multisync monitor. The next problem is that the video card has to hold the correct scan rate, and a computer graphics card without a crystal locking device is bound to go out of synchronization.

The next method of scan conversion allows the computer to make its usual signal and then to manipulate the signal with software to fit the desired shape. This can distort the image on the screen. A better method of scan conversion is to display an NTSC compatible-sized image. The computer scan frames are made to refresh at 60 Hz. The scan conversion software captures every other line to create 30-frame-per-second video. The problem with this method is that if there are very thin horizontal lines on the computer screen they will be effectively cut in half. If the line is only one pixel wide, the line could disappear. This problem can be remedied by using software to thicken the lines.

The more advanced scan conversion techniques use a method of interpolation. This type of scan converter has a buffer that stores frame information. Interpolation samples the lines of the computer image and then figures out what the adjacent pixels on new lines would look like. Even better scan converters can interpolate between frames, taking two adjacent frames and creating a new frame between the two. This method allows the computer's clock frequency to remain inaccurate, but it is beneficial if the computer's video is similar to that of NTSC. The better a scan converter performs interpolating, the less flicker there will be on the video image.

The size of the image captured from video does not always fill the whole screen. Video boards that can capture a full screen image are the best but also are very expensive. Full screen video is not always necessary; some boards offer partial screen capture, which shows the image in a smaller box on the computer screen. This box can vary from a small thumbnail size up to nearly a full screen. If you are making a video presentation on the computer, you may want only a portion of the screen to have the motion image while the rest of the screen shows text or other graphics. If you are doing nonlinear editing and want to create an edit decision list (EDL) you may want to save hard disk space by limiting the image size or color depth or both. Some video capture boards limit the maximum image size to 160 by 120 pixels with a color depth of 16 bits. For general video work, a video capture of 15 frames per second is the minimum recommended; any less and the image becomes far too jerky.

Another variable of frame capture boards is the maximum bit depth of the captured pictures. Most boards can capture 16 bits per pixel, but for better quality there are video cards that can deliver 24 bits or 32 bits per pixel. 16-bit video shows over 65,000 colors and 24-bit video is 16.7 million colors. The 32-bit cards use the extra 6 bits for image manipulation data.

Usually there is a trade-off between one of these three variables of frames per second, capture size, and number of colors captured. For example, the board will trade a larger image size for a lower pixel depth or lower frame rate. The boards that can produce full motion video with full screen display and high pixel depth often can only store the image in RAM. This is because the transfer rate to the hard disk is not fast enough to handle the incoming image. As little as one second of images can fill up 30 megabytes of RAM.

An expensive but optimal way to work around this is to buy a large RAM disk that can store video images, but even with this approach the memory is guaranteed to fill up quickly. To knock images down in size some sort of hardware or software compression is needed. Hardware compression is best because it is faster. With hardware compression the video board does all the work, leaving the computer's CPU free to do other tasks. Software compression relies on the computer's CPU to perform all the image compression. This can bog down the CPU, as this is a tremendous amount of data to handle.

The major players in compression are DVI, JPEG, MPEG, Cinepak, Indeo, MotiVE, and Captain Crunch. These are known as codecs, which is short for compression-decompression. Many boards use the Intel DVI (Digital Video Interactive) which claims better compression ratios than JPEG. The drawback with DVI and MPEG is they compress a series of frames together, making single frame editing inefficient. JPEG on the other hand individually compresses each frame, making editing and single frame manipulation a workable option.

Compression rates vary due to the complexity of the image being processed. The best rates are near 200:1, but do not expect this unless you are working with video pictures of the sky or some other uniform image. Higher compression rates can signify that a lossy compression method is being used. This means some of the data is being thrown away. If too much is thrown out the images will lose their definition.

The hot new compression technology is fractal compression. This type of compression takes a long time to compress, but the compressed images can be decompressed rapidly. Fractal compression can reduce the size of files much further than any other type of compression to date while remaining true to the clarity of the original image.

To be able to lay computer images over video, the computer must be precisely timed to the video devices. Video scan converters that do this have genlocking capabilities. The genlock circuitry synchronizes the computer image and the video frames. If the two get out of synchronization the genlocking can forward or reverse the video so it goes back in sync. In addition, a **time base corrector** (TBC) will keep the output of the video decks stabilized.

Multiple video inputs and outputs are desirable on a video capture card. Many boards can handle S-Video input, which is also known as Y/C input. This is named Y/C because the luminescence (Y) and the chrominance (C) levels are separated, producing a higher-quality image than composite video, which blends these two elements together. Y/C video is used with S-VHS and Hi8 tape decks and video recorders.

Video encoding takes the separated video elements that the computer stores and then translates them back into a composite video that can be recorded on a videotape recorder. Still frames can be stored in different file formats on the computer. Widely used file formats for graphic manipulation include TIFF, PIC, and TARGA. Integrated audio capture with video capture eliminates the need for a separate audio board. When editing video sound there is often more than one sound source. Narration, dialogue, music, and sound effects can all combine to form a soundtrack. Software controlled audio mixing capability is a good feature for video editing. Software control over bass and treble is also a important capability.

Video is reduced in size so the computer can handle it easier. Compression hardware that works on-the-fly can alleviate the strain of the immense data flow that is inherent in video capture. Compressing video reduces the storage and throughput problems. The next best thing to on-the-fly hardware compression is software compression. Using this method can halve the video data stream so the computer will be able to store twice the amount of video data on the hard disk.

Video overlay is a feature that allows you to send video images to the screen without first digitizing them. This allows you to preview the images before digitization. Some video boards allow for multiple board installation. This means more than one video window can be open on the screen at the same time.

Graphics cards in computers that comply with the Intel and ATI Shared Frame Buffer Interconnect (SFBI) standard will be able to combine full motion video and computer graphics on one card. Instead of two separate cards the computer will only need to have one card inside to control regular graphics and frame-capture. This cuts cost by eliminating redundant circuitry. Similar to SFBI is the VESA Media Channel, which provides a more multilevel design.

For professional video you will need a **waveform monitor**. When you look at the video on a television monitor you are not seeing exactly what everyone else sees at home. This is because every television is a little different. A waveform monitor is an oscilloscope that lets you display the video signal, allowing you to see the signal stability. Using a waveform monitor is the only way to ensure consistent quality when creating video productions. The waveform monitor essentially analyzes the shades of color in the video signal. A video signal is comprised of 1 volt DC, which is divided into 140 equal units called IRE (Institute of Radio Engineers). Luminance, chroma, and hue are all affected by the IRE. If the IRE is not at the right levels, the signal can be adjusted with a **processing amplifier**.

The active video signal falls between 7.5 and 100 IRE. If the peak luminescence signal is over 100 IRE, the video will be overmodulated. This means there will be distortion of the audio signal. The darkest part of the video image is called the pedestal and is usually set at 7.5 IRE. If the IRE falls below 0 the blacks on the screen will be crushed. All the detail in the black areas of the image will be lost. Having the pedestal fall below 0 IRE can also affect the sync pulse because the sysc pulse lies between 0 and -40 IRE. Waveform can be displayed on a computer monitor, but this method is not as easy to use as a traditional waveform vectorscope.

Broadcast video is designed to overscan the image viewing area. This means the image that is broadcast extends beyond the edge of the screen. When filming, television crews stick to guidelines for safe viewing area and safe title area for graphics so the main action remains within the boundaries of the screen. Computers tend to underscan, which means the image fits within the viewable area of the screen. Because of this difference, when you switch computer graphics to NTSC video you lose the outermost edges of the screen. If you reduce the size of the image on the computer screen to 512 by 384 (instead of 640 by 480) the whole image should fit on the video screen. It is a good idea to avoid using the outer 15 percent of the screen when keying titles or images onto video.

Images Going In

GIGO is a saying in the computer industry that stands for garbage in, garbage out. The quality of the video you can edit is limited by the quality of the video board's input and output ports. Most video capture boards will accept a variety of input and timing signals. The majority of video capture boards accept consumer-level composite video input, and some accept S-Video, which has separate brightness and color signals. The S-Video separate signals make for more brilliant images. Component video is used with SVGA and Hi-8 formats. Many of the video boards on the market are able to accept NTSC, SECAM, and PAL signals. Often professional video producers will shoot using Hi-8 format and then bump up to Betacam SP format when editing because it is a higher-quality format.

Audio input is an elusive element of video, and many boards handle it differently. Too many boards are built without audio support and must rely on an additional audio support board to do the job. For professional results look for boards that support SIMPTE and MIDI, standards that control the accurate editing of images and sound. These standards are essential for professional video editing.

Images Going Out

What good is a video capture board if it does not output to your desired medium? The more output possibilities, the better. Many professionals use Betacam SP as the desired tape format, so it is wise to make sure the video out on the capture board can deliver to a Betacam SP tape deck.

Multimedia Projection Systems

As multimedia hits mainstream the question arises "how do we display it?" The answer depends on whether you intend to show the production to small groups, such as in conference rooms, or large groups as you would in a seminar.

For displaying multimedia to small groups the two basic solutions are active-matrix liquid-crystal-display (LCD) projection panels, or cathode-ray tube (CRT) monitors. LCDs are much more portable than monitors, but the CRT shows images with better clarity. A good LCD panel should be able to show at least 256 colors and be able to handle both video and computer image sources.

To show the image on an LCD to a larger audience an overhead projector is required. The projector can take the image on the LCD screen and display it on a wall. To show the image well the projector needs to have an intensely bright and evenly lit surface. Projectors that are not bright enough will display disappointingly dim and dull images. The lumens output of the projection system is important. A lumen is a measurement of light and is a familiar term to anyone who has experimented with photography. A small dark meeting room may require a projector output of only 300 lumens, while a large conference room may require a projector output of 1,000 lumens or better.

An LCD panel often comes with a remote control with features that allow you to switch input sources and adjust the picture and audio. Some remotes can control the computer in addition to the LCD. The audio tracks are passed through the LCD to speakers without augmentation. To create displays that use a variety of audio sources you will need a sound mixing board to do the job.

Monitors used for presentations are usually 27 inches or larger. This is a reference to the diagonal measurement of the screen. The most flexible monitor needs to be multiscanning and able to handle input formats from NTSC, PAL, VCR, S-VHS, Hi8, S-video, laser disk, SVGA, and computer video sources. If you are planning on showing computer graphics, check to see if the monitor will display resolutions higher than 640 by 480. Some monitors come with remotes which let you control the display.

For large group demonstrations RGB projectors do the trick, but they are also quite expensive, running $50,000 and up. Compare this to the $3,000 to $10,000 price of LCDs and monitors. Three-lens projectors have higher light output than one-lens models and are great for permanent installations. If you plan on moving the projector often, a one-lens projector is more convenient, as the three-lens projectors require lengthy convergence tuning. For even sharper display, monitors can be stacked and used as a video wall. This is an expensive but powerful alternative. The expense comes from the cost of the monitors—usually there are four or more—and the cost of the computer to control and split the images.

Chapter 16

Beautiful Scanners

Everybody who uses a computer is bound to want a scanner at some point down the road. For example, you are typing a letter for your business and all of a sudden you realize how great it would be to put the company logo at the top of the letter. The problem is you have the logo on a business card but not in the computer. To display the artwork on the letter in the computer you need to get it into the computer, and this is what a scanner does.

Scanners are computer peripherals that capture images into a format that can be displayed on a computer monitor and stored on the hard disk. They operate using essentially the same technology that photocopiers use to capture images. Typically a fluorescent light floods the image and a lens registers how much light is reflected back. Dark areas reflect less light than white areas, and this reflection is measured by the scanner. Some scanners can only discern the difference between black and white. Other scanners are able to see **grayscale** or differing intensities of grays. Lighter gray reflects more light than darker gray, and the scanner measures the reflected quantity of light at numerous small intervals that together are combined to reform the entire image. Some scanners can differentiate between more levels of gray than others. Most 24-bit scanners can differentiate a total of 256 separate levels of gray.

Scanners are rated to capture a set maximum number of colors or levels of grayscale. The bit depth a scanner captures is similar in concept to the way graphics cards and monitors handle images. The 1-bit, 2-bit, and 4-bit scanners are generally low quality scanners that are only good for scanning line art or text. The 8-bit scanners are generally fine for scanning halftones or color images as long as high quality is not needed. The 15-bit and 16-bit scanners are fine for capturing illustrations, text, halftones, and color images but are still limited by the tones they can capture. Professionals will only consider a full 24-bit scanner for scanning photographs, continuous-tone images, and artwork.

Some professional quality scanners have 30-bit, 36-bit, or even 48-bit capture abilities. They cost from $20,000 to $250,000 and therefore are priced out of the consumer market. What do these scanners do that a 24-bit scanner cannot? They have better control over oversampling, registration, and grayscale. All scanners are susceptible to small distortions, and by oversampling a scanner reduces the effects of unwanted defects. The high sampling rates make these scanners able to more accurately capture levels of gray, plus, they use more precise controls for better alignment. They often use screw or worm gears instead of the motors and gears used in lower quality scanners. **Color scanners** scan an image three times using separate blue, green, and red filters. The image is created for the computer by combining the information taken in each of the three passes. High-end scanners can read 16.7 million colors.

Most scanners capture graphics or text on paper or other two-dimensional media, but scanners can scan a three-dimensional object by placing it on a platform and scanning from above.

Similar to printers and monitors, the higher the resolution a scanner can capture, the sharper the image. The higher resolution scanners that can relay accurate image detail are more expensive than low resolution printers. More memory will be needed to store the saved image when a scanner uses a higher resolution to capture an image. Your output device or requirements mandate the resolution you need to use to scan objects. To find the optimal resolution you need to know the height of the output image, the height of the original image, and the halftone resolution of the output device. Here is the formula for getting the right scan resolution:

Scanning resolution (Dots Per Inch) = (Lines per inch x 1.25 x final height of image) / Original Height

When printing, the quality is measured in resolution and lines per inch. For most business applications a 300 dpi scanner will suffice. For professional level printing, resolution is often referred to as lines of dots, or lines per inch. The number of lines per inch is also referred to as the line screen, or the line frequency. The screen frequency is the number of lines of dots per inch used to print an image. Most applications use between 65 to 150 lines per inch.

A printer with a resolution of 300 dpi is capable of producing 32 levels of gray and has about 53 lines per inch (lpi). A 600 dpi printer can produce about 64 levels of gray and has about 106 (lpi). For an ink-jet or dot matrix printer there are about 45 lines per inch.

Newspapers use between 65 to 85 lpi and magazines generally use 133 or 150 lpi. Books are printed from 150 lpi up to 300 lpi. Most people recommend using from 1.25:1 to 2:1 ratio of scan resolution to lpi. For printing at 150 lpi, the resolution at which most magazine are printed, a 300 dpi scan will do the job adequately. If a higher resolution scan is made, the extra captured information will be discarded when printing to the imagesetter.

If you have a 600-dpi printer, you want a 600-dpi scanner. Professional level scanners handle 1,200 dpi, 2,400 dpi, or even higher resolutions. If you plan to enlarge a photo with photo manipulation software, you will want to scan at a higher resolution. The more you enlarge the image the higher a scan you should use. If you are going to use an Optical Character Recognizer (OCR) with scanned text, use a scanner that does 400 dpi or better. When you scan in a page of text your computer stores it as graphics. To edit it as text an OCR will convert the graphics into text form. This process is not 100 percent foolproof but will provide better results at scans that are made at 400 dpi or higher.

When looking for a scanner make sure it adheres to the TWAIN standard. This standard makes scanners easy to operate and is supported by most scanning software. With TWAIN software you can import a scan directly into an application without hassle. The TWAIN drivers that accompany the scanner can have an impact on the capabilities for fine-tuning image capture. Better drivers can adjust gamma curves, RGB values, have automatic color correction, black point and white point setting capabilities, prescan zoom and image cropping, and highlight and shadow controls.

A scanner must have software to make it useful. Look for 24-bit editing software to be bundled with the scanner. Optical character recognition (OCR) software lets you scan text and then manipulate the words in a text editor. Look for external controls on the scanner that allow you to adjust brightness, resolution, contrast, and the color depth of the scan. If you are doing multipage scans, look for options like an automatic document feeder and transparency feeder. The autodocument feeder should handle a decent capacity and needs an output tray that can hold as many documents as can be put in the input tray.

Resolution

Many of the scanners on the market today scan at 400, 600, or 800 dots per inch. This is known as the optical resolution of the scanner. Scanners can achieve better-looking scans by using a method known as interpolation. A scanner that captures 400 dpi can interpolate using special software to achieve a scan that appears to have been captured by a 1,200-dpi scanner. When a scanner interpolates it creates extra pixels that have not been scanned by using information from the pixels that were scanned. In interpolation, the scanner looks to neighboring pixels and takes an average of their values and uses that information to add new pixels. For example, if a new pixel is to be added between an existing white and black pixel, the newly created pixel will be gray. This method works effectively up to twice the resolution of the original scan and is not always the best option as it can make hard edges in an image look fuzzy. You would not want to interpolate a scan of black text on a white background because by using interpolation the text would be outlined with gray pixels. If you need a high-resolution scan of text, the only way to get one is to use a scanner with high resolution hardware.

Scanning at the highest resolution possible is not always the best idea. Most business scanning can be done at 300 or 400 dpi. A 24-bit color image scanned at 1,200 dpi can take hours to scan and will eat up many megabytes of hard disk space. A 1,200-dpi scan is very demanding of a computer's resources. To make these scans you will need a fast computer with a large amount of RAM to manipulate such an image. Simply drawing the image on the screen can take the computer 15 or more minutes. If you need to work with such large images be sure to get a 17-inch or 20-inch monitor so the whole image can fit on the screen. If you use a smaller monitor the whole image will not fit on the screen in detail and every time you scroll the image to see different parts you will have to wait for the image to be completely redrawn on the screen.

The resolution at which you scan should have 1.4 times to 2 times as many pixels as the final printed output has lines per inch in the halftone screens. If you are planning to enlarge the image you are using before printing it, first figure out the enlargement percentage and then scan the image at the increased resolution needed. As a general rule you do not want to enlarge an image by a ratio of more than 3:1 or the defects and limitations of the scanner will be apparent. To scan an image that needs to be enlarged by more than 300 percent, take a picture with a camera and blow the print up to the right size and then scan it. Try not to scan at a resolution higher than is needed for the output or you will end up with files that are too big. All the extra unnecessary information will be thrown out by the printer anyway, so it is best to make scans at the correct resolution.

For reducing a image, do not shrink it by a ratio of more than 2:1. When shrinking the image, the computer has to throw away information, which can end up making the image appear distorted.

Scanning the Image

Flatbed scanners use a light source, usually a fluorescent light or quartz halogen lamp, to illuminate the image being scanned, which has been placed face down on the scanning bed. Some new scanners are using cold lamp Charged Coupled Devices (CCDs) to scan media. These scanners do not use the heat-producing CCDs and thereby avoid some heat-related problems. The cold lamp CCDs do not need cooling ventilation which means they are less susceptible to dust. They also do not have as many calibration problems as heat-producing CCDs have.

Inside the scanner a stepper motor moves the scan head under the image. The scan head is usually a charged coupled device (CCD), similar to the CCD used in camcorders. Color scanners often use three CCDs or they use one CCD and three filters, a green, blue, and red, that filter the light in three passes. Mirrors reflect the light from the image onto the CCD. The CCD views the image one line at a time, like reading a book, and sends the information it gathers to the scanner's processors. An analog-to-digital converter translates the CCD electrical charges into digital format. The image is then sent to the computer commonly via SCSI cable. In the computer the image is then usually stored as a TIFF file on your hard drive where it is ready to be manipulated in programs like Photoshop. High-end scanners use a photomultiplier tube (PMT) instead of a CCD. PMTs are more accurate than CCDs and can capture continuous tones better than CCDs. Detail in shadows and highlights are preserved with greater accuracy with PMTs.

Hand-held scanners work much like flatbed scanners but are less precise because you move the scan head manually. Hands are not as steady and smooth in operation as the flatbed scanner stepper motors, but hand-held scanners are more affordable than flatbed scanners and can be used for some elementary scanning. Some hand-held scanners come with a scanning tablet that holds the image in place and guides the scanner smoothly across the image.

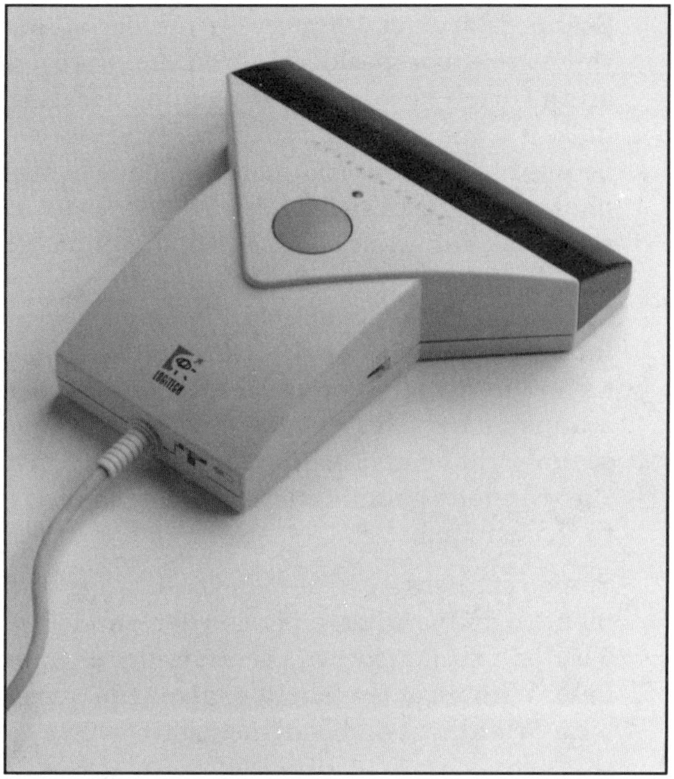

Logitech Handheld Scanner

The resolution of a flatbed scanner is dependent on the stepper motor that controls the CCD head. The smaller an increment the stepper motor can make, the higher a resolution a scanner can scan. For example, an 800-dpi scanner can move 800 increments within the space of one inch. The higher the scanner resolution, the slower the stepper motor, because to be extremely precise the motor needs to move very slowly.

Color scanners must capture RGB data (red, green, blue) and do this using one-pass or three-pass techniques. One-pass scanners generally use three lights—red, green, and blue—that flash on and off in sequence while the CCD scans the image. Three-pass scanners make the CCD actually scan the whole image three times. During each pass a different colored filter covers the scan head. The filters are for blue, green, and red.

Scanners are not 100 percent perfect at doing their job. Often there are extra speckled dots on the captured scan that were not on the original copy. This speckling is called noise, and the less noise a scanner generates the better. Image editing software can be used to clean up the noise made by a scanner. If you have a photograph of your friends and you want to use it in the computer you will want the colors in the photo and the colors on the screen to look the same. Friends do not look right when they appear to have purple skin unless they are from Mars. For image manipulation, the value of the colors scanned need to have the same color values on the screen. To ensure your scanner correctly captures the color values you will want a scanner that can be calibrated. Calibration allows you to adjust the scanner's gamma curves so the scanned image remains true to the original.

Some scanners have threshold settings that allow the adjustment to define when a pixel is determined to be black or white. This adjustment tunes the scanner to capture images at their best. Without a threshold control the same thing can be done with brightness and contrast controls but is not as easily.

The size of the documents a scanner can capture is an essential consideration, especially if you are using odd-sized originals. Most flatbed scanners can read images up to 8.5 by 14 inches. For larger scans you need to use a drum scanner, which can scan the larger formats. Drum scanners are made to scan both reflective media and transparencies. The images to be scanned are attached to a cylinder made of Plexiglas called the drum. Many drum scanners use a removable drum which allows you to save time by scanning one drum while mounting more media on a spare drum. Drum scanners traditionally use one to three Photo Multiplier Tubes (PMTs) which offer greater accuracy than the Charged Coupled Device (CCD) sensors used in handheld and flatbed scanners. The dynamic range a scanner can capture limits the quality of image that is captured. The dynamic range is the difference between the darkest blacks and the lightest whites and is measured on a scale of 0.0 to 4.0, with 4.0 representing the greatest ability to capture detail in dark and shadow regions of a scan. The highest density ratings of flatbed scanners are around 2.8, while the best drum scanners offer a maximum density of 3.9.

Drum Scanner vs. Flatbed Scanner

Drum Scanner	*Flatbed Scanner*
Excellent for extra high quality needs	Good for images of less than 150 lpi, like newsprint
Good for oversized work	Used for original images that are smaller than legal size
Good for enlarging images over 3x	Good for enlarging images under 3x
Good for scanning film or transparencies	Good for scanning images with limited range of quality
High quality is more important than cost	Cost is more important than quality
Original image is high image quality	Original image is low image quality
Original needs imperfections augmented	Original does not need much contrast or exposure changed

Drum scanners are primarily used at professional image capturing services and are quite expensive. If you only need to use one once in a while, it is probably a good idea to pay a service bureau to scan originals instead of buying a scanner.

Slide Scanners

Slide scanners are a specialized type of scanner that can capture images from film. Most slide scanners can capture a color depth of 24 bits or greater. Having a higher color depth gives the scanner a wider density range. This is measured on a scale from 0 to 4 and indicates the spread between the brightest white and the darkest black tones the scanner can record. In comparison, the average density range of color flatbed scanners is around 2.8, and the average density of drum scanners is around 3.6.

Some slide scanners offer extra features like automatic focus and calibration. Most film scanners can scan 35-mm film or strip film, and some specialized models can scan 2.25-inch, 4-by-5-inch, or other common film formats. Professional scanners use a color management system to calibrate the device. Look for software that can act as a densitometer tool enabling you to display the color values at various points on the image.

Ports

The majority of scanners use the SCSI interface. Others use a serial RS-488 interface which cannot send data as fast as SCSI. Portable computers that do not have a SCSI port can use a parallel-to-SCSI connector or a PCMCIA-to-SCSI connector. If the scanner has a SCSI connection, make sure it comes bundled with ASPI drivers so the SCSI controller can cohabitate with other SCSI controllers your computer may already have. For SCSI setup it is highly desirable to have pushbutton SCSI ID settings instead of jumpers or DIP switches, which are not as convenient to change.

Other Tips

For general scanning use a scanner capable of at least 300 dpi. Different scanners capturing 300 dpi scan a little differently, so it is best to see a sample from the scanners you are thinking of buying. Specially designed targets and test patterns can be scanned on paper to test for resolution handling of lines of differing sizes. This will give you a sense of the true capabilities of a scanner.

When scanning photographs you will need to convert the photos into transparencies which can then be scanned on a drum scanner or a scanner that is capable of dealing with the paper fiber and cast of the gelatin of the photographic stock.

The bulb that illuminates the scanned images should be replaced often to prevent a loss of quality. As the bulb grows old it does not illuminate with as great a degree of accuracy.

Software

Scanners usually come with software drivers and image manipulation software. Software included should be able to run the scanner, edit the image, and adjust the contrast and color of the image. Many scanners come bundled with Photoshop, which is an excellent image editing program.

Good software packages features include tonal curve control which controls the distribution of middle tones, brightness control, contrast control, and resolution control, and a preview mode that will let you zoom in on selected points of the image.

Can I Use My Fax as a Scanner?

If you have a fax machine and a fax-modem connected to your computer and they both have separate phone lines, you can easily fax a document to your computer. You could effectively use your fax machine like a scanner this way. The question is, do you want quality output? The best fax resolution is 200 by 200 dots per inch. This is low quality, and even the cheapest scanners on the market can scan at 300 dpi. Another factor is the fax scan will only produce a bi-level image. This means the fax will only be captured in black and white, not grayscale. This is fine for scanning text-only documents, but a grayscale image or photograph will not show any accurate detail. If you need to scan only text documents a fax might do the job, but it is a poor choice for use as a multipurpose scanner.

Chapter 17

The Systems of Choice

When considering a computer system it is important to decide what you want to do with it today and what you want to do with it in the future. If you buy a system before asking yourself these questions, the computer you get may not match the requirements the software demands of it. The demands of different software applications vary in regard to how much computing power is needed for the program to work appropriately. When choosing a computer, find the most demanding software application that will be run on it and use the minimum requirements of that software to guide any purchases. All of the systems should be equipped with a keyboard, a pointing device like a mouse, and at least one floppy drive. The system should also include at least one parallel port, two serial ports, and a keyboard port.

A word of advice that always holds true for computers: make sure the components purchased will have support in the future for driver updates. Updated drivers maximize the compatibility and performance of a computer with new software releases.

Keep in mind that the price of a computer is tied to both its storage capability and its overall performance. The faster computers with larger storage capacities require a bigger investment. Another fact to consider when buying is that the better the computer is, the longer it can be used before it needs to be upgraded or replaced. A computer is an investment for the future. Think of the cost as being spread over a several-year-period—that way the price between different models will seem less drastic.

If you are willing to spend about $2,500 you can get a system that is substantial and close to ideal for most needs. Buying a computer for $1,500 or less will require you to compromise by cutting corners in system performance. Try not to cut from the four major categories, which include CPU, memory, hard disk, and video. If you really have to cut down on one of these, buy a smaller hard disk, as a bigger hard disk can always be added later.

Software today is geared toward RISC chips, so don't invest in a system with CPU that is less advanced than a 486. Extra computing power is needed for Windows and future applications. Try to get the fastest MHz you can afford for the generation of CPU you purchase. Help the CPU from being unnecessarily slowed down by relieving its task load with an accelerated or coprocessed video card. The minimum amount of DRAM recommended for Windows 3.1 is 4 megabytes, for Windows 95 is 12 megabytes, and for Windows NT the minimum is 16 megabytes. More RAM is better if you like to multitask (work with many applications open simultaneously). With more DRAM you will be able to set up a bigger hard disk cache and manipulate larger graphics and programs up to 7,000 percent faster. This means the CPU does not have to wait for the relatively slow hard disk, and a greater degree of overall system responsiveness is achieved. Make sure the motherboard can be upgraded with at least 32 megabytes of DRAM. Anything less than 32 megabytes is substandard.

Monitors that diagonally measure 14 inches barely have enough screen space to work comfortably when using Windows. If you can, opt for a 15-inch monitor and you will be much more satisfied. If you want to work with a full page of a document on the screen, the smallest monitor you should consider is 21 inches or a 17-inch pivot screen.

To get a general idea of the minimum amount of hard disk space you will need, you can figure it like this:

- 3 megabytes for DOS
- 12 megabytes for Windows
- 60 megabytes for Windows NT
- 15 megabytes for documents and files

- 20 megabytes for each major application
- 10 megabytes for each minor application
- 100 megabytes for graphics files

Following this are descriptions of possible uses of computers and the computer hardware configurations that are most suitable.

Most new systems sold today come with Windows pre-loaded. Sometime the computer comes bundled with application programs like word processors or virus checkers. Look for good deals on the software you will be using, but don't let a computer bundled with a better software package sway you from buying a hardware package that will serve your needs better. The best new computer setup is one that has been pre-loaded with software and optimized for the software's demands. This optimizing includes the following:

- Putting Windows first in the path statement
- Loading DOS high
- Reorganizing the hard disk so directories are moved up front
- Defragmenting the hard disk
- Perfecting the amount of memory set aside for SMARTDrive and the operating system
- Making a swap file of the best size and placing it in the best location on the hard drive
- Creating program groups that are intuitive to find
- Designing a well thought-out program directory
- Installing the best and latest hardware drivers
- Loading the system with hardware and software documentation
- Setting up the programs

Make sure the retailer you choose to buy from has great technical support to help you with any questions or problems that might arise. Customer support often includes a fax-back service which provides helpful data sheets on frequently asked questions. A BBS that customers can call with a modem is excellent for support because it lets you download the most recent drivers and help files. Perhaps the most important support feature for a company is toll-free support phone lines, especially if the company is a mail-order outfit that is a long-distance call. Toll-free support will keep you from worrying about your phone charges when you are placed on hold. Round-the-clock 24-hour support is great and keeps you from having to wait for the next business day to resolve your urgent problem. This can be essential if your computer decides to go kaput on a Friday night.

Windows—General Purpose and Education

When buying a Windows system you should keep in mind the minimum DRAM requirements and realize more DRAM is recommended for multitasking or graphics work. Because Windows is graphical, it is more demanding and slower than just running DOS. Windows NT is a large program. The full installation requires about 60 megabytes compared to Windows 3.1, which is around 12 megabytes. To use Windows NT or Windows 95, buy a big hard disk.

Windows is a graphic environment and therefore is demanding of the computer's video capabilities. Choosing a faster video board can often improve performance better than choosing the next faster CPU. Unless you need the higher video quality for artwork or computer aided design, use a lower video resolution and a mode with fewer colors to speed up Windows and the system in general. For a typical video board, using a higher video quality means the system will perform slower.

Since Windows is a multitasking environment and such a big program, it is a hard-disk-intensive program. The faster the hard disk access time and transfer time, the better the system performance. Using a hard disk cache can speed things up to a average access time of near .03 ms.

Recommended general Windows system:

Low End

Processor:	486DX/2-66 MHz
Motherboard Type:	Local bus, 128 kilobyte cache
Floppy Drive(s):	3.5-inch, 1.44 megabytes
Hard Drive:	340 megabytes rated at 18 ms or less
System Memory:	12 megabytes DRAM

Video Board:	SVGA local bus
Monitor:	15-inch
Printer:	Ink-jet

High End

Processor:	Pentium 66 MHz
Motherboard	VL-Bus
System Cache	256 kilobytes
Hard Drive	500+ megabyte hard drive with 13 ms access speed or better
DRAM	16+ megabytes DRAM
Monitor	17-inch
Video Card	Local bus true color graphics card (16.7 million colors)
Printer	4-page-per-minute laser printer

Multimedia

Multimedia is a very loosely defined word. To some people multimedia means being able to play CD-ROM games with sound; to other people multimedia means being able to make movies with the computer. Each definition of multimedia has a different minimum hardware requirement. A low-end multimedia machine that is otherwise to be utilized as a general use Windows machine essentially has the same setup as the general Windows computers listed above. To make the Windows computer a multimedia system all that is needed is the addition of a sound card and a CD-ROM. If you intend to write music you need a sound board that has a MIDI interface to attach to keyboards or other MIDI instruments. High-end multimedia systems can be as demanding as a desktop video machine. This means plenty of computing power is needed. To record CD-ROMs make sure the computer's hard drive can support a transfer rate of twice that needed by the CD-R. The hard drive should be at least 1 Gb and have a seek time of 12 ms or better.

The following is the minimum recommended multimedia PC Level 2 specification, which reflects an industry-wide consensus for the needs of a multimedia computer system.

Minimum requirements for multimedia:

Microprocessor	486SX-25 MHz
DRAM	4 megabytes or 8 megabytes of RAM for more serious users
Hard Disk	160 megabytes
CD-ROM Drive	300 kilobytes per second sustained transfer rate and a maximum seek time of 400 ms. CD-ROM XA ready and multisession Photo CD capable. A 64-kilobyte onboard buffer on the CD-ROM drive. CD-ROM XA audio capability and support for IMA adopted ADPCM algorithm.
Sound Card	With 16-bit digital sound, an 8-note synthesizer, and MIDI playback
Graphics Card	Capable of displaying 640 by 480 pixels and 65,536 colors (high color). Graphics delivery of 1.2 megapixels per second at 40 percent of the CPU's possible bandwidth.
Ports	Include MIDI input and MIDI output, and a joystick port

Word Processing

Word processing is usually a fairly light task for the computer to handle, but many of the current high-end word processing systems offer as much power as desktop publishing programs, and therefore word processing will require a more powerful computer for more complex documents. The most powerful programs contain features such as a grammar checker, spelling checker, graphics capabilities, charting, and WYSIWYG (What You See Is What You Get) mode that will display exactly how the printed page will appear on the screen of the monitor. An optimal word processing computer system setup includes a full-page monitor, which allows for easy viewing of an 8.5-by-11-inch page. The color display should be at least in 256-color mode and the resolution 800 by 600. A moderate-sized hard drive will do. Additionally, the configuration should meet the requirements of a general use Windows computer.

Recommended word processing system:

Low End

Microprocessor	486DX/2-66 MHz
Motherboard	VL-Bus
DRAM	12 megabytes
Monitor	15-inch SVGA
Hard Drive	500 megabytes
Printer	Ink-jet

High End

Microprocessor	486D/X2-66 MHz or better
Motherboard	VL-Bus
DRAM	32 megabytes
Monitor	21-inch
Video Card	Accelerated SVGA
Hard Drive	500+ megabytes
Printer	600-dpi laser printer

Desktop Publishing

Desktop publishing demands a powerful computer system to run its applications. A fast CPU is needed to handle the application tasks. The system RAM must be able to hold both the programs and the open documents or the system performance falls drastically.

A hard disk with fast access time and transfer rate is needed for the demands of desktop publishing work. For best results a large hard disk cache is recommended. Desktop publishing requires a large hard disk to store the huge programs and documents that a desktop publisher manipulates. The best large disks are SCSI-controlled, and a SCSI controller is needed to connect other desktop publishing tools such as scanners and optical drives and CD-ROMs.

Video performance is a very significant consideration in desktop publishing. A full-page monitor or a two-page monitor is highly valued by desktop publishers and can prove to be a valuable investment because it eliminates time waiting for screen redraws. To be able to show illustrations, a true color board with the ability to show high resolutions is essential. A coprocessed graphics board is ideal because it relieves some of the burden from the CPU.

For input, a mouse or pen usually does an adequate job. Most detailed work with graphics is enhanced with a digitizing tablet for more control. Desktop publishing printing is usually done in color, so a color printer is needed for proofs and an imagesetter for final output. Since imagesetters are expensive, many desktop publishers use outside services for final printing.

Recommended desktop publishing system:

Low End

Microprocessor	486DX2-66MHz
Motherboard	VL-Bus
DRAM	32 megabytes
Monitor	17-inch
Hard Disk	500 MB
Video Card	True color local bus video
Storage	Removable hard drive
Storage	Tape backup

High End

Microprocessor	Pentium
DRAM	128+ megabytes
Motherboard	Local bus PCI and VL-Bus
Hard Drive	2 gigabytes
Video Card	Coprocessed true color
Controller Card	SCSI
Monitor	21-inch monitor, 0.28 mm dot pitch, and 1,280-by-1,024 resolution
Short Term Storage	SyQuest removable drive
Archival Storage	Tape backup
Printer	Laser printer with 600 dpi
Printing	Dye sublimation, thermal transfer, ink-jet
Scanner	600-dpi color scanner

Desktop Video

Desktop video is even more demanding than desktop publishing. Broadcast quality NTSC (National Television Standards Committee) video uses 30 frames per second. Capturing video using full-screen graphics in VGA mode at 30 frames per second in true color (16.7 million colors) produces about 45 megabytes per second. At this rate a feature-length film takes more than 243,000 megabytes (or 237.3 gigabytes) of hard disk space. The way to alleviate the problem of storing all this information is to use hardware or software compression, which reduces the size of the video data by up to a 1:1 ratio. For broadcast-quality video stored at a 20:1 compression level there is still about a 6-megabyte-per-second transfer rate.

NTSC (National Television Standards Committee) is the broadcast standard used in the United States. Other parts of the world use PAL (Phase Alternating Line signal) or SECAM. PAL is used in Europe and Australia. SECAM is used primarily in France.

Global Television Standards

Format	NTSC	PAL	SECAM
Total Vertical Lines	525	625	625
Frames Per Second	30	25	25
Fields Per Second	60	50	50
Interlaced	Yes	Yes	Yes
Aspect Ratio	4:3	4:3	4:3

The basic theory behind video manipulation has to do with the ability to harness two types of signals. The video picture signal carries the visual and audio elements of video. The video-controller signal controls the rewind, fast forward, record, and play functions of the videotape recorders.

There are several basic ways in which a desktop video system can be configured on depending on what type of video work is going to be done. The least demanding is video work is for a computer **presentation system**, which usually calls for a laser disk player, a video projector, and a computer controller to access the information on the laser disk. To make your own laser disk you can buy a $500-$2,000 CD recorder. If you need multiple copies it is cheaper to have a recording agency press them. Companies that perform this service usually charge about $300 per disk. Some computer presentation systems allow the overlaying of computer generated images, like graphics and animation, onto the images being played from the laser disk.

The next group of video systems is called animation stations. Animation stations can be subdivided into two specific groups: real time and single frame. A **real time system** will let you overlay computer animation onto videotape as it is displayed on the computer screen. To do this you need an incredibly fast computer that is capable of displaying 30 frames per second to meet the video requirements of the NTSC (National Television Standards Committee). Unfortunately, the stream of information is too large for a normal 486 system to handle uncompressed images in a full screen at 30 frames per second. This means there must be a compromise between one of these factors which results in a lower quality level.

The alternate and higher quality animation station to a real time system is a single frame video system. **Single frame systems**, as the name implies, let you record sequential images frame-by-frame onto videotape. To do this you need a video controller deck and a frame-accurate video deck. This enables the user to graphically manipulate full screen video at 30 frames per second and allows greater control over the visual elements than other methods.

A common type of video system is the **desktop editing system**. These systems are usually able to manipulate both video and audio. Professional sequencing protocols used for precisely manipulating audio and video are known as MIDI (Musical Instrument Digital Interface) and SMPTE (Society of Motion Pictures Timecode Emulation). Consumer-based protocols are VISCA, Control-S, Control-P, and Control-L. The minimally configured desktop editing system requires a computer, a black-and-white monitor, a video controller, and two video decks. This setup will allow the user to cut video frames together without the advanced capabilities of adding graphics or the ability to add transitions such as fades or dissolves.

An alternate video editing system is called an **A/X roll system**. This requires a color graphics adapter, a time-base corrector, two videotape recorders, a computer, and a video controller. With an A/X roll system you can cut between video images and computer-generated graphics. The drawbacks with this system are that the computer graphics can only be inserted between video segments, and there is no way to reorganize the sequence of video footage.

Better is an **A/B roll system**. This requires a computer, a time-base corrector, three videotape recorders, and special effects hardware. An A/B roll system setup allows the importing of computer graphics to videotape and the addition of transitions between edits. For a transition, the computer controlled video decks referred to as "A" and "B" play simultaneously and the signals are recorded onto video deck "C". The overall quality output you create depends a lot on the performance of the video decks used. Broadcast-quality output requires professional level tape decks.

The best type of system for video editing is called a **nonlinear editing disk based system**. These systems are the most demanding of the computer's performance. The video is stored on the hard disk and the stored footage is instantaneously available, similar to a video laser disk. With tape-based systems it can take several minutes to fast-forward or rewind to cue the footage needed next. The nonlinear editing suite allows the user to edit the video completely inside the computer, a studio-in-a-box. This type of editing can be up to ten times faster than traditional linear editing that works with videotape. This kind of editing suite requires a very fast hard drive with a minimum recommended spindle speed of 5,400 or 7,300 rpm. The hard drive used should not use thermal recalibration. Many hard drives make a periodic check to adjust head tracking in order to compensate for minute changes in hard drive dimensions due to changes in temperature. During thermal recalibration most hard drives stop all read and write activity to perform a series of track seeks. If this happens while recording to or from videotape, some frames may be dropped.

There are two basic varieties of nonlinear editing. The least expensive route captures time-coded video into the computer for editing. The video is not captured in full frame but instead only fills up a small window on the computer screen. Before capturing the video the footage must be time-coded to keep a point of reference for later editing. Since the images are not captured in full frame, they consume much less space on the hard drive. The video is then edited as normal. When finished you have an editing decision list (EDL) that can be used to control two or more videotape recorders to create broadcast quality footage.

Video Time Code Protocols

Professional Level Video Protocols	Consumer Level Video Protocols
SMPTE	VISCA
MIDI	Control-L
	Control-P
	Control-S

The second nonlinear editing route requires a super fast computer and tons of hard disk storage space. Video is captured from videotape to the computer at the highest quality possible. The footage is then completely edited in the computer. When production is finished the complete footage is then sent out to a videotape recorder. Get ready to shell out big bucks if you opt for this kind of editing suite.

Video signals are carried over one or more wires depending on the format used. There are a couple of standards that are used for transmitting video signals. NTSC's composite video signal combines brightness, color, and synchronizing data all within one wire. Professional level video products often support S-Video, a standard that uses two separate wires to produce a cleaner, higher-resolution picture. RGB signal transmission is a professional method that uses three signal wires for color and two signal wires for sync and brightness.

A nonlinear editing system requires a computer, compression hardware, and a genlocking scan converter. Genlocking allows synchronization of NTSC video and computer signals allowing the combination of computer graphics with video images. Video in the NTSC television format needs to be converted into a digital red-green-blue signal that can be displayed on the computer screen. The refresh rates for computers are not set at any specific rate, but the television refresh rate is always at a preset speed. The television video screen is refreshed in an interlaced mode at 60 times per second, and the computer screens can be refreshed in a non-interlaced mode at 60 to 100 plus times per second. Scan converters translate these electronic signals from composite video signals to RGB signals and vice versa. Scan converters range in price from around $400 to $30,000.

Quality of Motion Video Standards

Professional Level Video	Intermediate Level Video	Consumer Level Video
One-inch (Type C)	Hi-8	VHS
Betacam SP	S-VHS	Beta
D1	Laserdisc	8mm
D2		VHS-C
D3		
D5		
3/4-inch		
U-matic		
M II		

Tape decks used in video editing suites vary in quality due to the many standards available. Consumer level tape decks are usually VHS. Better quality taping formats are Hi-8 and S-VHS. Professional level tape decks are Betacam SP, D1, D2 and one-inch. The higher quality tape decks are the most expensive. It is a good idea to plan your video deck purchase before buying a computer video editor because the tape decks chosen often dictate what other hardware and software is needed. Many professionals use Hi-8 video cameras to tape footage and then bump up the tape to Betacam SP for editing because Betacam SP is a higher quality format and incurs less generation image loss than Hi-8.

A video camera is needed to capture images to tape that can later be edited. Some professionals use film cameras during production and transfer the film images to video for post-production, but most video producers use camcorders. Video camcorders use Charged Coupled Devices (CCDs) to capture the image and transform it into electrical signals. Some consumer camcorders have only one CCD but the better camcorders use three CCDs. The average consumer cameras offer a zoom lens with a 6:1 to 8:1 ratio. For professional level cameras, expect better zoom ratios near 10:1 to 12:1.

Television Video Standards

Format	*Horizontal Resolution*	*Number of Audio Tracks*	*Tape Used*	*Signal Type*	*Separate SMPTE or VISCA track supported*
VHS	240	2	1/2-inch Oxide	Composite	No
VHS-C	240	2	1/2-inch Oxide	Composite	No
S-VHS	400	4	1/2-inch Oxide	Y/C Component	Yes
S-VHS-C	400	4	1/2-inch Oxide	Y/C Component	Yes
8 mm	260	1	8mm Metal Particle	Composite	No
Hi-8	400	2	8mm Metal Particle	Y/C Component	Yes
3/4 Umatic	280	4	3/4-inch Oxide	Composite	Yes
3/4 Umatic SP	330	2	3/4-inch Oxide	Component	Yes
Betacam	330	2	1/2-inch Metal Particle	Component	Yes
Betacam SP	550	4	1/2-inch Metal Particle	Component	Yes
M II	550	4	1/2-inch Metal Particle	Component	Yes
One-Inch	330	4	1-inch Oxide	Composite	Yes
D1	460	2	19mm Oxide	Component	Yes
D2	440	4	19mm Oxide	Composite	Yes
D3	440	4	1/2-inch Metal Particle	Composite	Yes
HDTV	960	4	N/A	Composite	Yes
Unihi	575	4	3/4-inch Metal Particle	Composite	Yes
Pioneer Laserdisc	330	2	N/A	Component	Yes

Recommended desktop video system: (hardware only):

Low End

Microprocessor	Pentium
Computer Graphics	Coprocessed true color
Monitor	17-inch
Motherboard	VL local bus
Hard Drive	1 gigabyte

DRAM	64 megabytes
Other	Frame accurate video recorders VTR controller Video monitor

High End

Microprocessor	Pentium
Monitor	21-inch
Motherboard	PCI bus and VL-Bus
DRAM	256+ megabytes
Hard Drive	6 gigabyte RAID with 7,300 rpm or faster spindle speed
Controller	SCSI controller with hard disk cache
Other	Frame accurate video recorders VTR controller Video monitor Waveform monitor

Database

Databases are disk-intensive programs, so the faster the hard disk the better. A hard disk cache is recommended for heavy database work. There should be a moderate amount of system RAM and a fast CPU behind every database computer.

Databases are not excessively demanding of video, pointing devices, or printers. Most databases are not mathematics intensive, so a floating point coprocessor usually does not beneficially affect performance.

Recommended database systems:

Low End

Microprocessor	486DX/2-66MHz
DRAM	12 megabytes
Hard Drive	500 megabytes
Video Card	Accelerated SVGA
Monitor	15-inch
Printer	24-pin dot-matrix

High End	
Microprocessor	Pentium
DRAM	32 megabytes
Video Card	Accelerated card
Monitor	21-inch
Hard Drive	1+ gigabyte
Controller	Hard drive accelerator card
Printer	600-dpi laser printer

Computer Aided Design

The optimum configuration for a CAD (computer aided design) system depends on whether the computer will be used exclusively for CAD or as a multifunction computer. If the computer is to be a multifunction system, it is probably best to compromise between an ideal CAD setup and the setup for the other applications that will be used.

With CAD being an extremely demanding graphics program, a CAD system should have the best possible video performance. CAD work requires a large and high-resolution display. A large display allows the user to see more area of the drawing on the screen with enough necessary detail. Having most of the designed image on the screen eliminates excessive zooms and panning that take a long time, since the screen will need to be redrawn. A coprocessed graphics card speeds up redraws on smaller and larger screens and can help productivity by reducing the time needed to wait for the screen to redraw the picture. The professional CAD system monitor should be at least 19 inches diagonally with resolution of 1,024 by 768. Extensive color display is usually unnecessary, but there should be at least 256-color capability. Some CAD professionals find it helpful to have a two-monitor display with one showing the graphics and the other screen showing text commands.

Since most CAD programs are large and complex, they are also disk-intensive. CAD operations require a lot of DRAM. AutoCAD requires at least 16 megabytes to perform adequately. Most CAD programs require the computer system to have a math coprocessor to be able to run. The 486 and Pentium chips have a built-in math coprocessor, so they are a good choice. If purchasing a system without a math coprocessor make sure it can be upgraded to include one for the CAD work.

To achieve the precision control over drawing that is needed in CAD work a digitizer is necessary. Digitizers have templates that allow the user to carry out commands by pointing to different areas on the pad and clicking. Digitizers can also trace existing drawings, which is important if there is no scanner and tracing software available for converting pre-existing drawings.

For CAD graphics printing, a plotter is an invaluable tool. Plotters are capable of printing precise lines on very large sheets of paper. If you plan on using plotting services of another company, a removable hard disk drive like a SyQuest or Bernoulli drive is needed.

Recommended CAD systems:

Low End

Microprocessor	Pentium
DRAM	32 megabytes
System Cache	256 kilobytes
Monitor	17-inch
Hard Drive	600 megabytes
Video Card	Local bus video with resolution of 1,024 by 768 or better
Printer	Large format dot-matrix printer

High End

Microprocessor	Pentium
DRAM	128+ megabytes
System Cache	256 kilobytes
Removable Media	SyQuest removable drive
Controller Card	SCSI hard disk accelerator card
Monitor	21-inch monitor with .26 dot pitch
Video Card	Coprocessed true color video card
Motherboard	Local bus and PCI
Hard Drive	2+ gigabyte
Pointing Device	Digitizer tablet
Printer	Color plotter

Graphics

Graphics systems are demanding of just about every part of the computer system. First, a great video display is extremely important. A true color coprocessed display helps reduce redraw time. The system RAM needs to be large enough to hold the illustrations and the programs or the overall speed will certainly lag. A large and fast hard drive is essential for storing the big graphics files that are generated by graphics programs. For printing, a high-quality color printer is needed to do pre-press proofs. After the proofs are finalized the files can be sent to a service bureau to be professionally printed on the printing press. For illustrators and graphic artists the pointing device needs to be easy to handle and precise. Most artists choose the digitizer pen for drawing and painting. Traditional medium artists have known for years that holding a tool in your hand like a brush can give great artistic expression. Drawing with a mouse is like using a bar of soap; it is not accurate and natural enough for everyday graphics.

Recommended graphics systems:

Low End

Microprocessor	Pentium
DRAM	24 megabytes
System Cache	128 kilobytes
Monitor	15-inch
Hard Drive	600 megabytes
Video	Local bus accelerated video with 16.7 million color display
Backup	QIC 80 tape backup
Printer	Color ink-jet printer

High End

Microprocessor	Pentium
DRAM	128+ megabytes
System Cache	256 kilobytes
Removable Medium	SyQuest removable drive or PCMCIA hard drive
Controller Card	SCSI accelerated hard disk controller card

Monitor	21-inch high resolution with .26 dot pitch
Video Card	True color 16.7 million colors coprocessed video
Motherboard	PCI and VL-Bus
Hard Drive	2+ gigabyte
Printer	Imagesetter and dye sublimation
Backup	DAT tape backup

Spreadsheet

Spreadsheet programs are hard disk-intensive, so a hard disk cache will enhance system performance. Complex and large spreadsheets are demanding of the CPU, and a floating point math coprocessor is an important addition for a fast machine. The number of cells in the spreadsheet affects the amount of memory needed. The more cells a spreadsheet has, the more memory the computer system needs. A large, high-resolution monitor is necessary to show large spreadsheets on the screen. For printing spreadsheets a large carriage printer is needed to print wide or long spreadsheet tables.

Recommended Spreadsheet Systems:

Low End

Microprocessor	486DX/2-66 MHz
DRAM	12 megabytes
Video Card	SVGA accelerated
Monitor	15-inch
Hard Drive	500 megabytes
Printer	24-pin dot-matrix printer

(For wide spreadsheets buy a wide-carriage printer)

High End

Microprocessor	Pentium
DRAM	64+ megabytes
Video Card	SVGA video card, resolution 1,280 by 1,024
Hard Drive	1+ gigabyte

Monitor	21-inch
Printer	Tabloid-size laser printer

Big Daddy Mac

Some of you are probably wondering about what is on the other side of the fence and may think the grass is greener in the land of the Macintosh. This section is included for those of you who have to build onto a pre-existing Apple hardware system. It is also for all the curious Georges who are interested in the Apple systems. Apple computers are heavily used in some niche markets like desktop publishing, computer graphics, and video. The software companies that pioneered artistic programs on the Macintosh are now making packages that run on DOS-Windows-based machines that perform equally well.

Macs are a little easier to use than PCs. On a scale of 1 to 10 where 10 is the easiest to use, the Mac scores about a 9, and a PC with Windows scores about 8.6. Software installation sometimes is a little easier on Macs than PCs. To install a new program or feature, just drag and drop the icons into the appropriate folders on the hard disk. Windows installations are rarely as simple as this, and it can be difficult to uninstall a program if it is no longer wanted. A great feature of Macs is that most come standard with a SCSI port which makes adding peripherals, like CD-ROMs and scanners, as easy as plugging in a cable.

Apple offers toll-free support lines for any questions and a one-year warranty on the Macs. Apple also offers extensions to the warranties, which can be a good idea for portable computer.

The Apple Macintosh systems are all based on CPUs manufactured by Motorola. These chips are the 68000, 68020, 68030, 68040, and the PowerPC 601, 603, 604, 615, and 620. The power is comparable to the 8088, 286, 386, 486, and Pentium chips made by Intel.

Many Macintosh computers contain a **PMMU** (Paged Memory Management Unit). This is a coprocessor that takes some of the load off the CPU. The PMMU is specially designated to handle memory-related tasks and allow the Mac to use virtual memory.

Macintosh computers allow hardware additions to the computer via slots on the motherboard. The Macintosh computers use two main types of slots for hardware expansion that are known as the NuBus slot and the **Processor Direct Slot** (PDS). Not all NuBus or PDS slots are made equal; different computers have varying types of these expansion slots. These expansion slots allow for system upgrades to speed up the computer, fax/modems, sound cards, network cards, video cards, and graphics cards.

The **NuBus** slot in Mac computers allows for future expansion, like adding another video card or Ethernet card. This slot supports multiple processors, like video coprocessors, and allows bus mastering. The specialized coprocessors on NuBus boards can take control of the computer when the need arises.

NuBus cards are self-configuring. In the PC there often are little switches that need to be set to make a newly installed expansion board work with the computer system. NuBus cards come preset with a configuration utility ROM that notifies the computer what is being connected. The fastest NuBus standard is called **NuBus-90**, which can transfer two to four times the information as the earlier NuBus slots. The maximum NuBus transfer rate is around 40 megabytes per second.

One of the best associations that offer support for Macintosh computers is BMUG (Berkeley Mac User Group). BMUG has a great newsletter, excellent tech support, and tons of Mac shareware available to their members. They can be reached at 1442A Walnut Street, #62, Berkeley, CA 94709. The telephone number is (510) 849-BMUG or fax (510) 849-9026.

Apple Macintosh computers come with built-in networking known as LocalTalk, which allows two or more computers to be linked to share data and peripherals like printers. LocalTalk transmits data at 0.234 megabytes per second. Some Macintoshes have Ethernet, which is a more advanced networking system. Ethernet is about 400 percent faster than LocalTalk. This should all be superseded by FireWire, which has a transfer rate of 12.5 megabytes per second. FireWire will eliminate the need for SCSI, serial, and LocalTalk ports on future Macs.

Climb the Apple Tree

The Macintosh computers offered today fit into two main categories. The Performa line of computers are a compete kit including the monitor, keyboard, mouse, main computer system, and some bundled software. The Performas can be a good choice if the package includes everything you need. The Quadra line is the higher end of the Macintosh line. They are sold separately from the monitor, keyboard, and software. The Quadra line lets customers buy the exact setup to fit their needs. Essentially this is a more customized and better way of buying a computer system for most people. The newest Apple computers are called the Power PCs. These computers have a totally new CPU design and are much faster than the Quadra line. If you are looking at Apple computers, buy a Power PC so you get the benefits of new software.

Apple started licensing its technology to third-party developers, so you now have the choice of buying an Apple Power PC or a Radius Power PC (or a Power PC from numerous other manufacturers). For information about current Apple computers, contact Apple at (408) 996-1010.

Chapter 18

The Rest of the Story

Power Savers for a Green World

Many computers are turned on and left running for hours without being used. Thirty to forty percent of personal computers are left on during the day, night, and over the weekend. Just to keep these systems running costs about $105 a year. The power collectively wasted every day in the United States by idle computers could power a small country in Europe. The current power drawn by the 30 to 35 million computers in the U.S. adds up to around 5 percent of the total national power use.

To save our environment from excessive waste the EPA (Environmental Protection Agency) has announced its Energy Star program. The Energy Star designation applies to computers that incorporate power management and/or power-saving devices. Companies that meet the energy-saving standards will be awarded an Energy Star logo to display. Be kind to the earth by purchasing Energy Star computers.

The goal for manufacturers is to produce computer systems and monitors that will power down to 30 watts or less when idle. A system running on 30 watts uses, on the average, 50 to 75 percent less power. A standard system running 8 hours a day costs about $35 per year to power, while an Energy Star system will cost about $12 per year. This could add up to a collective energy savings of up to $1 billion per year and prevent the emission of 20 million tons of carbon dioxide into the atmosphere. Some companies signed on with the Energy Star program include IBM, Apple, Hewlett-Packard, Compaq, Acer, Digital, NEC, Nanao, Zenith, NCR, and AST.

A hidden savings benefit from using an energy-efficient computer system is the reduced air-conditioning cost in office buildings. Each watt of energy a computer consumes must be offset by 1.5 watts of air-conditioning power. The lower-powered computer means less cold air is needed.

Most computers sold today should operate at 3 volts instead of 5 volts. A lower-voltage computer coupled with power-saving features is the smart way to go. Printers and monitors are next on the list for power-saving features. Printers are often left on but are used only a small fraction of the time. An easy solution here is to not leave your printer on all day and night, or buy a printer with automatic power-down features. If you need it to print at a specific time every day, connect the printer to a timer that can turn it on and off automatically.

Laser printers have toner cartridges that can be refilled by returning the cartridge to a special service or to the manufacturer where the toner cartridge is disassembled and worn parts are replaced. The toner cartridge is then reassembled and returned for reuse. If you plan on refilling cartridges, keep an extra toner cartridge on hand so you can still print while one cartridge is being refilled.

Consider buying an ink-jet printer instead of a laser printer. Ink-jet printers use only 20 watts, much less than the average 100 watts that laser printers consume. When printing, use recycled paper. It is virtually impossible to visually differentiate a paper that uses 10 percent reused paper stock from virgin paper stock.

If your company publishes large volumes, consider alternatives to publishing on paper. The CD-ROM is an excellent medium on which to store large documents, as it takes up little space and can hold up to 300,000 pages of text. As a bonus, subjects stored on disk can be cross-referenced quickly, making research a breeze. Pressing CD-ROMs can be done in-house using a CD-R, or they can be sent to a service bureau to be mass-produced.

Some energy-saving monitors are being designed to sense the infrared heat that humans emit. Absence of infrared heat from the proximity of the monitor lets the sensors know you are not using the computer and signals the computer to switch the monitor from normal mode to standby mode. Turning it on should only take about 5 to 10 seconds, a small wait when the well-being of the earth is at hand. When powered down, the monitor runs on only 5 watts, which offers a great power savings. Another energy saver comes from the Video Electronics Standard Association (VESA) which has devised the Display Power Management Signaling specification. DPMS allows a motherboard level power controller to shut down an attached monitor to a sleep mode. The cathodes inside the picture tube remain partially charged and fire up immediately when computing is resumed.

Internal peripherals are more efficient than external ones because they do not require an extra power supply and transformer for energy. Internal peripherals use the computer's power supply and transformer; external peripherals need separate power supplies to operate.

Portable computers by design consume a great deal less energy than their desktop counterparts, so consider buying a portable for energy efficiency. Plus you can get solar panels to charge a portable computer's batteries. Kick back and let the sun do the all the work.

A source for "green" floppy disks is MicroDiskServices, a company that reclaims floppy disks from outdated software packages. The paper from the packages is recycled and the floppy disks are erased, reformatted, and quality checked. These disks include a lifetime replacement guarantee.

For more information on retail green consumer products, contact the catalog retailers Real Goods or Jade Mountain. They offer a wide variety of products that keep the environment happy. Governmental organizations that act as clearinghouses for conservation issues include National Appropriate Technology Assistance Service (NATAS) and Conservation and Renewable Energy Inquiry and Referral Service (CAREIRS).

Software Choices

Without software a computer is just a hunk of metal and silicon. To make a computer useful it needs to be paired with one or more software programs. Let's explore the three main types of software distribution: commercial, shareware, and freeware. **Commercial** software is found in most computer stores, and to evaluate the software you usually have to buy it first. If it turns out that it is not what you are looking for and the store does not have a return policy, then this can be an expensive problem. Most of the best advanced software is commercial.

Shareware is software that can be obtained free from friends or on BBSs (Bulletin Board Services) or usually for a distribution fee from shareware distributors. The programmers of shareware software will let you evaluate it free of charge, and if you like it they request that you send them compensation, usually in the form of green paper with pictures of presidents on it. Some of the available shareware is great and some is not, but you do not pay until the fat lady sings, meaning you do not have to pay if you find the program useless. There are shareware programs in distribution that are as good or better than commercial programs on the market. Many shareware programs are too specialized to have a commercial audience but fill a void for productive software.

Freeware is software that those blessed programmers have made and unleashed upon the computing world for free. Freeware is in the public domain, and you do not have to pay a dime for it even if you want to use the program. Freeware is distributed through the same avenues as shareware.

The ASP (Association of Shareware Professionals) is a worldwide non-profit organization of authors, publishers, vendors, user groups, and BBSs. They maintain a great on-disk catalog containing a list of the shareware programs, with descriptions and names and addresses of the program authors. If you would like a copy of this catalog, contact the ASP at the following address:

Jan Abbott—Executive Director
Association of Shareware Professionals
545 Grover Road
Muskington Road, MI 49442-9427
Telephone: (616) 788-5131

Commercial Programs

New programs are released onto the market practically every day. The best place to keep up on the newest releases is in the many periodicals that cater to computer users. It is important to fill out and return the warranty and registration cards that accompany new products, because many manufacturers offer free upgrades or other benefits to registered users of their programs. Before filling in the registration cards, make certain you bought the right program and are satisfied with it, because many stores will not accept returned software without the warranty and registration card, even if they are filled out but not sent in.

Many software companies offer demonstration versions of their programs to give you a sense of how good their programs are without having to buy them first. These demos usually have examples of the type of work that can be done with the software program. Some demos look and act like the real program but are missing main features like the ability to save or print any of the work done using the demo.

Commercial software is usually bundled with manuals that explain how to install and use the software. If you want to get your money's worth, read the manuals. If you have a problem, look in the manual or at the help file included in the software. If you still cannot find the answer, call the technical support line at the software company. If the manual is not well-written, check the bookstores for after-market books.

The Source of Your Future

The 1990s are touted as the service decade. A personal computer is something you'll only purchase once every few years, so make sure you buy it from a good source. When choosing a vendor look for one that is stable and has been in business for a few years. Computer companies that go belly-up do not offer technical support and have a hard time honoring warranties. Before making a final decision, call the Better Business Bureau for a background check to see if any complaints have been filed against the business in question.

Sources for new computers include superstores, mail order companies, chain stores, warehouse clubs, value-added resellers, electronic and office supply chains, and direct purchase from the manufacturer. Each of these sources offers different features. Superstores carry an extensive line of products at low prices. They usually offer on-site service and in-house technical service. A drawback of superstores is the sales force may not know enough to really help you, and superstores may not carry specialty items. To get to these stores often requires a long trip because they like to choose real estate sites that have low overhead.

Catalogs and mail order offer the largest selection of products delivered right to your door. The prices are often the lowest around, and out-of-state purchases can exclude sales tax. Many of the larger mail order firms offer great technical support. The drawback of shopping by mail is you cannot examine the products before you buy. You need to know exactly what you are looking for or completely depend on the salesperson's judgment. Returns to mail order businesses are not as quick and easy as driving to the local computer store. If your product is defective it may take several days before you get a replacement. The cost of shipping defects and returns is often born by the shopper, but this is a point to check with each business. Make sure before you buy that the dealer is authorized by the manufacturer or your warranty may be void.

Chain stores carry a wide and solid selection of products that rivals the superstore. The drawback to these stores is they cannot stock everything, but they are usually able to special-order any product you might need. These stores usually have limited technical support, but since most product support is offered via the manufacturer this is not always a critical point. Don't expect the sales staff at these stores to know everything, especially regarding products they do not regularly stock. Many of the salespeople at these stores work on commission, and it is unfair to expect free consulting from them on products that you intend buy through mail order or warehouse clubs. If you have been helped by the salespeople, treat them justly by making your final purchase from them. Some of the smaller chain stores are unable to get volume discounts from the manufacturer and therefore are not too flexible with their prices. A great offering made by some chain stores is a loaner program if your computer needs service. This will keep you productive if your monitor or computer decides to stop working.

Warehouse clubs are known for their low prices, but the product selection is usually pretty random and limited. Warehouse clubs tend to stock older equipment and they usually do not have a service department. If you need help at one of these stores, forget it.

Electronic and office supply chain stores are usually limited in their selection of computer software and hardware. In general, the salespeople are not as knowledgeable as those at dedicated computer stores. If you know what you are looking for and can bargain on the price, these stores may be a good source for your computer needs.

Buying direct from the manufacturer will limit your product selection. Often niche markets offer direct buying, and these prices are high due to lack of competition. Direct marketers usually are extremely knowledgeable about their products and can help you customize them to meet your specific needs.

Value-added resellers (VARs) are typically not set in a retail store environment. They are experts in vertical markets like data collection or point of sale equipment. VARs usually work on large projects in the corporate world and they are extremely knowledgeable about the custom-designed systems they offer. Their prices are usually on the high end, but you are paying for their expert level of knowledge that cannot be found in retail stores.

The following are some inside tips on buying a computer. When making the purchase use a credit card. Under the Fair Credit Billing Act there are certain protections applicable to buying items over $50 in value within 100 miles of your home. The advantage of using a credit card instead of a check is if you do not receive exactly what you ordered, or if you received defective merchandise, you have a better defense with a credit card. You can refuse to pay the bill and then the credit companies will step in to mediate and resolve the issue. If you order something from a retailer using a credit card and it does not arrive on time, contact your credit card company immediately and let them know about the delay. After contacting the credit company, cancel your order with the vendor. If your order is canceled the seller is required to credit your account within one billing cycle.

Before you make a purchase ask about the store return policy and get its policy in writing. Can you return items? Is there a restocking fee? Is there a money back guarantee? How long is the special offer valid? Find out about the support supplied to customers after buying the computer. Does the company offer 24-hour technical help, and if the call is long distance is the telephone number toll-free? What are the weekend support hours? Is there unlimited free support or do you have to pay after a specified period of time? Can you get on-site repair and how much will it cost? What is the store turnaround time for replacing defective parts?

The seller is obligated to ship your merchandise to you within 30 days of receiving your order. If the order is not shipped in this time period the seller must notify you in writing in advance and provide a new shipping date if known. If the seller does not hear from you it is assumed that you accept the new conditions offered. In this case you may cancel the outstanding order at any time, even if you have given your consent for the delay.

Find out the terms the warranty offers. How long does the warranty last for both parts and for labor? Can they fix the product in-house or do they ship it out for repair? In-house repair is usually faster. Does the company have staff dedicated to handle support? Some vendors offer on-site repair; it is a good idea to find out the specifics of these plans. Listen carefully because some vendors say they offer on-site repair but what they really do is send you a replacement part with instructions on how to install it yourself. Sure, this is on-site repair, but you are the repair person. Some companies offer a fax-back system that sends troubleshooting data sheets to you to help solve any questions at any time of the day or night. When dealing with retailers always remember the golden rule to "get everything in writing." Ask whether the equipment is new or reconditioned, especially when buying from mail order, and make sure the manufacturer, model, size, and other specifications are all clarified.

Some vendors offer BBS support for their products that can be connected to using a modem. A BBS lets you get updated drivers and technical support quickly and on your own time schedule. An alternative to having direct BBS support is alternative support access via forums on major commercial services like CompuServe or America Online.

When you receive your equipment make sure you got exactly what you ordered. Some times mixups occur. If the wrong equipment is sent or if it is defective, get a return merchandise authorization (RMA) from the vendor before you send it back. Do not throw away the boxes just in case you need to ship the units back to the manufacturer or in case you decide to move.

If you do have problem with your purchase, there are a couple of avenues you can use to take action. Keep a copy of all correspondence you have regarding the matter. Contact the store directly to see if you can iron out any problems and notify them in writing of all relevant information. If that does not work, contact your credit card company and they will mediate the dispute. If you get burned on a deal, contact the local Better

Business Bureau and Department of Consumer Affairs. The Federal Trade Commission produces consumer help booklets like "Facts for Consumers" and "Facts for Businesses" which you can obtain by writing to the FTC in care of Public Reference Branch, Room 130, Washington, DC 20508.

The Direct Marketing Association maintains information about companies that operate in the mail-order business. They have a Mail Order Action Line that attempts to resolve disputes with vendors. For help, mail copies of all disputed information to the DMA at 1101 17th Street NW, Suite 705, Washington, DC 20036.

If you are returning a product, keep both the shipper's receipt and packing slip. If the product is non-defective some business charge a restocking fee that is a percentage of the merchandise value. This is because they cannot sell the product again as new and would therefore take a loss. The vendor often requires that you obtain a restocking code number before returning the product for a repair or refund. If a mail-order company uses the words "specification subject to change," this means the seller reserves the right to replace the product with another of equal or greater value. It is a good idea to obtain the vendor's return policies in writing so there are no unwanted surprises in the event that you need to return an item.

Renting or Leasing

There are alternative options open to businesses other than buying computer equipment outright. If you run a company, business leasing or rental may be the way to go. Each buying route has its own advantages and drawbacks.

Renting equipment is usually done on a very short-term basis. An example of a company that might consider renting is one that needs computers for temporary employees who are doing extra work for a limited period of time. A person who is planning a business trip or vacation may want to rent a portable computer to take along on a temporary basis. Most major metropolitan areas have desktop publishing services that rent computers by the hour, but if a business trip takes you to the backroads it is probably better to rent a portable computer. Because the cost per month for renting equipment can be more than 10 percent of the equipment's value, renting equipment is usually done for a term of less than three months, and it is probably uneconomical for most businesses to rent for more than six months.

For equipment needs over longer periods of time, leasing is a viable alternative to renting or outright purchasing. Leasing keeps companies up on the current technology and helps them get rid of old technology by making the leasing company responsible for reselling used equipment. Leasing takes a financial burden off companies by spreading the purchase cost over an extended period of time. In addition, leasing keeps capital depreciation off the balance sheets. Leasing is an expense on the books and thereby can reduce the company's taxable income. Loans are viewed on the books as liabilities. Since banks use debt ratios to determine a company's financial stability, any liability on the books will adversely affect the chances of being approved. By leasing, the company is flexible in its ability to qualify for new loans because the value of the leased equipment does not affect the debt ratio.

The two major types of leasing available are capital leases and operating leases. A **capital lease**, also called a financial lease, is treated as a financing method. The cost of the leased equipment is put on the lessee's balance sheet just as if the equipment had been purchased. This type of lease most often extends the useful life of the equipment and the monthly payments generally are lower than for an operating lease.

The **operating lease** is a shorter-term lease than a capital lease. It usually is for a period of three to five years. In an operating lease the owner of the equipment is the leasing company, and therefore the depreciation for the capital is taken on their books and not the lessee's. This account balancing is good in the event that when the equipment is sold, if it is sold at a loss, the balance sheet of the lessee does not show the loss. The burden of risk is completely shifted to the leasing company, which must ensure the equipment is resold at the end of the lease term. The drawback here is that because the leasing company assumes all the risk, the cost of an operating lease is usually higher than a capital lease.

A company that can afford to simply purchase equipment may prefer to do this because purchasing increases the company's equity base. There are bigger tax advantages to purchasing equipment in the first few years than there are in leasing. This is not a simple decision to make because forecasts must be made to estimate the residual value of the equipment when it is past its term of value to the company. Other items of consideration when weighing options to lease or purchase computer equipment include depreciation schedules, tax rates, interest percentages, and lease costs. This process is best left to an accountant who has a firm grip on how to estimate value to the company.

Our Disabled Friends

For our friends who are challenged with disabilities, there are resources to help get them on the road to friendly computing. Calling the National Institute on Disability Rehabilitation and Research is a good place to start. They are located in Washington, D.C., and can be reached at 1-800-949-4232. The Internet has news groups that cover disability-related issues. You can make contact via the Internet at misc.handicap and alt.education.disabled. The major online services like CompuServe, Delphi, and BIS have forums dedicated to adaptive technology.

Free handbooks are available in hard copy and/or electronic form that cover how to add adaptive technology to computers from the Clearinghouse on Computer Accommodation (COCA) of the Information Resource Management Service, General Service Administration. For this booklet write to Susan A. Brummel, Director, COCA, c/o GSA, Room 2022, KGDO, 18th and F Streets NW, Washington, DC 20405.

For a huge information source, try the CD-ROM database regarding disabilities available from the Trace Center in Madison, Wisconsin. It is available direct from the center for $25 or can be accessed by modem from the Massachussets Commission for the Blind BBS at (617) 451-5327, or via the Project Enable BBS at (304) 766-7842. Other resources follow:

- **Computers and The Americans with Disabilities Act: A Manager's Guide**
  John A. McCormick, 1994, Windcrest/McGraw Hill, ISBN: 0-8306-4445-8
  This book is an excellent source of information to help those with disabilities integrate into society and the workplace better through using computers.
- **ABLEDATA-REHAB DATA:** National Rehabilitation Information Center (NARIC) (301) 588-9284 or 1-800-346-2742
- **Trace Research & Development Center**
  They maintain a database of every adaptive product available. (608) 262-6966

What to Do with Your Old Computer

An obsolete computer can be used as a decorative object, be given away, or sold. If you want to donate the equipment to a worthy cause there are several nonprofit organizations like the East West Foundation, Non-Profit Computing, Educational Assistance, and the National Cristina Foundation. They will find new settings that breathe life into an old computer.

The **National Cristina Foundation** redirects used computer equipment to educational use, use for the handicaped, and job retraining use. The **East West Foundation** recycles computer donations to American schools and charities. They support democratic government and refurbish computers for use in Eastern Europe, the former Soviet Union, and other countries. They also place computers with domestic organizations with social service agendas.

The **Educational Assistance** group redirects computer donations to U.S. colleges and universities. It runs the College Opportunity Program which assists "at risk" high school students in completing school and continuing on to college. **Non-Profit Computing** serves as a database for non-profit and government organizations that are in need of used computers and telecommunications equipment. The other functions of Non-Profit Computing include training classes, volunteer consulting, problem solving, and information assistance for people with disabilities.

If you think your computer may have "antique" value, the **Historical Computer Society** could be its new home. The Historical Computer Society takes the relics to schools to display while helping people learn the history of computing. They also publish a newsletter called *Historically Brewed*. The **Computer Recycling Center** will redirect used computers to new homes as educational tools for California students. They also offer support for the equipment after it is installed in its new environment.

The Detwiler Foundation accepts volume donations of computer equipment and redirects it to school districts. **Gifts In Kind** donates products to over 50,000 charities across the country. The recipients of Gifts In Kind work include the American Red Cross, Boys and Girls Clubs of America, Habitat for Humanity International, Special Olympics, and the Nature Conservatory.

Computers 4 Kids takes outdated computers and puts them to use in schools that otherwise could not afford them. They want to educate a new generation of computer-literate Americans. **Computers and You** helps disadvantaged children and adults who live in San Francisco's Tenderloin District. If it is software programs or computer books that you need to unload, **CompuMentor** runs a program that makes these items available to nonprofit agencies.

If you would rather sell the computer there are several routes to take including retail stores that buy used equipment, exchanges, and classifieds. Remember that when you sell your computer you probably will not get close to what you paid originally. Selling to a used computer dealer is probably the easiest method but will leave you with the least amount of cash. Selling through the classifieds, on a computer bulletin board system, through a local computer user's group, or word-of-mouth can be the most financially rewarding method.

Computer exchanges keep national directories of computers for sale and possible buyers. Exchanges operate by taking a certain percentage of the sale. The United Computer Exchange is a national clearinghouse for sellers and buyers of used computer equipment. They can be reached at 1-800-755-3033 or (404) 612-1205. Other exchanges include the National Computer Exchange at 1-800-622-6639, the Boston Computer Exchange at 1-800-262-6399, and Second Source at (215) 886-9092.

Keeping Informed

Reading is software for the brain. There are magazines that are geared toward more specific interests such as multimedia, artificial intelligence, and desktop publishing. A book called *The Computer Industry Almanac* contains an exhaustive list of magazines that explore almost every special interest imaginable.

Joining a computer support group can be rewarding. Many offer services, technical support, and classes to help you get the most out of your computer programs. To find the nearest PC user group, contact the Association of Computer User Groups at (914) 876-6678, or if you are a Macintosh user call the User Group Connection at (408) 461-5700.

Appendix

Directory of Resources

American Computer Exchange
6065 Roswell Road, Suite 535
Atlanta, GA 30328
Tel: 1-800-786-0717
Tel: (404) 250-0050
Call them if you want to use a computer exchange.

Association of Personal Computer User Groups
1730 M Street NW, Suite 700
Washington, DC 20036
Tel: (914) 876-6678
Umbrella organization for PC user groups

Boston Computer Exchange
Box 1177
Boston, MA 02103
Tel: 1-800-262-6399
Tel: (617) 542-4414
Used computer exchange

CAREIRS
P.O. Box 3048
Merrifield, VA 22116
Tel: 1-800-523-2929

CD-ROM, Inc.
1667 Cole Boulevard, Suite 400
Golden, CO 80401
Voice: (303) 231-9373
CD-ROM mastering

CD-ROM Services
14567 Big Basin Way, Suite 4B
Saratoga, CA 95070
Voice: (408) 867-0514
CD-ROM mastering

Closing The Gap, Inc.
P.O. Box 68
Henderson, MN 56044
Tel: (612) 248-3294

CompuMentor
89 Stillman Street
San Francisco, CA 94107
Tel: (415) 512-7784
Redistributes donated software

Computers 4 Kids
150 Brookside Road
Waterbury, CT 06708
Tel: (203) 754-5560
Fax: (203) 756-6312
Redistributes donated computer equipment to schools

Computer Recycling Center
1245 Terra Bella Avenue
Mountain View, CA 94043
Tel: (415) 428-3700
Redistributor of donated computers

CP+
16351 Gothard Street
Huntington Beach, CA 92647
Voice: (714) 847-1799
Voice: 1-800-274-4277
Portable computer modem phone line connectivity kit

Cristina Foundation
591 W. Putnam Avenue
Greenwich, CT 06830-6095
Tel: (203) 622-6000

Educational Assistance Ltd. (EAL)
P.O. Box 3021
Glen Ellyn, IL 60138
Voice: (708) 690-0010
Fax: (708) 690-0565

East West Foundation Education Development Foundation
49 Temple Pl.
Boston, MA 02111
Voice: (617) 542-1234
Fax: (617) 542-3333

Gifts In Kind
700 North Fairfax Street, Suite 300
Alexandria, VA 22314
Tel: (703) 836-2121
Fax: (703) 549-1481
Donates used computers to nonprofit organizations

Jade Mountain
P.O. Box 4616
Boulder, CO 80306-4616
Tel: 1-800-442-1972
Tel: (303) 449-6601
Green energy solutions mail-order company

Magellan's
Box 5485
Santa Barbara, CA 93150-5485
Tel: 1-800-962-4943
Catalog of travel products great for the mobile computer user

MicroDiskServices
15530 Woodenville-Redmond Road
Woodenville, WA 98072
Tel: 1-800-624-7273 ext. 4057
Recycled floppy disks

National Computer Exchange
118 East 25th Street
New York, NY 10010
Tel: 1-800-622-6639
Tel: (212) 614-0700
A used computer exchange

National Cristina Foundation
591 West Putnam Avenue
Greenwich, CT 06830
Voice: (203) 622-6000
Fax: (203) 622-6270

Non-Profit Computing, Inc. (NPC)
40 Wall Street, Suite 2124
New York, NY 10005
Voice: (718) 357-3416

Optical Media International
180 Knowles Drive
Los Gatos, CA 95030
Voice: (408) 376-3511
Fax: (408) 376-3519
CD-ROM mastering

Real Goods
966 Mazzani Street
Ukaih, CA 95482
Tel: 1-800-762-7325
Green goods mail-order company

Second Source
479 Old York Road
Jenkinstown, PA 19046
Tel: (215) 886-9092
A used computer exchange

Safeware, The Insurance Agency Inc.
2929 N. High Street
P.O. Box 02211
Columbus, OH 43202-2211
Voice: 1-800-848-3469
Insures computer equipment against loss or damage

TechPool Software
1463 Warrensville Center Rd.
Cleveland, OH 44121
Voice: (216) 382-1234
Voice: 1-800-925-6998
Fax: (216) 328-1915

The Computer Insurance Agency
6150 Old Millersport Road NE
Pleasantville, OH 43148-9900
Voice: 1-800-722-0385
Fax: (614) 263-5109
Computer insurance provider

Traveling Software
18702 N. Creek Pkwy.
Bothell, WA 98011
Voice: (206) 483-8088
Voice: 1-800-343-8080
Fax: (206) 487-1284

United Computer Exchange
2110 Powers Ferry Road, Suite 307
Atlanta, GA 30339
Tel: 1-800-775-3033
Tel: (404) 612-1205
Used computer exchange

User Group Connection
P.O. Box 67249
Scott Valley, CA 95067
Tel: (408) 461-5700
Tel: 1-800-538-9696 ext. 500

Index